THE
WORLD
ATLAS
OF GIN

JOEL
HARRISON
& NEIL
RIDLEY

THE
WORLD
ATLAS
OF GIN

EXPLORE
THE GINS
OF MORE
THAN 50
COUNTRIES

MITCHELL
BEAZLEY

This book is dedicated to all the hard-working people in the
world of gin, who each make their own unique product infused
with passion, dedication, hard work and skill.

An Hachette UK Company
www.hachette.co.uk

First published in Great Britain in 2019
by Mitchell Beazley, an imprint of
Octopus Publishing Group Ltd
Carmelite House
50 Victoria Embankment
London EC4Y 0DZ
www.octopusbooks.co.uk
www.octopusbooksusa.com

Distributed in the US by
Hachette Book Group
1290 Avenue of the Americas
4th and 5th Floors
New York, NY 10104

Distributed in Canada by
Canadian Manda Group
664 Annette St.
Toronto, Ontario, Canada M6S 2C8

UK ISBN 978-1-78472-531-0
US ISBN 978-1-78472-654-6

A CIP catalogue record for this book is available from the British Library.

Printed and bound in China.

1 3 5 7 9 10 8 6 4 2

Group Publishing Director: Denise Bates
Art Director: Juliette Norsworthy
Senior Editor: Leanne Bryan and Louise McKeever
Designer: Ben Brannan
Picture Research Manager: Giulia Hetherington
Picture Research: Sally Claxton
Cartographer: Encompass Graphics
Illustrator: Emma Russell
Cover Design: Luke Bird
Production Controllers: Gemma John & Nic Jones

CONTENTS

INTRODUCTION

A *World Atlas of Gin*. How is this possible for a spirit that is, surely, as British as a cup of tea and a cucumber sandwich? Gin is strongly identified with London partly due to the term "London Dry" that defines a category of gin and certainly because of the infamous "gin craze" that swept through the streets of the city from the late 1600s to the mid-1700s. However, much like the aforementioned tea and cucumber combo where the former hails from China and the latter from India, the concept of gin, a juniper-forward spirit, was imported to the UK from Netherlands in the 17th century. And it quickly made itself at home. Such were the captivating charms of this early form of gin that the innocent folk of London were soon in its thrall and unable to tear themselves away for well over a century.

From that period of time onwards, gin become a well-travelled spirit, as the range of cocktails on pages 52–53 bears testament to, with gin-based concoctions being developed in India and the USA in the 1800s, and then Italy and Singapore in the 1900s.

Now well into the 21st century we are witnessing a truly global gin boom. Our work as professional drinks writers takes us on many trips to countries far and wide where, over the last decade, we have seen gin become a citizen of the world, reflected in this Atlas encompassing, astonishingly, over 50 gin-producing nations.

From heritage brands such as Tanqueray found in hotel bars worldwide to sachets of gin consumed neat on street corners in Nigeria, and with new craft distillers from Mexico's Yucatán to Australia's Tasmania exploring indigenous botanicals, gin is seriously big business. And there is an increasing trend overall for distillers to make their gin a distinct embodiment of the locality and terroir by scouring the local landscape for unique and unusual botanicals.

This book is a curated guide to the world of gin, focusing on only those producers who are making their own products, either where they control the whole gin production process from field to glass or redistil spirit using a unique mix of botanicals. The result is not just about the spirit in the bottle but the interesting and engaging tale of how it got there. Creating a good gin with a balanced botanical recipe is an art form, and as such we have also highlighted those expressions that – we hope – you'll love as much as we do.

With many of these gins available in different markets across the world through an ever-growing network of specialist distributors and retailers, this Atlas provides you with the inspiration and opportunity to become a gin explorer. Be it from the comfort of your own home with a G&T, on a hotel rooftop bar with a well-made Martini, or – and the very best option – while visiting the distillers themselves.

So, pack your suitcase and come on a juniper journey with us. Let us know your favourites @WorldsBestSpirits and we'll see you all for a Negroni soon.

Creating a good gin
with a balanced
botanical recipe
is an art form.

PART 1

GIN: A WELL-TRAVELLED SPIRIT

As distilled drinks go, gin is unquestionably one of the most distinctive yet widely enjoyed spirits in the world. It has truly escaped from its humble European origins to gain a global footprint, demonstrated by the consistently swelling numbers of distilleries of all sizes that are crafting it.

In this first section of the book, we define what gin is, how it is made and explore some of the best ways to enjoy it.

SO WHAT IS GIN?

◔ *Juniper, the key ingredient in every gin*

As unassuming as it may sound, gin is simply defined as a spirit that "has the predominant flavour of juniper berries". However, there is a complex world of gin styles to navigate, each with differing production techniques and origins. In the EU, the legal regulations state that gin must start with a "neutral" base spirit that is distilled to no less than 96% ABV, while in the USA a lower ABV of 95% (190° proof) is permitted. But all gins in Europe must be bottled at no less than 37.5% ABV, or 40% ABV (80° proof) in the USA.

The key challenge in the global gin business today is that it is extremely difficult to define accurately just how far the phrase "predominant flavour of juniper" relates to modern gin production, as it relies on the discretion of the distiller rather than a scientific measure.

One thing is for sure though: such ambiguity has opened up the spirit to an unprecedented level of innovation and consumer excitement over the last decade, which will no doubt continue at a frenetic pace for years to come.

> There is a complex world of gin styles to navigate, each with differing techniques and origins.

◑ *Copper pot still distillation in progress*

◉ *Gin has always been an egalitarian drink*

A HISTORY OF GIN

Gin has been on a five-hundred-year journey of self-discovery and refinement, ending up as the clear, juniper-led spirit we know today. The first mention of a juniper-based elixir was in the Dutch publication *Der Naturen Bloeme* by Jacob van Maerlant te Damme in 1269, highlighting the medicinal benefits of a drink infused with the berry's flavour. But it wasn't until 1495 when the first recipe for a juniper spirit was recorded in a Dutch cookbook entitled *Making Burned Wine*, "burned wine" being the term for a distilled spirit, which later became the basis for the term "brandy" or fruit-wine distillate. This original recipe used a wine base in which cardamom, cinnamon, cloves, galangal, ginger, grains of paradise, juniper and nutmeg were heat infused before the mixture was cut with either clean water or local beer.

The popularity of distilled spirits in the Netherlands became so great that by 1497, *korenbrandewijn*, a distillate from grain and the forerunner to genever (*see* page 18), was designated as a taxable product in Amsterdam. References to "genever aqua vitae", a grape brandy flavoured with juniper, appeared throughout the 1500s, juniper winning out over other botanicals presumably because of its abundance as well as its reputed medicinal properties. By the end of the century, however, distilled spirits had become grain- rather than grape-based, as most notably observed by Dutchman Casper Jansz. Coolhaes in *A Guide To Distilling*. In 1575, the Bulsius family set up their genever distillery in Amsterdam, drawing on their family name to create what is now the oldest-recorded brand of spirits in the world, Bols (*see* page 95).

Due to religious turbulence in the Low Countries of Europe, by 1570, an estimated 6,000 Flemish Protestants had made their way to London, taking their passion for juniper-flavoured spirits with them.

The origins of Dutch genever

As trade routes around the world began to be established by the nautical nations of Great Britain, France, Spain, Italy and Holland, it was the growth of the Dutch East India Company, or Vereenigde Oostindische Compagnie (VOC), eventually becoming the world's largest at the time, that provided a ready-made global distribution network for Dutch-made genever, while also bringing exotic herbs, spices and botanicals into the Netherlands for distillers to experiment with.

By 1623, genever was appearing in English texts, with a mention in Philip Massinger's London play *The Duke of Milan*, at a time when many British mercenaries went to fight in the Thirty Years' War (1618–48). Having discovered the juniper-flavoured spirit, the troops used it as fortification before battle, giving rise to the term "Dutch courage" still used today for those in need of a small motivational kick. Sixty-five years after Massinger's play, Dutch prince Willem invaded England and along with his English wife Mary Stuart seized the throne in 1689.

With the Distilling Act of 1690 both reducing foreign imports and lowering licence costs for distilling, the English – and Londoners in particular – turned their own hands to making spirit flavoured with juniper and other botanicals, and in so doing came up with a new word for it: gin. In this hothouse environment for the growth of gin, pretty much anyone who wished to distil simply needed to post a notice of intention outside their property ten days in advance. But despite the ease of distilling, a trend soon emerged for infusing or macerating poorly produced base spirit with juniper and other botanicals to help make it more palatable, known as "bathtub gin". It was also often sweetened for a better

◔ *Gin was often consumed in place of beer*

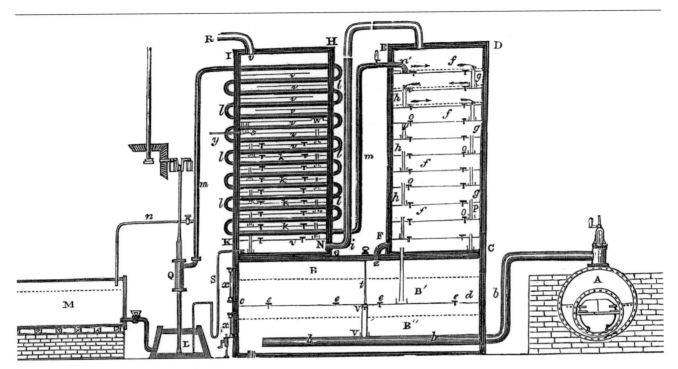

● *Early plans for continuous distillation*

flavour, most likely with honey due to the high cost of sugar at the time, and sold under the name Old Tom gin (*see* page 21).

Such was the problem of home-produced gin in London in the early 1700s that it earned the nicknames "mother's ruin" and "Madam Geneva". As the price of gin dipped below that of beer and ale, it made the drink even more popular, especially with the poor. It is estimated that a staggering 50 million litres (13 million US gallons), or the equivalent of 90 bottles for every adult resident of the city, was being consumed per year at that time.

It was in 1751 that gin became the subject of one of the most famous works of art from that time, William Hogarth's *Gin Lane*, in which he depicts a London street scene where the community is ravaged by illness, starvation and death. Hogarth contrasted this engraving with another, *Beer Street*, which shows jolly, industrious men and women enjoying good health and prosperity.

The late 1700s and early 1800s saw the Industrial Revolution drive efficiency in manufacturing, and distilling was not immune from this process. With the development of the column (or continuous) still (*see* page 24) in 1831, high-grade neutral base spirit could be produced quickly and inexpensively, and many of the famous gin brands we know today, such as Gordon's (*see* page 82), Plymouth (*see* page 72), Tanqueray (*see* page 79), Beefeater (*see* page 63) and Fleischmann's in America (*see* page 156), built a reputation on consistent quality.

Today, gin has truly conquered the world, with 54 different countries listed in this Atlas as producing gin or a style thereof. Not only has gin proved to have an enduring legacy with over half a millennium of history behind it, but also an exciting future as the number of producers continues to grow, along with a widening diversity of styles, flavours and bottles, attracting an ever greater fan base around the world.

● *An early gin bottle*

GLOBAL STYLES OF GIN

As we explained earlier, there are loose regulations concerning the flavour definitions of gin. Nevertheless, there are several defined styles of gin – and its forerunner genever – produced around the world.

COMPOUND GIN

Also known as "bathtub gin" (*see* page 16), this style is where botanicals, either fresh, dried or as pre-extracted oils, are simply added to a neutral base spirit. It is the easiest way to construct a gin and can even be done at home; all you need is a high-strength vodka or potable base spirit (a high level of alcohol helps to extract the oils and flavours in the botanicals) and a vessel in which to macerate (steep) them. During the maceration process, some colour will seep into the spirit, giving it a light, golden hue. After a few hours or a few days, you will have yourself a gin.

COLD COMPOUNDED GIN

In this case, botanical essences are added to the base spirit post-distillation and then reduced in strength by diluting with water and finally bottled. Because of this process, the resulting gin is not classed as a distilled gin.

GENEVER

This spirit (also spelled jenever or simply known as "Hollands") is the original incarnation of gin (*see* page 15), *genever* being the Dutch for "juniper". The base spirit – a malt wine made from rye, corn and malted barley – is first double distilled to between 46–48% ABV and then some of this spirit (the rest being held in reserve) distilled for a third time with botanicals – juniper, hops and sometimes coriander seeds – before being blended back into the reserved spirit (sometimes after being cut with neutral spirit) and reduced down to around 38% ABV, dependent on the style. Due to the more flavourful base spirit, genever can come across as almost savoury in comparison to traditional distilled or compounded gins.

There are three main styles of genever, defined by law:
oude – the older, more traditional style, which must contain at least 15% malt wine in addition to neutral spirit and bottled at no lower than 30% ABV
jonge – must contain no more than 15% malt wine and bottled no lower than 30% ABV
corenwyn or *korenwijn* – must contain at least 51% malt wine and bottled no lower than 38% ABV (there are also 100% malt wine genevers).

Any style can have a certain amount of sugar added (up to 20g/¾ oz per litre/2 US pints for *oude* and *korenwijn*, and up to 10g/¼oz per litre/2 US pints for *jonge*. Genever can be aged in oak, too, for a minimum of one year and in casks no larger than 700 litres (185 US gallons) (*see* Focus: Genever, page 97).

WACHOLDER AND STEINHÄGER

A German variant of gin, *Wacholder* (which translates as "juniper") is commonly used as an umbrella term for numerous juniper-based spirits distilled in Germany, predominantly in Westphalia and the Rhineland. Despite having a provenance dating back to the early 19th century, this distinctly juniper-heavy style of spirit, consumed as a chilled shot or a chaser, has remained a German favourite and is rarely seen internationally. *Steinhäger* comes specifically from the Westphalia region of Steinhagen, which became protected under EU Geographical Indication (GI) regulations in 1989. (*See* Focus: Wacholder and Steinhäger Styles, page 103.)

◔ *Bols, one of the most enduring spirits brands in the world*

BOROVIČKA

Unique to Slovakia and also protected by a GI, this is a single botanical (juniper) style of gin, and by law has to be made from a grain spirit base (*see* page 143 for some examples).

FLANDERS GENEVER ARTOIS

This juniper-based, genever-style spirit, protected by EU regulation and produced solely in Northern France, must be made using a grain base of rye, barley, wheat and oats (*see* page 109 for more on this).

DISTILLED GIN

This is made by redistilling a neutral base spirit with juniper and other botanicals in a still (*see* page 22), in which the spirit is boiled, vaporized and condensed back into a liquid. Distilling captures the flavours of the botanical recipe using one of two methods:

1. Steeping and boiling, where the botanicals are first macerated in the spirit before distilling the spirit with or without the botanicals present.

2. Vapour infusion, where a basket of botanicals is hung inside the still (*see* page 22), allowing the spirit's vapours to pass through them before being turned back into a liquid.

 Botanical tray in a copper pot still

The variables are multiple: the length of steeping time; splitting the botanicals between both methods in one distillation; distilling all the botanicals together or doing the process separately for each or groups of them, then blending the resulting distillates together before the gin is bottled. A distilled gin may also have natural flavourings added after distillation, so long as these flavours have been extracted through distillation as well, for example the rose and cucumber in Hendrick's Gin (*see* page 79).

LONDON DRY GIN

London Dry gin must exclusively be a distilled gin in which all the botanicals used have been involved in the distillation process, with the resulting distillation being at least 70% ABV, and only water added before it is bottled.

Despite its name, London Dry gin can be made anywhere in the world with many countries using the term but in some cases modifying it to reflect where their gin is made, such as Japan's Ki No Bi Kyoto Dry Gin (*see* page 229).

It is also not a requirement for a gin producer to create its own base spirit, with most buying it in, distilled to their own specifications. The minority of producers that insist on making their own will often speak of the additional quality, in both flavour and texture, that this brings to their gin (*see* page 48).

FACT WORTH NOTING

In any distillation run, it is the citrus oils that come through first, followed later by notes of juniper and more earthy tones.

OTHER GIN STYLES

AGED GIN

Gin can be matured in casks, usually oak but sometimes chestnut or other woods, and from ex-whisky barrels to wine barriques and ginger beer barrels, which contributes both colour and additional flavour (*see* page 48).

OLD TOM GIN

As gin is essentially a "dry"-tasting spirit, some gins have sugar or honey added to sweeten them up and to give the spirit more viscosity, and a proportion of these are also a simpler botanical style of gin known as Old Tom. This nickname reputedly originates from the prevalence of public houses marked with the sign of a cat selling sweetened gins during the 1700s in London.

NAVY-STRENGTH GIN

This style of gin has an alcohol content of 57% (114° proof in the USA) or higher, making it flammable. This term relates to spirits carried on naval ships that even if they leaked on to gunpowder onboard would not prevent its ignition. It was a way of ensuring that ships were not supplied with watered-down gin.

FRUIT AND SPICED GIN

Over recent years, a trend toward gin containing fruit and spice flavours has exploded, largely kicked off by the popularity of British sloe gin, traditionally made by harvesting sloe berries from hedgerows, pricking them and macerating in gin for a lengthy period of time before adding sugar and finally bottling. A wave of these macerated-style fruit gins has swept around the globe, including citrus, strawberry, cherry, wine grape (*see* page 217 for Australia's Four Pillars Bloody Shiraz gin), pears (*see* Portugal's Tinto Gin on page 119) and plum gins, as well as other styles flavoured with spices such as saffron and vanilla.

George Cruikshank

COLOURED GIN

In addition to fruit gins, a new range of coloured gins has become immensely popular. From the classic pink gin consisting of a few dashes of Angostura bitters added to a glass of gin that originated as an early 19th-century naval remedy for sea sickness but soon became a fashionable pink-hued cocktail, the concept has gone into overdrive with new-style pink gins containing fruit flavours, alongside a multitude of other shades of gin.

GIN PRODUCTION: TYPES
OF GIN STILL

Distilled gin and London Dry gin must be produced using natural botanicals, predominantly through the use of a still, although freeze distillation can be used, where the temperature of the macerated spirit allows the water and alcohol to separate due to the lower freezing point of alcohol (for example, *see* Collesi Gin, page 123). Stills come in all sizes, from small desktop-style stills holding around 3–5 litres (6–10½ US pints) to much larger stills that can hold thousands of litres (US gallons). There is no defined legal limit for the size of still in which to produce gin.

CLASSIC POT OR ALEMBIC STILL

This is a copper pot, or kettle, that is heated from below. The stills come in a variety of sizes, with some distillers even designing and building their own. There are a few manufacturers that dominate the market, with some designs being more popular than others. Arnold Holstein, Kothe and Christian Carl stills are built in Germany, while Hoga copper pot stills come from Spain and Frilli from Italy. Forsyths stills are Scottish built and frequently used by whisky distillers who also produce gin using the same equipment.

The botanicals are either placed directly in the pot, a process referred to as direct charged, along with high-strength alcohol (over 95% ABV in the USA, 96% ABV in Europe) and often left to macerate (steep) in the alcohol for a period of time before redistillation. Alternatively, the botanicals are hung in a basket above the alcohol to enable its vapours to pass through, picking up essential oils and flavours along the way, known as vapour infusion. In some cases, both techniques are employed in the same still.

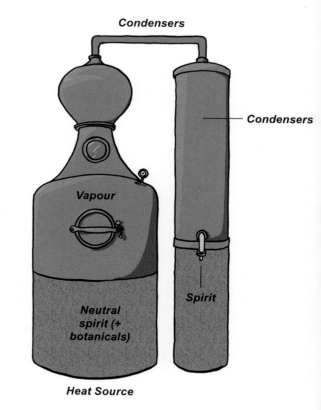

Condensers

Condensers

Vapour

Spirit

Neutral spirit (+ botanicals)

Heat Source

◔ *Classic Pot Still, external view*

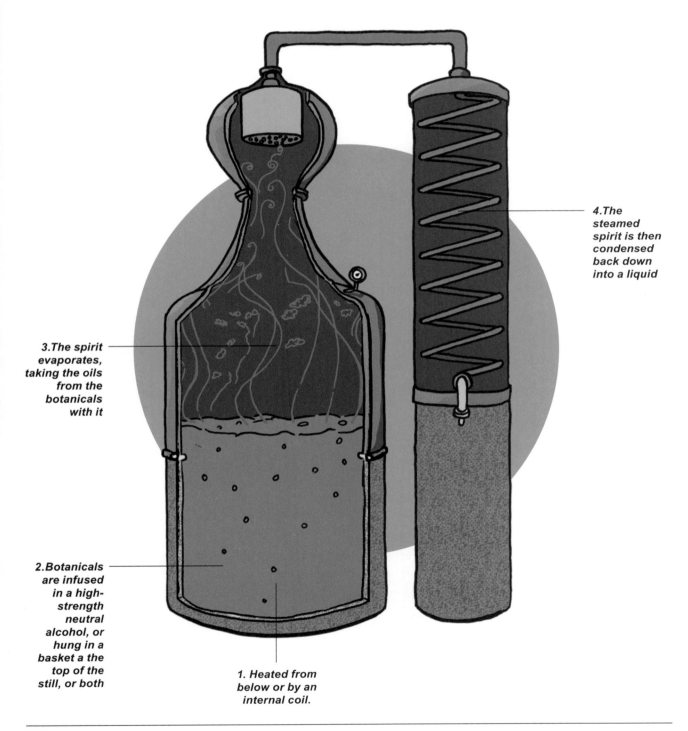

4.The steamed spirit is then condensed back down into a liquid

3.The spirit evaporates, taking the oils from the botanicals with it

2.Botanicals are infused in a high-strength neutral alcohol, or hung in a basket a the top of the still, or both

1. Heated from below or by an internal coil.

◉ *Classic Pot Still, internal view*

COLUMN STILL

This type of still is used for the rectification of alcohol – that is, to increase the alcohol content of the spirit. Column stills are narrow and tall, and the alcohol passes through a series of plates, each in turn working to separate the water from the alcohol, in a process known as fractional distillation (*see* page 246). Producers often use these stills for making their own base spirit to ensure that the neutral alcohol is distilled to the specific percentage of ABV that the regulations require.

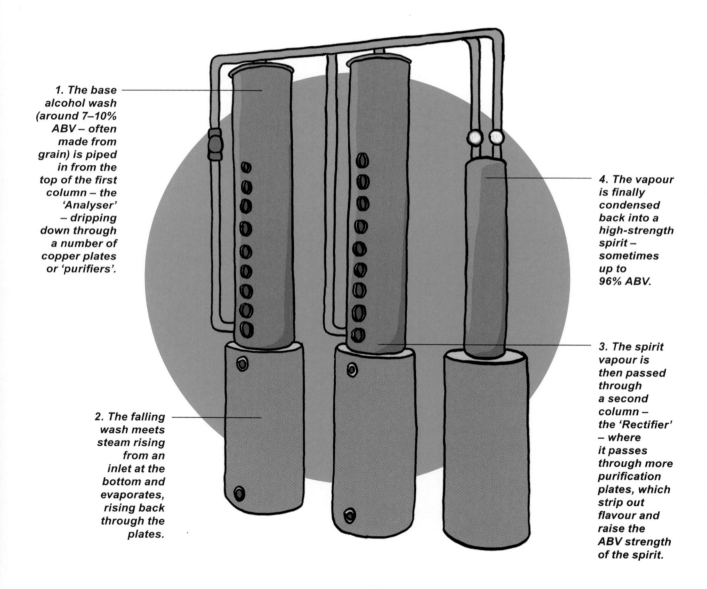

1. The base alcohol wash (around 7–10% ABV – often made from grain) is piped in from the top of the first column – the 'Analyser' – dripping down through a number of copper plates or 'purifiers'.

4. The vapour is finally condensed back into a high-strength spirit – sometimes up to 96% ABV.

3. The spirit vapour is then passed through a second column – the 'Rectifier' – where it passes through more purification plates, which strip out flavour and raise the ABV strength of the spirit.

2. The falling wash meets steam rising from an inlet at the bottom and evaporates, rising back through the plates.

Column Still

HYBRID STILL

A combination of a pot still base and a column still top, this type of still creates a lighter spirit and botanicals can be placed directly in the column part of the still.

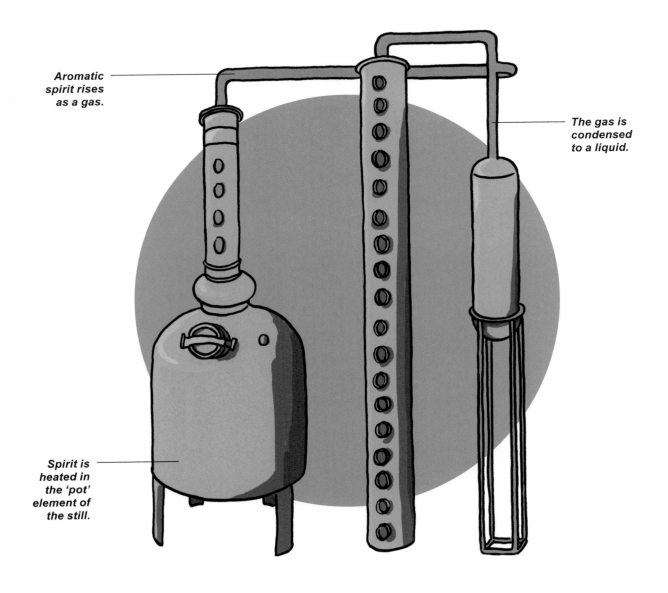

Aromatic spirit rises as a gas.

The gas is condensed to a liquid.

Spirit is heated in the 'pot' element of the still.

● *Hybrid Still*

CARTER-HEAD STILL

This type of style allows for a botanical basket to be hung between the still and the condenser.

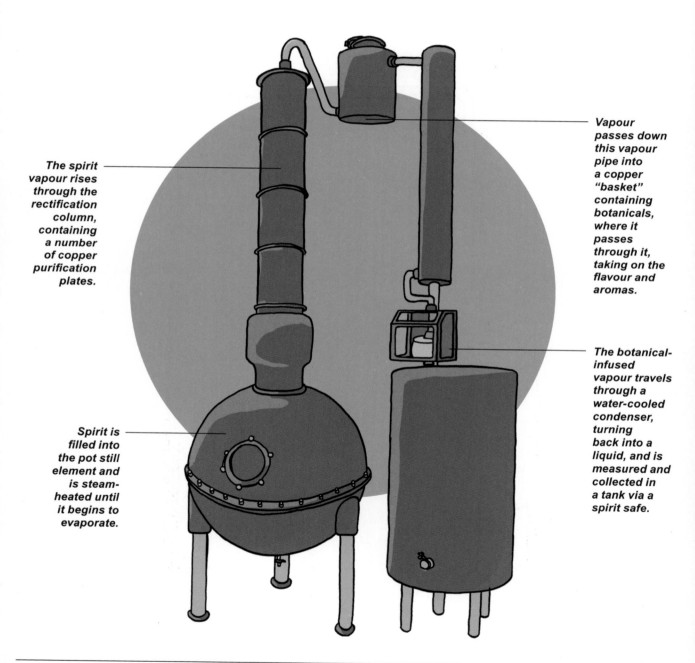

The spirit vapour rises through the rectification column, containing a number of copper purification plates.

Vapour passes down this vapour pipe into a copper "basket" containing botanicals, where it passes through it, taking on the flavour and aromas.

Spirit is filled into the pot still element and is steam-heated until it begins to evaporate.

The botanical-infused vapour travels through a water-cooled condenser, turning back into a liquid, and is measured and collected in a tank via a spirit safe.

◉ *Carter Head Still*

iSTILL

The iStill is a modern style of still that has taken the concept of ease and efficiency to a new level. It works with computers rather than the more traditional copper stills, which are more manual in their operation.

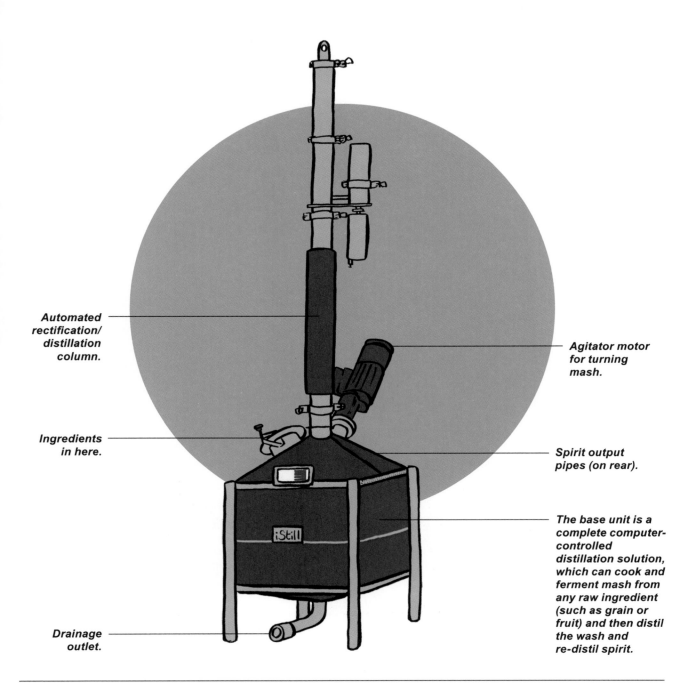

Automated rectification/ distillation column.

Agitator motor for turning mash.

Ingredients in here.

Spirit output pipes (on rear).

The base unit is a complete computer-controlled distillation solution, which can cook and ferment mash from any raw ingredient (such as grain or fruit) and then distil the wash and re-distil spirit.

Drainage outlet.

iStill

ROTOVAP/ROTAVAP OR ROTARY EVAPORATOR

This miniature still was originally designed for use on the desktops of laboratories for scientific testing, but became increasingly popular in the production of spirits about a decade ago for distilling on a small scale. These stills operate on a vacuum principle whereby the atmospheric pressure within the vacuum is reduced, which enables the spirit in the vacuum to distil at a much lower temperature than under normal atmospheric conditions. This is particularly useful for distilling delicate botanicals that would become tainted or "cooked" at high temperatures. The still has a glass flask in which a high-strength base spirit is placed along with the botanicals, often one at a time in gin production.

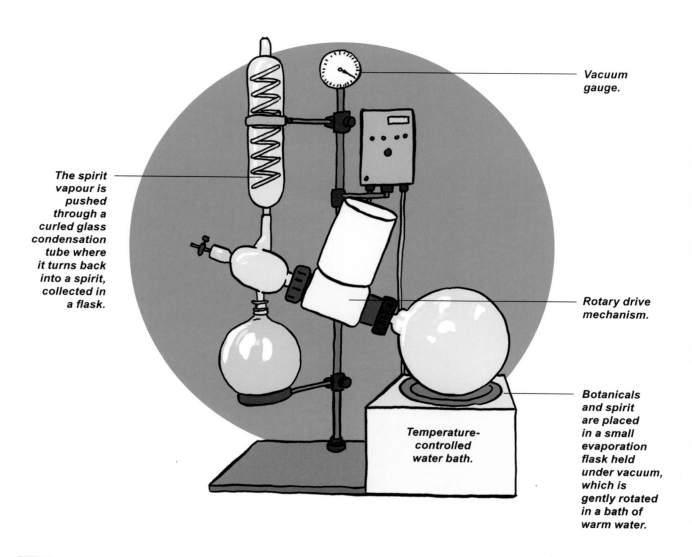

Vacuum gauge.

The spirit vapour is pushed through a curled glass condensation tube where it turns back into a spirit, collected in a flask.

Rotary drive mechanism.

Botanicals and spirit are placed in a small evaporation flask held under vacuum, which is gently rotated in a bath of warm water.

Temperature-controlled water bath.

Rotovap

Rare Stills

There are a few examples of old, specialized stills in use today. Hendrick's, for instance, employs an original Bennett still (*see* page 79), built in 1860 by Bennett, Sons & Shears, which produces a very robust, high-strength gin spirit. This is thanks to its spherical copper pot shape, with a pronounced copper bulb beneath the neck of the still, which allows a high degree of copper contact.

The Florentine is another rare type of still with a peculiar design: a copper ball atop a squat cylindrical structure that is connected to a copper neck pipe. The copper ball aids spirit "reflux", whereby the spirit vapours are forced to work harder to escape the still – they hit the ball and condense into a liquid before running back down into the pot still – resulting in a more intense flavour.

OTHER TYPES OF STILL

These include:

Lomond Still

The distiller is able to add or remove plates within the still to create different styles and strengths of spirit.

Genio

Developed in Poland and similar in concept to the iStill (*see* page 27), this new type of still is computer controlled and offers a more precise, analytical approach to distillation, designed to maximize efficiency, speed, size and spirit purity.

STEAM HEATING VERSUS DIRECT FIRING

Stills are generally steam heated nowadays for distilling, as it maximizes efficiency and ensures a consistent temperature, as well as being a safer way to distil. Only a few distillers use the traditional method of direct firing (*see* GINSTR, page 104), because it is more difficult to control and maintain the temperature of the distillation process, and carries a far greater degree of risk, given the flammability of alcohol.

Stills come in all sizes, from small desktop-style stills to much larger stills that can hold thousands of litres.

ONE/SINGLE-SHOT AND MULTI-SHOT PROCESSES

In the one- or single-shot process of distilling gin, the proportions of botanicals and neutral spirit are balanced to create a distillate that can either be directly bottled or cut with water before bottling. In the multi-shot process, on the other hand, the ratio of botanicals to base spirit is increased, resulting in a concentrated, high-strength "gin cordial" that is then cut with neutral spirit and water before bottling. Therefore, a single run from a multi-shot distillation will produce more bottles than a one-shot distillation.

CHILL FILTRATION

Some gins undergo this process in order to remove certain fatty compounds (lipids) that cause gin to turn cloudy when exposed to cold temperatures. There are, however, some distillers who claim that these compounds give additional flavour to the gin and so are keen to retain them.

GIN PRODUCTION: THE IMPACT ON TASTE

SO YOU WANT TO MAKE A GIN?

The first step is to devise a recipe for your gin, from what base spirit to use to which combination of botanicals to select.

Next, there are three routes to choose from:

1 The simplest option is to buy some neutral alcohol (e.g. vodka) as your base spirit and steep or infuse your botanicals in the spirit. Strain and bottle the resulting liquid and you have what is called a compound gin (see page 18).

2 If you want to create a distilled gin, the easiest way is to find a producer who can make and bottle it for you, at what is known as a contract distillery such as Thames Distillers (see page 67).

3 The remaining option is to buy and set up your own still and obtain a licence to distil.

If you go down route 3, you need to either make your own base spirit or buy in a base spirit from a distillery.

Once you have your base spirit, you can move on to redistilling it with your selected botanicals.

You can either add your botanicals to the spirit just before distillation or leave them to macerate (steep) in the alcohol for a period of time before distilling, or hang the botanicals in a basket in the neck of the still for the vapours to pass through during distillation, or a combination of both.

You can opt for a one/single-shot process, where a given quantity of base spirit is distilled with the chosen proportion of botanicals as per your original recipe, or a multi-shot process, where the ratio of botanicals to base spirit is increased to make a concentrated botanical distillate.

Post-distillation, you can choose to flavour your gin with botanical essences if you wish.

Finally, if you have gone for one-shot production, dilute your distillate with water to your chosen bottling strength, or in the case of the multi-shot process, add neutral spirit and water to rebalance the botanical proportion before bottling.

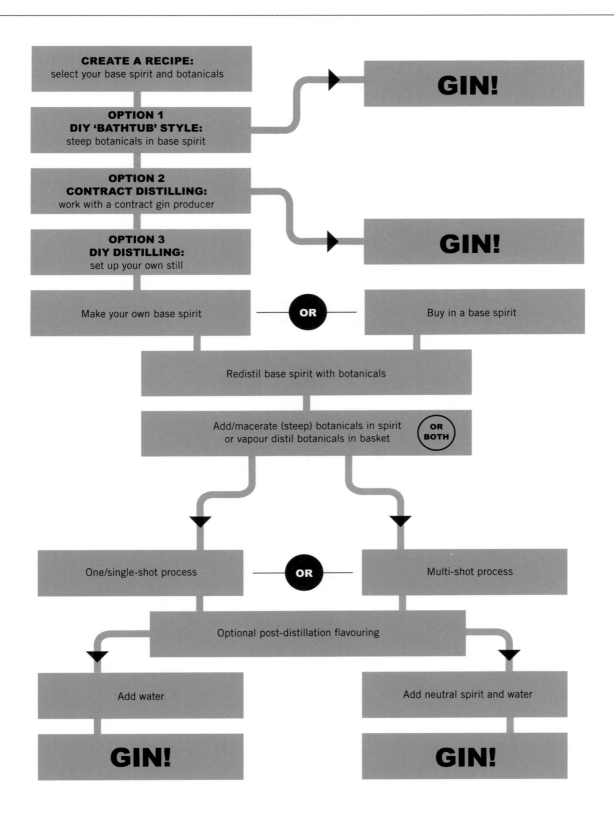

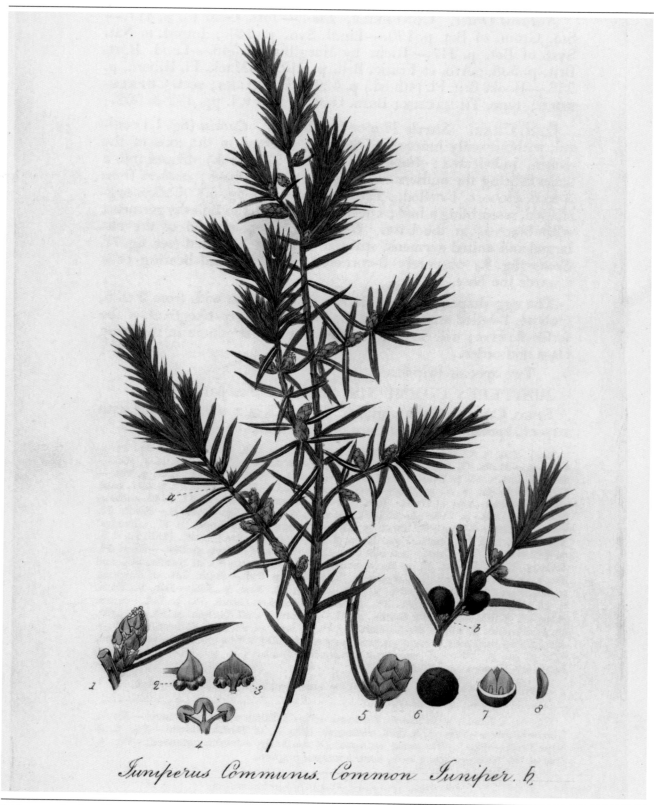

Juniperus Communis. Common Juniper. ♄

⬤ *Common juniper illustration*

JUNIPER:
THE AROMATIC HEART OF EVERY GIN

With its heady mix of botanical aromas and flavours, gin is without doubt one of the most highly complex spirits in the world. In fact, as we will explore over these pages in greater detail, obtaining such a balancing act of assertive botanical characteristics is the key to creating an enduring, unique and above all delicious gin recipe.

At the heart of every gin, though, there is one botanical whose name needs little introduction to anyone who has ever enjoyed a gin. But what is juniper exactly and just how have distillers and consumers come to covet this tiny pearl of flavour so much?

Common juniper or *Juniperus communis* is, as its name indicates, the most commonly found and used culinary species of juniper, growing widely in the Northern Hemisphere in as diverse climatic conditions as the Arctic, the mountains of North America and the warmer climate of Southern Europe. It is a hardy evergreen whose prickly green thorns have done little to deter those in pursuit of the unique aroma and flavour of its tiny dark "berries"– actually small, deceptively fleshly "cones" that bear a resemblance to embryonic pine cones – down the centuries. It is, however, estimated that there are as many as 67 different *Juniperus* species, part of the cypress or Cupressaceae family, found growing globally, including *Juniperus californica*, *Juniperus deppeana* and *Juniperus phoenicea*.

THE CULTIVATION OF JUNIPER

The juniper plant can take on various guises and sizes: from rambling, twisted trees growing up to 16m (52ft) in height, through to the more commonly occurring low-lying shrubs, which thrive in colder, barren areas of scrubland. The plant doesn't take well to artificial cultivation and as a result it is rarely "farmed", meaning that juniper harvesters will scour and forage many locations to find the best wild crops to monitor. The berries take around 18 months to fully mature from hard green buds into the ripe stock that a distiller is looking for: plump but firm and purple in colour, with a slightly wrinkled, leathery outer skin. Underneath this skin is an oily, fleshy interior peppered with small, triangular seeds. Harvest time of the more common varieties depends largely on the specific climate of the location, but usually takes place between September and January.

● *Early juniper harvest*

SPECIES OF JUNIPER AND TERROIR

The most well-known sources of *Juniperus communis* are in Italy, Macedonia, Albania, Kosovo, Serbia and Croatia. One UK-based distiller and retailer, Master of Malt, has highlighted the nuances in flavour arising from the different terroir of juniper in a series of single-botanical gins called Origins, each using juniper alone and from one location only.

Similarly, a number of craft distillers are turning to more uncommon, local species of juniper, such as the western juniper *Juniperus occidentalis* native to the Western United States, including Cascade Alchemy Oregon Gin (*see* page 175), Massachusetts's Berkshire Mountain (*see* page 158), Bully Boy near Boston (*see* page 158) and Ironworks Gin in Canada's Nova Scotia (*see* page 185), which are all exploring whether terroir has a significant impact on the resulting gin. The Pacific Northwest is now a region rich in *Juniperus occidentalis*, but also the Rocky Mountain juniper *Juniperus scopulorum*, mainly found in the drier, more inland mountainous areas, and *Juniperus maritima*, which thrives in coastal environments. In addition, Death's Door Distilling in Wisconsin (*see* page 162) harvests a species of wild juniper from Washington Island called *Juniperus virginiana*, showcasing it in a simple three-botanical gin recipe. However, the District Distilling Co. in Washington, DC (*see* page 158) has taken this development once step further by working with a juniper foraging expert and using even more unusual indigenous species such as wild redberry juniper, *Juniperus pinchotii*, and checkerbark or alligator juniper, *Juniperus deppeana*, to delve deeply into the botanical's subtle, diverse characteristics.

In Japan, the concept of using domestic juniper is also beginning to take off, with the Sakurao Distillery in Hiroshima (*see* page 233) being one of the first in the country to use juniper native to the southern region in its gin. Similarly, in India, the Goan distillery NÄO Spirits (*see* page 241) has gone to great lengths to source Himalayan juniper, *Juniperus recurva*, for its brand Hapusa, Sanskrit for "juniper". In Mallorca, Gin EVA features locally grown coastal juniper (*see* page 118), while the Moorland Spirit Co. in the north of England (*see* page 74) and Scotland's Arbikie distillery (*see* page 83) are actively propagating juniper in a bid to regenerate local species.

HARVESTING JUNIPER

Harvesting juniper berries is almost entirely done by hand and is perhaps one of the most skilful, labour-intensive aspects of the gin-making process. The reason for this is the particular way the berries develop on the plant. Two years' worth of harvest will be growing on

Juniper harvest

the same bush, which means that the branches cannot simply be cut off and the ripe berries extracted. Instead, the bushes are beaten with sticks, releasing those that are ready and enabling the rest still growing to safely stay on the plant until the following year. As many harvesters work independently, they then supply juniper cooperatives that deal with suppliers or international spice suppliers directly. Once harvested, the berries are processed to remove any extraneous twigs or thorns, then graded by colour and size before being dried. This latter aspect of production is hugely important, as the berries must not be allowed to dry out entirely, but just enough to remove any surface moisture that would result in them rotting in transit. Fortunately, the skin of a juniper berry is thick, enabling its oily core to remain intact on the journey between the cold of the outdoors and the warmth of the distillery.

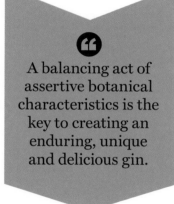

A balancing act of assertive botanical characteristics is the key to creating an enduring, unique and delicious gin.

Wild juniper in the USA

○ *Grading different styles of juniper in Europe*

THE PROPERTIES AND QUALITY OF JUNIPER

The aroma of juniper shares certain similarities with the fruit and resin of the pine family. However, its peppery, musky/herbaceous note is truly distinct and derives from the oily heart of each berry. The oil content can vary from location to location (*see* page 34), but it is generally believed that juniper grown in warmer climes, particularly in Italy and other Southern European countries, yields a higher oil content. It is this that the distiller is looking for, leading to a greater concentration of aroma and flavour once it is incorporated into the recipe of a specific gin.

Large-scale distillers, such as UK-based Beefeater (*see* page 63), G&J Distillers (*see* page 75), Thames Distillers (*see* page 67) and Scotland's Cameronbridge Distillery (*see* page 82) and Spanish gin giants Larios (*see* page 116) will use vast amounts of juniper in the annual out-turn of each gin – in the case of Beefeater, as much as 50 tonnes/tons (55 US tons) every year.

This gives head distillers such as Desmond Payne MBE (*see* page 63) a challenge to create a consistent balance of the specific properties he is looking for in the juniper that will finally enter the stills. His team typically spend one day a year examining 100–200 samples of juniper from various locations across Southern Europe to construct the juniper blueprint for Beefeater.

WHAT IS THE DISTILLER LOOKING FOR?

As with every gin, each recipe possesses a unique botanical DNA. Similarly, each distiller will be looking for something slightly different from their juniper, so it is probably easier to point to what are the undesirable characteristics of juniper. Most distillers will avoid an overly oily/almost petrol-like and turpentine aroma, alongside typically overripe fruit notes such as those found in mango and pineapple. (For a more detailed breakdown of the aromatic characteristics of the juniper berry, *see* the aroma map on page 45.)

First, the individual samples of berries are crushed between the fingers and sniffed to assess the overall quality of the sample. Next, the oil is extracted through small-scale lab distillation, which is then added to a measure of neutral alcohol as a compound to see how the oil will effectively translate into the final gin recipe. It is only after this "big sniff" that the agreed quantity can be ordered from the supplier.

THE MEDICINAL QUALITIES OF JUNIPER

Throughout history, juniper has been considered a remarkably valuable botanical, possessing a range of medicinal properties, and is still regarded as worthy of therapeutic use today to treat various complaints, especially in homeopathy. It was claimed that juniper was used as far back as 1500 BC to treat ailments such as tapeworm infection. Documents dating from 1055 reveal that Italian Benedictine monks were exploring juniper-infused tonics and ferments for their health benefits. From here, the art of distillation would have been widely practised across monasteries in Europe, with aqua vitae often infused with various locally sourced herbs, including juniper, to ward off various ailments.

It is likely that spice traders would have been picking up juniper on their travels throughout Europe to trade at port cities, such as Rotterdam in the 16th and 17th centuries, whence it made its way into the UK, particularly for its highly valued medicinal qualities. Indeed, around the time of the Great Plague of London (1665–6), the Royal College of Physicians suggested steeping juniper berries in vinegar and inhaling the resulting aromas as a preventative medicine.

The final word must go to physician Nicholas Culpeper (1616–54), described by Dr Johnson as "the man that first ranged the woods and climbed the mountains in search of medicinal and salutary herbs...", which rather aptly sums up the truly significant attraction of the humble juniper berry. In his *Complete Herbal and English Physician*, first published in 1653, Culpeper writes of juniper: "This admirable solar shrub is scarce to be paralleled for its virtues... being a most admirable counter-poison, and as great a resister of the pestilence

as any grows; they are also excellent good against the bitings of venomous beasts...". He explains how juniper is a wonderful diuretic, strengthener of the stomach and wind expellant, besides proving an effective remedy for coughs, constipation, colic, cramps and convulsions. A cure-all indeed!

Each distiller will be looking for something slightly different from their juniper.

MAP OF THE PRINCIPAL JUNIPER-GROWING COUNTRIES

Juniper is a remarkably hardy botanical plant, which can be cultivated all over the world, with an estimated 67 species growing abundantly in the wild in a multitude of different climates. The widely accepted heartland is Central–Eastern Europe, which exports the majority of juniper berries to distillers as far afield as the USA and Australia. The map below details some of the key growing locations, as well as a few notable varieties that grow wild.

JUNIPER-GROWING REGION

- Main countries which supply juniper
- Secondary countries

BOTANICALS:
THE DISTINCT DNA OF EVERY GIN

To earn the title of gin, the requirement of every distiller is to ensure that the product they make has the predominant flavour of juniper. So using juniper as the lone botanical element still secures the gin classification, and there are numerous examples on the market that take this "naked" approach. However, the regulations are fairly inexact as to the interpretation of "predominant flavour", and at the time of writing, no scientific testing is necessary to prove otherwise.

But where would gin be without the enormous array of other complex flavours and aromas that give the spirit its unique character? One way is to think of gin as an orchestra: the juniper is the star performer, the soloist or the conductor that provides the lead for all the other players. The rest of the botanicals are there to provide the dynamics; the light and shade that support the central flavour, enhancing the character and complexity of the spirit but never overstepping the mark and becoming too dominant.

Almost mirroring the history of gin's travels around the world, the range of different botanicals used in gin today has largely come about as a consequence of the overseas spice trade into Europe, particularly via the ports of Amsterdam, Rotterdam, La Rochelle and southern England, when both the Dutch and British East India Company of the early 1600s had a virtual monopoly on the ocean-going trade. Since spices, sweeteners and other botanicals masked the harsh taste of the early gin and genever spirits, more elaborate recipes began to take shape during the 18th and 19th centuries, leading us to the present day where certain botanicals used in the majority of gin recipes have become almost indispensable "classics" in the arsenal of the distiller.

TYPES OF BOTANICAL
The broad yet subtle spectrum of flavour found in gin comes from a carefully composed balanced recipe of key groups: earthy, bitter and dry; sweet and fruity; spicy and savoury; citrusy and floral. Each botanical plays its individual part when its characteristic essential oils or flavour compounds are extracted through the maceration and distillation process (*see* page 22). Sometimes these elements are profound and distinct, providing a foundation and support for the juniper to take its central role, while some serve to bring out complementary flavours, building character and body, whereas others are there to provide lighter top notes. Distillers are often looking for a perfect core blend, house style or DNA on which they can then build other recipes to highlight the versatility of their gins. In other cases, distillers are seeking to make bolder, more extreme statements and will skew a recipe in a certain direction, such as citrus led, for a distinctive, memorable gin expression.

JUNIPER AROMA AND FLAVOUR DIAGRAM

Finding the right balance of flavour from juniper is the key to consistency and quality. With gin being so heavily focused on this distinctive botanical, distillers pay much attention to assessing their batches of the berries for specific taste and aroma notes, which can be as diverse as woody through to a more fruity and floral character. This diagram below illustrates the subtle variations and combinations in aroma and flavour that can be found in each individual batch of berries.

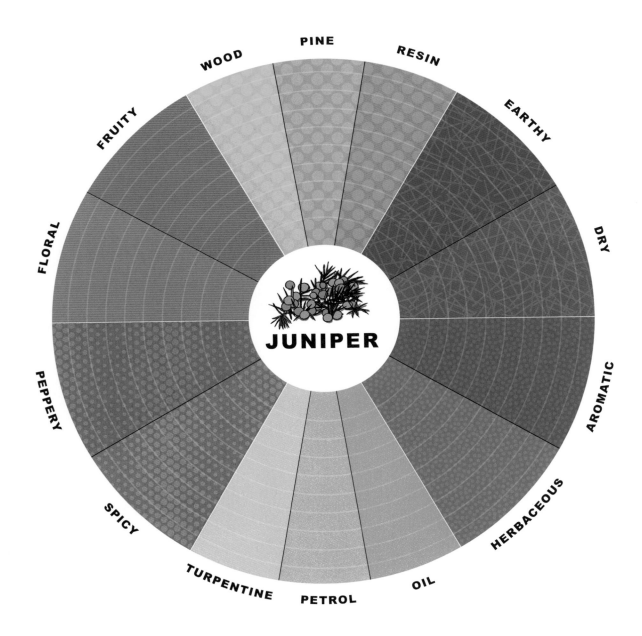

CLASSIC BOTANICALS

In addition to the all-important juniper, the following are generally considered to be the classic gin botanicals, providing the backbone to a vast number of gin recipes around the world.

The botanicals provide the dynamics; the light and shade that support the central flavour.

GRAINS OF PARADISE
(*Aframomum melegueta*)
Origin: West Africa and Ethiopia
Characteristic: Peppery, piquant and menthol notes.

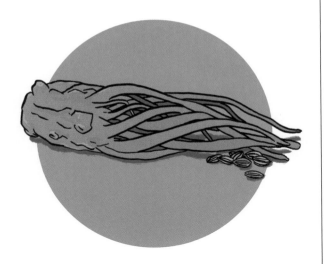

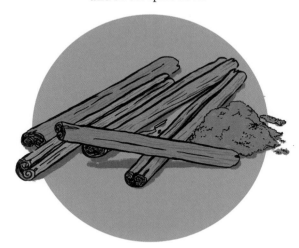

CINNAMON
(*Cinnamomum*)
Origin: China, Sri Lanka
and Indonesia
Characteristic: Warming, woody
and sweet spice notes

ANGELICA SEEDS AND ROOT
(*Angelica archangelica*)
Origin: Belgium and Saxony
Characteristic: Woody, musky
aroma and flavour; provide the
foundation for a botanical recipe.

LIME PEEL
(*Citrus latifolia*)
Origin: Mexico and Iran
Characteristic: Fresh, green,
zesty, tart notes.

CASSIA BARK
(*Cinnamomum cassia*)
Origin: Southern China and
Eastern Asia
Characteristic: Aromatic bark
that contributes woody, dry notes.

LEMON PEEL
(*Citrus limonum*)
Origin: Southern Spain
and Turkey
Characteristic: Tangy, zesty, tart,
fresh notes.

GRAPEFRUIT PEEL
(*Citrus paradisi*)
Origin: China, USA, Mexico
and Spain
Characteristic: Fragrant, tangy,
zesty perfumed, fresh notes.

ORANGE PEEL
(*Citrus sinensis – sweet; Citrus
aurantium – bitter*)
Origin: Spain, North America
and Turkey
Characteristic: Tangy, fresh, zesty,
fruity, sweet/tart, drying bitter notes.

CORIANDER SEEDS AND LEAF
(*Coriandrum sativum*)
Origin: Eastern Europe and India
Characteristic: Fragrant, citrus,
aromatic and spicy.

BOTANICAL FLAVOUR MAP

The wide variety of botanicals used in the recipe of a gin can be bewildering, but the Flavour Map below, developed by the authors and Desmond Payne MBE, master distiller for Beefeater, helps to pinpoint the style and intensity of aroma and flavour of some key botanicals often found at the heart of many gin recipes.

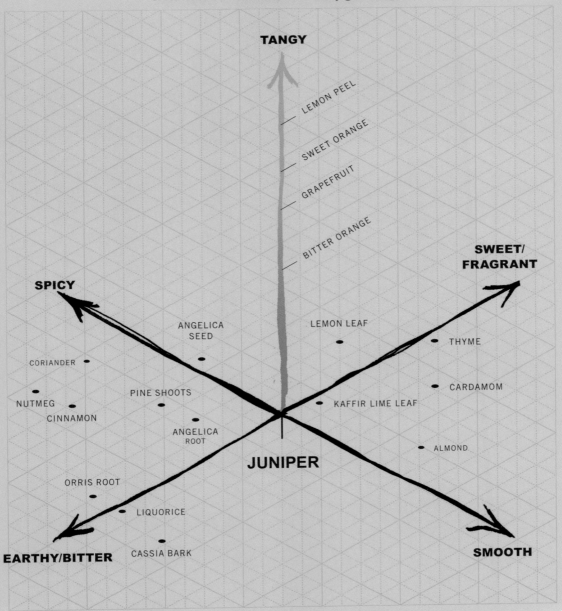

TANGY

LEMON PEEL
SWEET ORANGE
GRAPEFRUIT
BITTER ORANGE

SWEET/FRAGRANT

SPICY

ANGELICA SEED
LEMON LEAF
THYME
CORIANDER
CARDAMOM
NUTMEG
PINE SHOOTS
KAFFIR LIME LEAF
CINNAMON
ANGELICA ROOT
ALMOND

JUNIPER

ORRIS ROOT
LIQUORICE
SMOOTH
EARTHY/BITTER
CASSIA BARK

CARDAMOM
(*Elletaria cardamomum*)
Origin: Southern India, Sri Lanka
Characteristic: Perfumed, aromatic spice and menthol/eucalyptus notes.

LIQUORICE ROOT
(*Glycyrrhiza glabra*)
Origin: China, Turkey and Middle East
Characteristic: Earthy, aromatic and sweet flavour.

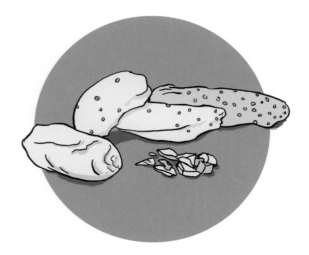

BAY LEAF
(*Laurus nobilis*)
Origin: Mediterranean and California
Characteristic: Sharp, bitter, eucalyptus notes.

ORRIS ROOT
(*Iris florentina*)
Origin: Italy and Morocco
Characteristic: Dry, bitter flavour and slightly perfumed aroma. Binds botanical recipes together.

NUTMEG
(*Myristica fragrans*)
Origin: Indonesia and South East Asia
Characteristic: Warmth, menthol, medicinal flavour; spicy and pungent aroma.

CUBEB BERRIES
(*Piper cubeba*)
Origin: Indonesia, Java and Sumatra
Characteristic: Dry, spicy, piquant pepper notes.

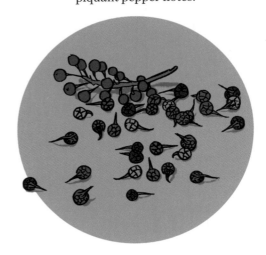

ALMOND
(*Prunus dulcis*)
Origin: California, Spain, Australia and Iran
Characteristic: Bittersweet; adds smoothness and viscosity.

Key groups: earthy, bitter and dry; sweet and fruity; spicy and savoury; citrusy and floral.

CLOVE
(*Syzygium aromaticum*)
Origin: South East Asia
Characteristic: Bold, aromatic
herbal, menthol spice.

GINGER ROOT
(*Zingiber officinale*)
Origin: India, China, Nigeria
and Indonesia
Characteristics: Warming, sweet
spice with piquant flavour.

BASE SPIRITS:
AN ADDITIONAL SOURCE OF FLAVOUR?

The base spirit of a gin has become a particularly hot topic internationally in recent years, with more distillers, especially in North America, adopting a field-to-glass approach where instead of using a bought-in, completely neutral, flavourless high-strength spirit (190° proof in the USA; 96% ABV in the EU), they choose to distil their base spirits to a slightly lower strength, often only a single degree or two less. The difference might sound slight and inconsequential, but distillers will tell you that more of the spirit base character, be it sugar, grapes, fruit, potato or grain (wheat, rye or corn) and so on, comes through in the flavour, aroma and texture of the spirit, which will ultimately have a significant impact on the resulting gin.

CITRUS FRESH OR DRIED?

When it comes to citrus fruit, the amount of essential oil within the peel is key to how it reacts within a botanical recipe. Some distillers prefer using pre-dried, chopped peels, which, when macerated in alcohol, distilled directly or vapour infused (*see* page 22), will release a more consistent result in the end product. Fresh peels contain more essential oils and are often brought in as whole fruits, before being hand peeled to preserve the fragrant, vibrant zing they give to the gin. As a result, the emphasis is on the quality of the fruit as to how much a distiller should use in a particular batch of gin.

> **"**
> Hand-foraging
> botanicals has
> become a natural
> way to distinguish
> gins from their
> competitors.

OTHER BOTANICALS

The list of botanicals used in modern gins is exhaustive, with smaller craft distillers during the last decade looking far beyond the aforementioned classics to create styles that reflect the location of the distillery, a historical style or culinary movement. Hand-foraging botanicals has become a natural way to distinguish gins from their competitors and give a sense of transparency and regionality to the recipe.

FLORAL ELEMENTS
Rose petals, lavender, elderflower, chamomile, vanilla pods and bergamot are commonly used to add perfumed top notes to a gin. Examples include Warner Distillery's Elderflower Gin (see page 70), Nolet's Silver Dry Gin from Holland (see page 97) and Northern Ireland's Shortcross Gin (see page 91.)

HERBACEOUS ELEMENTS
Olives, rosemary, celery, fennel, thyme, pine needles, spruce tips and hops develop distinct savoury, herbaceous notes in a gin. Notable examples here include Spain's Gin Mare (see page 15), Japan's Kozue Gin (see page 233), Canada's Phillips Fermentorium STUMP Coastal Forest Gin (see page 184), Wales's Dyfi (see page 84), Denmark's Nordisk Gin (see page 131), Oregon's Rogue Spirits Spruce Gin (see page 176), California's St. George Gin (see page 169) and Holland's Rutte Celery Gin (see page 99).

SPICY/WARMING ELEMENTS
Because the actual "heat" from a chilli pepper is not a distillable characteristic, some distillers substitute the piquant bite with others such as allspice or black cardamom (a more pungent, smoky variety than green cardamom), or dial up the individual spice elements, such as star anise and clove. Peddlers Gin from China (see page 235), Opihr Oriental Spiced Gin, produced by G&J Distillers (see page 75), Jaisalmer Indian Craft Gin (see page 241), Brass Lion Singapore Dry Gin (see page 242) Pink Pepper Gin (see page 112) and Mexico's Pierde Almas (see page 190) are all warming, spice-laden gins.

CITRUS-HEAVY ELEMENTS
A number of New Western-style distillers (see Essential Terms, page 249) are producing gins that use citrus fruits, some of which are very unusual, seasonal or indigenous to one location, such as Buddha's hand, finger lime, yuzu peel and amanatsu, as the core botanical, often sharing joint limelight or effectively putting the juniper slightly in the shade, but very tangy and fresh on the palate. Examples include Japan's Nikka Coffey Gin (see page 232), Italy's Malfy Gin (see page 121), Wheadon's Gin from Guernsey (see page 77) and US Ironroot Texas Drought Gin (see page 167).

EXOTIC AND FRUITY ELEMENTS
There are some incredible fruit-infused gins or gins distilled with fruit, such as Ferdinand's Saar Dry Gin from Germany using sloes (see page 105), Australia's Four Pillars Bloody Shiraz Gin using grapes (see page 217), Portugal's Sharish Blue Magic Gin using apples (see page 119) and Eau Claire Distillery's Saskatoon berry-infused Parlour Gin from Canada (see page 185). Other examples display distinct fruity elements from the base spirit, including Thailand's Iron Balls Gin using pineapples (see page 245) and Israel's Pelter Winery gin distilled from Pink Lady apples (see page 203).

SALINE AND SMOKY ELEMENTS
Some distillers have looked to the sea in search of unusual botanicals, which result in almost salty/briny qualities, such as Cornwall's Curio Wild Coast Gin (see page 74), Canada's St. Laurent Gin with laminaria seaweed (kombu) (see page 182), Scotland's Isle of Harris Gin that has sugar kelp in the recipe (see page 82), while others pursue a distinctly smoky note including Sweden's Hernö Gin using ex-whisky casks (see page 82) and Estonia's Flavorwood Smoky Gin, smoking the botanicals pre-distillation (see page 139).

◉ *Gin, direct from the still, carries a high viscosity*

HOW TO TASTE GIN

As with any spirit, spending a little time finding the right glassware to unlock the complex balance of flavours in a gin is a rewarding experience. Until recently, exploring a gin neat without the addition of a mixer, water or ice has mainly been the domain of professional assessment, but given the huge range of styles and botanical recipes now available, it is something that can be undertaken very easily at home.

To get the most out of the gin you are tasting, it is important to consider the following points.

> Spend a little time finding the right glassware to unlock the complex balance of flavours.

GLASSWARE

To enjoy a great Gin and Tonic, choose a highball glass or large bulbous stemmed glass, which will provide the gin with the ideal environment to interact with the tonic, ice and garnish. However, for a true assessment of the spirit, it is worth purchasing a small tulip-shaped glass, often referred to as a nosing glass, which is wider at the base with tall, tapering sides that narrow to a small diameter top, helping to concentrate the aromas of the gin.

THE TASTING PROCESS

Add a measure of gin to your nosing glass and give it a quick swirl. The spirit will form a ring around the sides and then begin to roll back down, forming "tears", or "legs" as they are also known. This will give you an indication of the gin's viscosity: do they run back down quickly and dissipate, indicating a finer viscosity, or do they move slowly, suggesting a more oily spirit?

Check the ABV of the gin on the label. In Europe, gin cannot be bottled under 37.5% ABV, or less than 40% ABV in the USA, and there are now a number of gins that are bottled at a much higher ABV, including navy-strength varieties (typically 57% ABV). Gin with a higher ABV will deliver a more intense flavour. When assessing higher-strength gin, it is worth having a small sip first, then adding a small splash of water to reduce the strength to a more palatable level.

Professional spirits tasters look for three particular elements when assessing a spirit for the first time: the nose (aroma), the palate (taste) and the finish (the length of time the flavour of the spirit lingers and evolves in the mouth once it has been swallowed). Occasionally, the colour of a gin is examined: a slight tint may reveal that the gin is compounded or macerated (*see* page 18) or that it has been aged in wood, taking on additional character and colour (*see* page 21).

The Nose

Try to place your nose at the very top of the inside of the glass – the 12 o'clock position – and take a long sniff. Then repeat at the bottom of the inside of the glass – the 6 o'clock position. The aroma intensity will be different, with more delicate aromas at the top and heavier, more alcoholic/spiritous notes at the bottom, so it is worth moving your nose around as much as possible to get a full picture of the aroma. A well-balanced gin will give an immediate note of juniper, often a herbaceous, pine/resinous aroma first, which should then be perfectly counterbalanced by other aromas – drier, spicy notes, softer floral notes and sharper, zesty aromas. A true London Dry-style gin should always centre on a juniper-forward note, while other gin styles may pair the juniper aroma with another dominant botanical (*see* page 42).

The Palate

As mentioned earlier, look at the strength of the gin first before diving straight in. Take a small sip and try to coat the whole of your mouth in the gin for a few seconds before swallowing. Again, look for a well-balanced flavour: the herbaceous, piney juniper should take the lead role, supported by spices, floral notes and zesty flavours. In the case of Old Tom gin (*see* page 21), additional sweetener will have been added, but a quality, well-balanced example shouldn't be too cloying or overly sweet, still allowing the botanicals to shine through.

The Finish

After you have swallowed the gin, how long does the flavour linger in the mouth, and which flavours remain? Another indication of a well-balanced recipe is a resulting echo of all the key botanicals: dry, piney juniper, subtle spice, perhaps some hot/peppery notes and a tangy zestiness.

CREATING THE PERFECT GIN AND TONIC

While arguably there is no right or wrong way to make a Gin and Tonic, there are unquestionably some ways to enhance the experience and bring out the best in the gins in your collection. Here are our top tips:

Chill your glass first. Although a highball glass is the classic vessel for a great Gin and Tonic, using a large, thin-stemmed balloon glass straight from the freezer gives the drink a wonderful frosted appearance.

Use plenty of good-quality ice. The quality and quantity of ice will determine how your drink dilutes and whether it remains enjoyable down to the last sip. Try to use large, solid cubes of ice made from filtered water, which will have a greater clarity to them and fewer impurities that may impair the flavour of your drink as it dilutes. The larger the cubes, the more chilling effect they will

◔ *Nosing*

◔ *Tasting*

◔ *Checking for impurities*

have and the longer they will take to melt and dilute the drink. It is also worth exploring with a single very large chunk of ice that can be carved from a big block of ice. There are companies that now offer delivery of perfectly clear blocks of ice to give any drink that professional bartender quality.

Know your gin choice. Using 50–60ml (around 1¾–2oz) of a 57% ABV (114° proof) gin is going to have a profoundly different result from a regular-strength gin, so adjust your recipe accordingly. Our favoured ratio of gin to tonic is 1:3 using a gin of around 40–43% ABV, and this guideline can be adapted for different gin strengths or styles.

Try the tonic before using it. With such a wealth of tonic waters now available in a variety of flavour styles and levels of sweetness, it is always worth sampling it first to give you an idea of how much or how little to use. The best tonics should always have an underlying dry, bitter note and a well-balanced, natural sweetness, along with plenty of carbonation. Fever-Tree, Franklin & Sons, Double Dutch, Fentimans, Thomas Henry, Three Cents, 1724 and Merchant's Heart are all highly reputable brands to explore. The most important point here is to choose smaller-sized glass bottles or cans of tonic as opposed to larger plastic bottles, which lose their carbonation almost immediately after they are opened.

◔ *Lime or lemon? The classic Gin and Tonic*

Mixing and garnishing. With your tonic poured over the gin and ice, slowly stir and "lift" the gin within the glass so that it is evenly distributed. Matching the garnish to the gin is important, as the aroma of the garnish can quite easily overpower the elements in the gin that you don't want to overlook. Classic recipes work well with either a wedge of lime or lemon; our preference is lemon. Either way, avoid squeezing it into the glass – its purpose is to contribute an additional uplift of citrus aroma and create a more appealing aesthetic, rather than introducing sourness from the juice. A quality gin should have a perfect citrus balance already. Also try using a thin strip of citrus peel instead of a whole wedge, with as much of the white pith removed as possible, as this can add unwanted bitterness to a drink. Drier, more savoury gins (Gin Mare, page 115, for example) work well with herbaceous garnishes such as a sprig of rosemary or thyme or even an olive. More floral gins tend to work with lighter, fragrant garnishes like cucumber, basil, grapefruit or freshly sliced green or pink apple. Some bartenders favour adding dry botanicals to the glass, such as juniper berries, star anise, cardamom pods or cinnamon. Just be aware that the longer they sit in the drink, the more additional flavour they impart to it, altering the botanical balance of the actual gin.

◔ *Double Dutch tonic waters push the boundaries of flavour*

AN ATLAS OF GIN COCKTAILS

INDIA

Gin and Tonic
This quintessential long drink was developed by the British in India during the late 1800s when tonic water was heavily laced with quinine, a bitter-tasting extract from the South American cinchona tree believed to both cure and prevent malaria. But when mixed with gin, sweeteners, ice and a slice of citrus, it made a palatable drink and became a classic cocktail.

ITALY

Negroni
A simple mix of equal parts gin, Campari and sweet vermouth, served over ice with a wedge of orange, this drink was reputedly first ordered by Count Negroni at Caffè Casoni in Florence, Italy, in 1919.

USA

Martini
The origins of this iconic gin and dry vermouth drink are uncertain, but the legendary bartender "The Professor" Jerry Thomas included a recipe for the Martinez cocktail in his cocktail book *The Bar-Tenders Guide* of 1887, attributed to his residency at San Francisco's Occidental Hotel. Thomas was also the first person to write about the Tom Collins.

UK

Vesper Martini
Created by James Bond author Ian Fleming, this cocktail featured in his 1953 book *Casino Royale* where 007 asks for a drink with three measures of gin, one of vodka and half a measure of French dry vermouth, such as Lillet. This was likely to have been invented at Fleming's regular drinking den, now the Dukes Hotel in London, where today Alessandro Palazzi makes one of the most famous gin Martinis in the world.

SINGAPORE

Singapore Sling
A mix of gin, cherry liqueur, triple sec, Bénédictine, pineapple and lime juices and some Angostura bitters, this long drink was developed in the early 1900s by Ngiam Tong Boon, a bartender working at the Long Bar in Raffles Hotel, Singapore.

FRANCE

French 75
Gin lengthened with Champagne and sweetened with sugar, plus lemon juice and a dash of bitters, the origins of this cocktail can be traced back to the early 1900s and the New York Bar (now Harry's New York Bar) in Paris.

GIN COCKTAILS
AROUND THE WORLD

French 75

Vesper Martini

Negroni

UK

FRANCE

USA

ITALY

INDIA

SINGAPORE

Martini

Gin and Tonic

Singapore Sling

PART 2

THE WORLD OF GIN

In this main section of the book, we explore the world of gin even further, covering every continent (except Antarctica) in as much detail as possible, unearthing sub-styles and categories, different techniques and unusual, exotic botanicals and base spirit ingredients across no fewer than 54 different countries.

With the incredible pace at which the world of gin is growing, it would have been an impossible task to make this a complete guide to every gin brand. The increasing number of contract gins has compounded the problem: specific customer brands made to bespoke specifications by larger distilleries (*see* Thames Distillers, page 67, for more on this). It was decided to omit this style of product from the Atlas (save for a few key brands) to give us room to focus on a diverse range of gins where an actual distillery could be identified – no matter how big or small – and a distinct style or array of local flavours showcased.

EUROPE

GREAT BRITAIN AND IRELAND

It is hard to imagine an atlas of gin that didn't begin with Great Britain, which has, in many respects, adopted the spirit as its national drink despite gin's historical roots in the Netherlands. Over the past decade, gin has undergone a complete reinvention in the British Isles. Once the domain of only a few major brands, the UK has become a craft distilling powerhouse, with The Gin Guild estimating at the time of writing that there are more than 600 gin brands and around 200 distilleries producing gin. And the renaissance of gin hasn't stopped at the Irish border, with the Irish craft distilling scene now growing at an equally impressive pace.

LONDON

The history of London and the origins of gin are intertwined, so much so that the premium style of gin – London Dry – even takes its name from the city. Yet until Sipsmith (*see* page 64) started distilling in 2009, there had been no new distilleries in London for nearly two hundred years. Today, however, there is a kaleidoscopic collection of distilleries making a huge variety of different styles of gin.

● *Beefeater 24, still made in London*

BEEFEATER

The Beefeater Gin Distillery could not be located in a more quintessentially British part of London. That is because the distillery boasts as its neighbour the home of Surrey Cricket Club and regular international cricket venue The Oval. From the rooftop of Beefeater, you can see over the stands and on to the square. What a place to enjoy a summertime Gin and Tonic, soundtracked by polite handclaps from spectators, supported by the thwack of leather on willow.

As for the distillery itself, its current home in Kennington, just south of the river but still very much in Central London, is not the original location for this iconic London gin. The key man in the history of Beefeater was James Burrough. A pharmacist by trade, in 1863 he purchased Chelsea-based John Taylor & Son who were well established in the world of gin and other mixable beverages. After Burrough's death in 1897, the growing business was taken over by his sons and moved south of the River Thames to Lambeth. The distillery's continued success and growth meant a third and final move to its current location.

Today, Beefeater Gin is presided over by a man who many consider to be the "godfather of gin", Desmond Payne MBE. Payne has been involved in gin for over 50 years and began his career in 1967 at Seager Evans & Co. Wine Merchants and Gin Distillers before spending a quarter of a century at Plymouth Gin (*see* page 72) and later, in 1995, moving to Beefeater.

The custodian of their classic London Dry Gin (juniper led, with Seville orange and lemon peels; bottled at 40% ABV), Payne was responsible for creating the super-premium Beefeater 24 (45% ABV), which draws on 12 hand-selected botanicals including Japanese sencha and Chinese green teas that are steeped for 24 hours before distillation. The core range from Beefeater also includes an oak-aged version, Burrough's Reserve (43% ABV), which is made on James Burrough's original 268-litre (71-US-gallon) copper pot still before being rested in Bordeaux wine casks.

Today, Beefeater boasts a new visitor centre for tastings and tours, as well as a shop that sells limited, distillery-only versions of the Beefeater Gin.
beefeatergin.com

SIPSMITH

London's love affair with gin runs deep, with a history that spans more than five hundred years. Yet between the mid-1900s and the turn of the century, the number of producers in Central London had dropped to just one: Beefeater (*see* page 63). And it was this opportunity to reignite slumbering spirits production in the capital that led to a group of friends setting up Sipsmith Distillery, the first copper pot still distillery to open in the city for 189 years. This decision kick-started the modern-day gin trend for "producer distillers".

Originally established by childhood friends Fairfax Hall and Sam Galsworthy, Sipsmith found a home in an old garage-cum-studio nestled between Victorian houses in a street in Hammersmith, West London. Here, in the former office of the late drinks writer Michael Jackson, which they later discovered also housed a small brewery, they installed Prudence, a copper pot still from Germany, and at the start of 2009 distilled the first drops of a new London gin.

With a prototype gin being honed, Hall and Galsworthy turned to acclaimed drinks writers and historians Jared Brown and Anistatia Miller for help in refining their product. Brown soon joined as master distiller and the recipe for their mainstay product, a classic London Dry gin, was born, delicately balancing classic juniper notes with a distinct floral sweetness and forward citrus notes. It all finishes off with a spicy, woody flurry.

By the end of 2014, demand for Sipsmith required the team to move their operations from the streets of Hammersmith to a venue more befitting their brand and growth – a new site in Chiswick, just a stone's throw from the iconic London brewery Fuller's.

⌾ *The founders of Sipsmith Gin*

Having already added a second still while in Hammersmith (Prudence was followed, fittingly, by Patience), the increased size of the new premises allowed the team to add another new still, Constance. Later, a smaller "baby" still, Cygnet, was commissioned.

⌾ *Sipsmith started the UK gin revolution*

Today, Sipsmith's core range consists of the classic London Dry Gin (41.6% ABV), which boasts ground almonds, lemon and orange peels, liquorice root and cinnamon bark as key flavour components, Lemon Drizzle Gin (40.4% ABV), with the addition of lemon verbena and vanilla pods adding a brightness to the flavour, Sloe Gin (29% ABV) and London Cup (29.5% ABV). Perhaps their most interesting product, however, is V.J.O.P. – Very Junipery Overproof Gin – which they describe as having taken the "lead instrument in an orchestra (juniper) and amplified its presence in the ensemble, then raised the decibels by increasing the proof alcohol". At 57.7% ABV it makes a mean Martini.

Keep an eye out for seasonal limited editions, such as a Christmas-released Mince Pie Gin (40% ABV) and their individual rose, lime or strawberries and cream summer syrups.
sipsmith.com

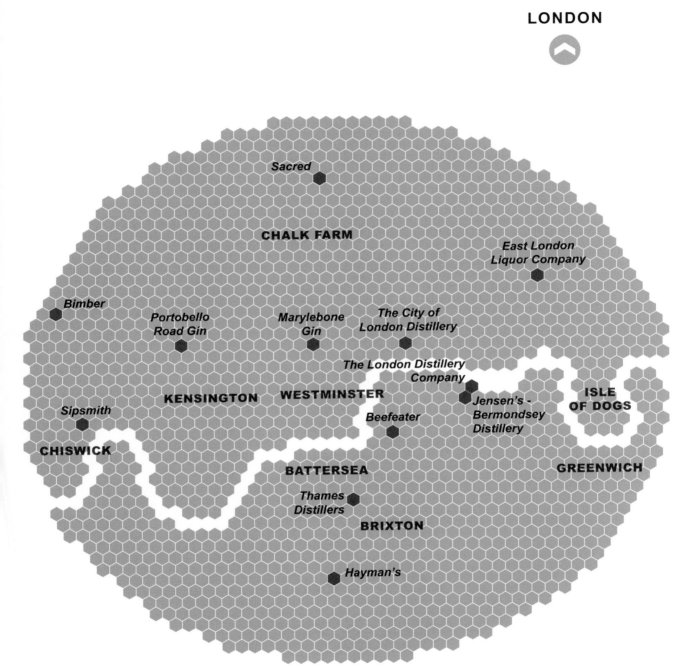

LONDON

Sacred

CHALK FARM

East London
Liquor Company

Bimber

Portobello
Road Gin

Marylebone
Gin

The City of
London Distillery

The London Distillery
Company

Sipsmith

KENSINGTON

WESTMINSTER

Jensen's -
Bermondsey
Distillery

ISLE
OF DOGS

Beefeater

CHISWICK

BATTERSEA

GREENWICH

Thames
Distillers

BRIXTON

Hayman's

EAST LONDON LIQUOR COMPANY

The East End of London may have had a fairly torrid gin history with its multitude of gin parlours profoundly limiting the life expectancy of its citizens in the 18th-century, but today it is in rude health, thanks to the ingenuity and dedication of a new breed of young distillers. Among them is the 30-strong team behind the East London Liquor Company, located near Victoria Park, the first new distillers in the area for a hundred years. Hidden away on a small industrial site next to a gym, founder Alex Wolpert, former head distiller Jamie Baxter and current head distiller Tom Hills have created a distilling playground, producing gin, vodka and rye whisky – in fact, when you visit the bar on the site, you can see an actual playground through a huge window behind the gleaming copper stills, built by the renowned German distilling experts Arnold Holstein.

The two gins currently produced by ELLCo. comprise the "standard" signature release bottled at 40% ABV and a series of "premium" batched products with a slightly higher ABV (45%), both distilled using a wheat-based spirit. The signature is a mixture of both vapour- and direct-infused botanicals, including fresh lemon and grapefruit peel, coriander, angelica root, juniper, cubeb berries and cardamom, with a distinctly earthy, spicy touch of the angelica developing first. The premium batches play around with the botanical balance and are direct infused (*see* page 22), with a broader range of flavours coming from the likes of Darjeeling tea, cassia bark and pink grapefruit peel, along with distinct herb garden notes including thyme, sage, bay leaves and lavender. In essence, they give Wolpert and Hills a blank canvas to play with,

> The distillery has now added sherry, bourbon, chardonnay, cider and ginger beer cask releases.

so expect future batches to differ accordingly.

One of the most exciting areas that the distillery has started to develop is a barrel-ageing programme, which began in January 2016, exploring the nuances in flavour that oak casks can contribute to a gin. The first of these was a French oak offering matured for 14 weeks, which brought a spicy, dried fruit element to the gin. The distillery has now added sherry, bourbon, chardonnay, cider and ginger beer cask releases to the series as well as a highly distinctive peated whisky cask-matured for 47 weeks, giving the resulting gin a superb earthy smokiness, but is still very much juniper led.

Alongside the distillery and bar is a new microbrewery, craft spirits bottle shop and an Italian-themed restaurant, helping to bring a touch of something unique to both East London and to the UK gin category. Anticipate great things to continue. *eastlondonliquorcompany.com*

◉ *The East London Liquor Company range*

OTHER LONDON-BASED GINS TO TRY

THAMES DISTILLERS

Thames Distillers is led by Charles Maxwell, an eighth-generation distiller who has undoubtedly had one of the greatest impacts on the gin scene, not just in London but across the UK, over the last two decades. From his base in Clapham, he produces contract gins for those looking to start up their own brands but who don't yet have the capital or space to buy their own stills. Thames has given birth to many gins that today have their own distillery, such as Jensen (now housed in Bermondsey, South London), Portobello (in their "Ginstitute" on Portobello Road, Notting Hill), Darnley's (now distilled in St Andrews in Scotland), to mention just a few.
thamesdistillers.co.uk

DODD'S GIN/THE LONDON DISTILLERY COMPANY

Originally based in Battersea, The London Distillery Company now has a home under the railway arches of Bermondsey. It produces Dodd's Gin (bottled at 49.9% ABV) using a neutral grain base and London honey as a key botanical, as well as a range of gins in partnership with Kew Gardens, including an organic gin (46% ABV), featuring over 20 botanicals such as passion flower, lavender, lemon, lime, grapefruit, orange and bergamot peel, wild bilberries and eucalyptus. These are all distilled in Christina, a traditional 140-litre (37-US-gallon) copper alembic still, with the more delicate botanicals cold vacuum distilled in their so-named Little Albion still (*see* pages 22–3).
londondistillery.com

CITY OF LONDON DISTILLERY

Based just off Fleet Street, the City of London Distillery has two German Carl stills. Here, you can make your own gin, or sample one of their own creations such as their City of London Authentic Dry Gin, a classic mix with added pink grapefruit, bottled at 41.3% ABV, or their Christopher Wren gin, named in homage to the architect who designed the nearby St Paul's Cathedral, which showcases sweet orange and bottled at a punchy 45.3% ABV.
cityoflondondistillery.com

SACRED GIN

Ian Hart has been making gin in his living room in North London, now known as the Sacred Spirits distillery, since 2009 using glass vacuum stills (*see* page 28). His core gin draws flavours from Spanish and Italian pink grapefruit, sweet orange, lemon and lime, along with cinnamon and frankincense, and is bottled at 40% ABV.
sacredgin.com

BIMBER GIN

Across in Park Royal, Bimber Distillery is producing a host of spirits, with gin being a major focus. They make theirs using their own four-times distilled wheat vodka, infused with ten botanicals (think warming cinnamon) overnight before distillation in Astraeus, a 600-litre (159-US-gallon) copper pot still before being bottled at 42% ABV.
bimberdistillery.co.uk

NO.3 GIN

Two Central London areas that boast gins linked to their history are St James's and Marylebone. The former is home to Berry Bros. & Rudd, the oldest wine and spirits merchant in the world. Their gin, No.3 London Dry Gin, is served opposite the shop in Dukes Hotel (*see* page 54) and is actually made in the Netherlands, but it is a superb example of a great Martini gin (bottled at 46% ABV), using just six botanicals: the three fruits of juniper, orange peel and grapefruit peel balanced with the three spices of angelica root, coriander seeds and cardamom.
no3gin.com

MARYLEBONE GIN

Another eighth-generation distiller, Johnny Neill (the man also behind Whitley Neill gin) makes Marylebone Gin on Marylebone Lane using a mixture of 13 botanicals including lemon balm and lime flower in a curious still that runs from a wall plug, designed by a coppersmith in the USA. Neill bottles his gin at a decent 50.2% ABV.
marylebonegin.com

HAYMAN'S GIN

South of the river, keeping the Beefeater and Thames distilleries company, is Hayman's, which uses a two-day process to make their gins to a family recipe dating back over 150 years and distilled using 100% English wheat. Their classic London Dry (41.2% ABV) uses ten botanicals for a fresh, bright and balanced gin, while their Gently Rested Gin (41.3% ABV) draws flavours from a three-week resting period in old Scotch whisky barrels.
haymansgin.com

REST OF ENGLAND

London's indelible influence on both the history of gin consumption and the boom in craft gin distillation in recent times has effectively led to a country wide explosion in brand-new distilleries. Rather like craft beer, almost every county and region has a gin made for it by a larger contract distillery, or a distillery in situ producing something that aims to represent the sheer versatility and distinctiveness of this botanically diverse spirit.

BOMBAY SAPPHIRE
HAMPSHIRE

When gin was in the doldrums, there was little innovation coming from any of the established gin brands in a category that was deemed to be dying. Gin was the domain of the Queen Mother, not hipsters, and the world was awash with flavoured vodka, aromatized wines and lager. Cocktails were sugary and brightly coloured, and certainly didn't contain gin.

This context made the development of Bombay Sapphire in 1987 by International Distillers and Vintners, now a major part of Gordon's and Tanqueray Gin owner Diageo, a distinctly brave move. Owned by Bacardi since 1997, it has been at the forefront of the new gin revolution, changing perspectives on the category with its distinctive blue bottle and a light, approachable flavour, becoming part of the gin establishment in the process.

What made Bombay Sapphire truly unique and gave it the light botanical flavours for which it has become so famous was the pioneering vapour infusion method (*see* page 20) employed in the distilling, drawing on a technique developed by Thomas Dakin and his family in the early 1800s using

◉ *The glasshouses at Laverstoke Mill*

a Carter-Head still (*see* page 26). This design of still enables a basket containing the botanicals to be placed at the top of the still through which the spirit vapours can pass, rather than adding the botanicals directly to the boiling spirit in the base of a pot still. The result is a delicate "one-shot" spirit (*see* page 29) that plays toward a more floral and perfumed style of gin.

Despite ownership in its short lifetime by two major drinks companies, Bombay Sapphire was made at Greenall's distillery (*see* page 75) until a dedicated brand home was opened in 2014 at a former paper mill in Hampshire, which in the past printed bank notes for the UK and, fittingly, India, and dates back as far as the 1086 Doomsday Book. Not only does Laverstoke Mill, as it is known, house the stills that make Bombay Sapphire (as well as producing Oxley Gin using the unusual process of vacuum distillation – *see* page 28), but the architect Thomas Heatherwick installed two trumpet-shaped glasshouses, one cool and one warm, in which some of the key botanicals used in the production of the gin are grown. Such is the modern nature of the processes at the distillery (in contrast with their distillation methods) that these glasshouses are even heated using air warmed through the recovery of heat created in the running of the facility.

Among the balanced mix of ten botanicals in the signature edition of Bombay Sapphire (40% ABV) are lemon peel, grains of paradise, cubeb berries and almonds. For a little more oomph in your glass, try the Star of Bombay (47.5% ABV), drawing on a total of 12 botanicals including ambrette seeds, solely sourced from Ecuador, and dried bergamot orange peel hand-picked in Calabria.
bombaysapphire.com

WARNER'S DISTILLERY
NORTHAMPTONSHIRE

English gin production is focusing evermore on regionality, and one of the first distilleries to produce a gin that drew on distinctive local flavours was Warner's Distillery.

Based in a 200-year-old barn on Falls Farm in the village of Harrington, Warner's Distillery uses local natural spring water, grain spirit and home-grown ingredients to create a range of gins in small batches by hand that boast flavour at the fore.

The business is the brainchild of Tom Warner and Sion Edwards, who met at agricultural college. Their initial aim was to distil essential oils from local, farm-grown and hedgerow-foraged botanicals, but this quickly turned to thoughts of gin and in December 2012 their first product was born.

The classic Dry is made on their 500-litre (132-US-gallon) still called Curiosity, named after cat's paw prints found in the cement floor of the barn, using a one-shot distillation method (*see* page 29) through a copper catalyser, which Warner's Distillery says "turbo

● *The ever popular Warner's gin*

charges the removal of impurities from the base spirit and botanical recipe so that we end up with a much purer and cleaner spirit". In November 2016, a new small 50-litre (13¼-US-gallon) copper pot still named Satisfaction arrived at the farm. Introduced to ease some of the workload of Curiosity, Satisfaction allows Warner's Distillery to experiment with new flavour creations, including their Honeybee Gin (43% ABV) launched in 2017, using honey from hives on the farm. Cleverly, the gin comes with a pouch of wild flower, bee-friendly seeds attached to the neck.

The base for Warner's Distillery gin is neutral grain spirit from Langley Distillery (*see* page 75), and once their range of gins are individually distilled, they are cut back with local spring water from the farm before being bottled.

Harrington Dry Gin (44% ABV) features juniper, coriander and cardamom to mix well in a Martini or with tonic, with two flavoured expressions supporting the range. The elderflower (40% ABV) builds on the base of the standard Dry by infusing it with fresh elderflowers handpicked from the farm, resulting in a sweeter, more floral gin. Victoria's Rhubarb Gin (40% ABV) is, however, an altogether different product. Made using a variety of rhubarb originally grown in the kitchen garden of Buckingham Palace during the reign of Queen Victoria, rhubarb juice is extracted using a traditional fruit press and blended with a base of the classic Dry gin. The outcome is pale pink in hue and sweet yet tangy flavour, which is easily drunk neat, over ice or mixed with ginger ale.
warnersdistillery.com

REST OF ENGLAND

Moorland Spirit Co.

The Lakes Gin

Masons Dry Yorkshire Gin

Brindle Distillery

Manchester Gin

G&J Distillers

True North Distillery

Langley Distillery

Two Birds

Warners Distillery

Adnams, Southwold

Chase Distillery

Cotswolds Distillery

Cambridge Distillery

TOAD (The Oxford Artisan Distillery)

The Bath Gin Company

Bombay Sapphire

Silent Pool

Langley's

Brighton Gin

Conker

Mermaid Isle of Wight Distillery

Southwestern Distillery

Dartmoor Distillery

Plymouth Gin

Salcombe Gin

Curio Spirits Company

Three Fingers Distillery

Wheadon's Gin

PLYMOUTH GIN
DEVON

The South West region is a thriving hub of UK gin distillation, and one of the most exciting locations to discover an array of local botanicals. An emphasis on more coastal, mineralic flavours, such as rock samphire, seaweed, bog myrtle and spignel, has almost given the region a recognizable terroir of its own and many new distilleries are capitalizing on a unique combination of locally foraged coastal ingredients to provide a backbone to their gin recipes.

Historically, Plymouth Gin Distillery, also known as the Black Friars Distillery, has led the way in the region, which was established way back in 1793 and can arguably lay claim to being one of the oldest continuously run gin distilleries in the UK. Until recently, Plymouth was also the only UK gin to have a Protected Geographical Indication (PGI), meaning that under EU regulations no other distiller could produce a "Plymouth"-style gin or indeed distil a gin in the town of Plymouth. However, current owners Pernod Ricard have since relinquished this status.

Thankfully, Plymouth is still one of the most respected and valued gins on the market and its distillation style has not been hugely tampered with for the last two decades, now under the diligent and highly skilled management of master distiller Sean Harrison. It is a decidedly simple and classic approach, using a single copper pot still with a steam heating coil (*see* page 29) that has been in place for more than 150 years, which is filled with grain spirit and seven botanicals, namely juniper, coriander seeds, cardamom and orris and angelica root for a distinctly earthy note, plus sweet orange and dried lemon peels. The juniper notes are soft but backed by a very

◐ *The historic Plymouth gin distillery*

balanced spice and root/earthiness, with a top note of fragrant sweet cardamom developing more strongly on the palate. A one-shot method (*see* page 29) produces batches of around 5,000 litres (1,320 US gallons) of gin per batch, which is then reduced with pure Dartmoor water to a variety of different strengths: 41.2% ABV for the Original and the Navy Strength at a potent but remarkably sophisticated-tasting 57% ABV. What is fascinating here is that while today many distilleries offer a navy-strength edition, association with the British naval fleet is part of Plymouth Gin's DNA, Plymouth being one of the primary ports used by the Royal Navy as well as a commercial trading hub, so a high-proof gin designed for seafaring was essential. The recipe for Plymouth Sloe Gin (26% ABV) dates back to 1883, with sloe

berries and sugar infusing the gin for around four months.

The distillery recently established one of the very first distillery schools, where visitors can learn about the gin-making process and create a bespoke version of their very own Plymouth Gin, an undisputed British classic that has unquestionably helped to reinforce and maintain the UK's love affair with gin through both the bad times and the good. *plymouthgin.com*

TARQUIN'S CORNISH GIN
CORNWALL

As Britain's fascination with craft gin distilling began to gain confidence in 2012, Tarquin Leadbetter, a former classically trained Cordon Bleu chef, began to explore the possibility of establishing the first Cornish distillery in more than a hundred years in Wadebridge. Armed with a 0.7-litre (1½-US-pint) still, he began producing a library of botanical distillates and combined them to form around 100 different recipes until he found one containing 12 that struck a chord. In 2013, using a 250-litre (65-US-gallon) direct-fired (*see* page 29) Portuguese copper still called Tamara (after the River Tamar that marks the border between Devon and Cornwall) sealed with bread dough in the traditional fashion, the first bottle of Tarquin's Cornish Dry Gin was sold to a local hotel. Fast forward to 2017 and Tarquin's SeaDog Navy Strength Gin (57% ABV) won the World's Best Gin prize at the San Francisco World Spirits Competition. Today, Southwestern Distillery runs a mixture of three traditional dough-sealed pot stills (alongside Tamara lie sisters Senara and Tressa) as well as a modern Italian-made pot still called Ferarra. The botanicals – Italian juniper (and Kosovan in the navy strength), Bulgarian coriander seeds, liquorice root from Uzbekistan, Polish angelica, Moroccan orris root, Guatemalan green cardamom, Madagascan cinnamon, bitter almonds from Morocco and fresh orange, lemon and grapefruit peel – are macerated for 12 hours in a wheat base spirit before locally grown violets are added. Once distilled, the spirit heart is collected at 78% ABV and then cut with demineralized Cornish spring water and bottled at 42% ABV.

Tarquin has produced a number of limited-edition fruit gins, including Blackberry and Rhubarb & Raspberry (both 38% ABV), along with The Hopster Dry Gin (42% ABV) in collaboration with Sharp's Brewery, which sees the addition of Pilot, Cascade and Crystal hops bringing out a distinct floral herby note in the gin. *tarquinsgin.com*

◔ *Checking Tarquin's alembic copper stills*

CURIO SPIRITS COMPANY
CORNWALL

A newcomer to the burgeoning South West scene, but certainly a distillery making plenty of noise in a short space of time, Curio was set up by husband and wife team William and Rubina Tyler-Street at the end of 2014, with a base in Mullion on the Lizard peninsula in Cornwall. Taking inspiration from their unique coastal location with its notably mild climate and abundance of sub-tropical plants, the Curio Wild Coast Gin (41% ABV) features 15 botanicals including hand-picked rock samphire, Cornish seaweed, lime flower tea, angelica, lime and lemon peel and cinnamon, and is distilled using a variety of stills including a 60-litre (16-US-gallon) copper pot and glass Rotovap vacuum still (*see* page 28). Wild Coast is as dramatic in flavour as the coastline that inspired it: a balanced floral top note meets a distinctive sea-spray saltiness, all rooted in a pine fresh juniper note and plenty of citrus zest. The recent addition of a blueberry gin (41% ABV) has seen the couple sourcing the fruit from the site of a former local monastery, where historians have traced cultivation of blueberries as far back as the 12th century.
curiospiritscompany.co.uk

SALCOMBE GIN
DEVON

While the story may sound familiar – two friends meet over a mutual love of gin – Salcombe's origins lie in the once-thriving fruit trade that this small Devonshire port used to support by building remarkably fast schooner ships to transport perishable fruit from as far afield as the Azores and the Mediterranean to ports in London, Liverpool, Bristol and Hull. With this history firmly in mind, the distillery founders Howard Davies and Angus Lugsdin launched their first gin back in 2016, which is a citrus-heavy recipe using fresh lime, lemon and ruby grapefruit, bottled at 44% ABV.
salcombegin.com

DARTMOOR DISTILLERY
DEVON

Like its contemporaries in Salcombe, the Dartmoor Distillery brings a distinct sense of locality into the mix for its two gins, Black Dog Gin (46% ABV) and navy strength (57% ABV) Dartmoor Beast Gin, both using Dartmoor water and hand-foraged botanicals from the local moorland. Distiller and founder John Lawton worked with his cousins, who have owned and run the Lawton Tube Co. for over a century, to develop a unique copper still amusingly named Ethyl Ethel.
dartmoordistilleryltd.com

CONKER GIN
DORSET

The prospect of a working life in chartered surveying, or rather the reality of pursuing a career path that isn't known for its high levels of passion, led Rupert Holloway, founder of the Conker Spirit distillery, to a creative alternative: training as a distiller and producing Dorset's first gin distillery, based in the town of Bournemouth. Using ten botanicals rooted in the classics, Conker (which it has to be noted doesn't contain conkers or, for those non-British readers, horse chestnuts) also has a delicate floral side, thanks in part to the addition of New Forest gorse, elderberries and samphire. It is bottled at 40% ABV.
conkerspirit.co.uk

THE BATH GIN COMPANY
SOMERSET

The first distillery in the city for 250 years, The Bath Gin Company has developed three distinctly different expressions in the cellar of its Canary Gin Bar in the centre of town: Classic, a pot still style using 11 botanicals including bitter orange, kaffir lime leaves and English coriander, Hopped Rhubarb and Orange Sloe Gin, all bottled at 40% ABV.
thebathgincompany.co.uk

HEPPLE GIN
NORTHUMBERLAND

The Moorland Spirit Co., a hugely ambitious project based in one of the last great wildernesses of the UK, was established by three of the brightest minds in drinks: chef and forager Valentine Warner, renowned mixologst Nick Strangeway and Walter Riddell, who lives on the Hepple Estate and maintains the land on which the botanicals are largely foraged and selectively hand-picked. The distillery produces its Hepple Gin using their unique "Triple Technique" three-stage process: supercritical CO_2 extraction, which is often used in the perfume industry to collect highly concentrated and complex aromas; copper pot distillation, for a more

traditional smoothness of flavour in the spirit; and glass vacuum distillation (*see* page 28), bringing an additional vibrancy to the botanical flavours. It has also developed a juniper rejuvenation programme in cooperation with the Northumberland National Park to replant more than 200 juniper seedlings every year. Hepple, bottled at 45% ABV, is distinctly juniper forward, with a bold, pine-led aroma and fresh fruitiness.
moorlandspirit.co

THE LAKES GIN
CUMBRIA

A whisky, gin and vodka hybrid, The Lakes Distillery is perhaps a little too large to be classed as a craft operation, but nonetheless focuses on all the key aspects of crafting fine spirits. Their core gin is London Dry in production style, distilled in batches in a 1,200-litre (317-US-gallon) copper pot still and bottled at 43.7% ABV. It brings together 14 botanicals, six of which are foraged from the breathtaking countryside in the Lake District, including a local juniper, heather, hawthorn and mint, alongside a more widely available juniper, angelica, liquorice, orris and orange and lemon peel.
lakesdistillery.com

MANCHESTER GIN
MANCHESTER
Inspired by the old saying that the industrious Mancunian workforce of the city were like "worker bees", the distillery, run by partners Jen Wiggins and Seb Heeley, make their gin using three small stills named Wendy, Victoria and Emmeline, producing batches of just 500 bottles at a time, each bottle monikered with a bee, at between 40–42% ABV depending on their style. Dandelion and burdock root are both hand foraged from the city surroundings, and the gin has a smooth, sweet earthy delivery thanks to the use of ground almonds and liquorice in the botanical mix.
manchestergin.co.uk

CUCKOO GIN
LANCASHIRE
On the outskirts of the small village of Brindle lies Holmes Farm, the home of Cuckoo Gin, produced with a focus on sustainability and ethically sourced botanicals. The signature expression, bottled at 43% ABV, includes juniper, coriander, grapefruit and orange peel, oats, almonds, cardamom, chamomile and cinnamon, with a spiced edition bringing in clove, ginger, cinnamon, fennel, lemongrass and spicy Tellicherry black pepper for a warming, well-rounded gin to sip over ice, bottled at 42% ABV.
brindledistillery.co.uk/cuckoo-gin/

MASONS DRY YORKSHIRE GIN
YORKSHIRE
Husband and wife team Karl and Cathy Mason have been producing a no-nonsense, slow-distilled juniper-, citrus- and cardamom-forward gin in a 200-litre (53-US-gallon) copper alembic still (see page 22) in Harrogate since 19 June 2013 – World Gin Day, to be precise. Alongside a floral, slightly perfumed Lavender Edition, in true Yorkshire fashion the couple has released a Yorkshire Tea Edition, which is broad-shouldered, with tannic notes and an underlying grassy freshness. All are bottled at 42% ABV.
masonsyorkshiregin.com

SHEFFIED DRY GIN
SHEFFIELD
This gin is the project of the keen minds at the True North Brewing Co, led by head distiller Ben Schulze, and it is the first to be distilled and bottled in the city for more than a hundred years. Alongside the classic selection of botanicals including coriander, angelica and cardamom, a very earthy, dry note develops thanks to the addition of gentian root, which is swiftly balanced out by a sweet honey note and topped off with something wholly original – a dash of Henderson's Relish, a local spicy delicacy that has been produced in Sheffield since the end of the 19th century. It is bottled at 42% ABV.
truenorthbrewco.uk/

G&J DISTILLERS
CHESHIRE
One of the undisputed powerhouses of British gin distillation, G&J – formerly Greenall's – has the lofty accolade of being the oldest continuously gin-distilling facility in the world, operating in Warrington since 1761, when a 25-year-old Thomas Dakin opened his distillery on Bridge Street. In that time, only seven master distillers have served the company, with the current incumbent, Joanne Moore, working for the company for more than 20 years and credited with the creation of such gins as Bloom, Opihr and Thomas Dakin, as well as the continued development of the Greenall's gin brand. In fact, Bombay Sapphire was also distilled by Moore until 2013, when production was moved by owners Bacardi to the Laverstoke Mill site, where it has built replicas of the traditional Carter-Head stills employed by Greenall's in Warrington (see page 69). Today, G&J Distillers are one of the country's key contract gin producers, the go-to for many an aspiring start-up with a concept and recipe in mind.
gjdistillers.com

LANGLEY DISTILLERY
WEST MIDLANDS
Another legendary company whose place in the annals of UK gin history cannot be underestimated, the Langley facility, based on the outskirts of the city of Birmingham, may not have the same stature as the likes of Beefeater (see page 63), or the relatively new Bombay Sapphire site (see page 69), but behind the Victorian brick buildings lies a wealth of history. The distillery is situated at the historic Crosswells Brewery site, which dates back to the early 1800s and was built over an ancient underground water source. Gin has been distilled at Langley Distillery since 1920, and the remarkable stills that remain in daily use include Angela, the 1,000-litre (265-US-gallon) "grandmother" (as master distiller Rob Dorsett affectionately refers to her), dating back to 1903, alongside the slightly larger Constance at 3,000 litres (790 US gallons) from 1950, the voluptuous Jenny at 12,000 litres (3,170 US gallons), 1994, and McKay, the tiny 200-litre (53-US-gallon) pot still, the oldest of its kind, built by Bennett, Sons & Shears in 1865. Two other truly ancient and now unused stills, No. 3 and No. 5, actually predate these, with one estimate placing their manufacture as early as the late 1700s. Langley distils around 300 different contract gins, about 70 million bottles a year, shipped all over the world as far afield as Fiji, South Africa and the Philippines. However, one of its highlights must be Palmers Distillers Cut: a sensational, broad-shouldered classic London Dry bottled at 44% ABV containing 15 botanicals including lily bulb, orris root, grains of paradise and grapefruit peel, designed by Dorsett and only available from the distillery website.
langleydistillery.co.uk
palmersgin.com

TWO BIRDS GIN
LEICESTERSHIRE
Established in Market Harborough, back in 2013, Two Birds was originally a project for engineer and gin enthusiast Mark Gamble to run out of his home workshop. After creating his first gin, he soon won a gold award from the Craft Distillers Alliance, which opened Gamble's eyes to the true potential of the brand. Now operating on a purpose-built site, his classic London Dry Gin is still produced in 100-bottle batches in Gerard, a 30-litre (8-US-gallon) still that Gamble designed and built himself, plus his identical, unnamed brother. A mix of just five botanicals – juniper, orris root, coriander, fresh lemon zest and an undisclosed secret ingredient – gives a very dry, juniper-forward gin, bottled at 40% ABV. Alongside this, Two Birds has created an Old Tom (also 40% ABV) and a cask-aged variety (47.3% ABV), matured for three months in virgin oak casks with additional pecan wood staves. The most recent development is the commissioning of two 300-litre (80-US-gallon) Chinese-made column/pot stills, which will enable Two Birds's larger parent company, Union Distillers, to develop and distil a greater variety of spirits for contract customers.
twobirdsspirits.co.uk

COTSWOLDS DRY GIN
WARWICKSHIRE
Since 2014, Daniel Szor and his team have been bringing award-winning gin and, latterly, a single malt whisky to the beautiful surroundings of the Cotswolds Distillery in Stourton in the North Cotswolds. The gin is a single-shot (*see* page 29), London Dry style (46% ABV), using

around ten times the quantity of raw botanicals as is usually called for, with the recipe combining Macedonian juniper, Polish angelica, locally grown lavender and Egyptian bay leaves, along with fresh lime and grapefruit peel. The gin is surprisingly oily and non-chill filtered, giving a slight haze when tonic or ice is added.
cotswoldsdistillery.com

TOAD
OXFORD
Not far away from the Cotswold Distillery, there is the The Oxford Artisan Distillery, or TOAD for short. TOAD is on a mission to revive ancient species of grain for use in its spirits. Opening in July 2017, TOAD has employed an archaeo-botanist, John Letts, who spent 25 years researching, farming and sourcing historic grains, and the grain that the distillery uses to create its own spirit (in extraordinary-looking column stills) is harvested within a 80 km (50-mile) radius of the distillery. Besides the classic Oxford Dry Gin (46% ABV), TOAD has recently collaborated with Oxford University to create

its Physic Gin (40% ABV), which contains botanicals grown in the University's 17th-century Botanic Garden.
spiritoftoad.com

CHASE DISTILLERY
HEREFORDSHIRE
Chase Distillery in many respects almost grew out of an ingenious necessity, when founder William Chase, a potato farmer who launched the hugely successful Tyrells potato crisp brand, decided to begin distilling the unused and unwanted supermarket-reject potatoes. Chase potato vodka came initially in 2008, followed by the first gin, using the same potato-based spirit, carrying a hint of creamy, buttery flavour, which brings together ten botanicals, part vapour infused and part pot still macerated (*see* page 22) in Ginny, Chase's dedicated gin still. Alongside the original GB Extra Dry gin (40% ABV), the distillery also produces four other gins, including Williams Elegant 48 Gin (48% ABV) – a profoundly different spirit that uses apples from the farm's 200-year-old orchard, as well as hops, elderflower and a mixture of other botanicals grown in the surrounding countryside.
chasedistillery.co.uk/

CAMBRIDGE DISTILLERY
CAMBRIDGE
Hailing from one of the most traditional cities hasn't stopped William Lowe from becoming one of if not *the* most innovative gin distiller in the UK. Along with his partner Lucy, Will established arguably the world's first gin "tailoring" service, whereby an individual or corporate client can have a truly bespoke small-batch gin developed for them, the recipe devised by selecting from an extensive library of individual single-botanical spirits. In addition,

Lowe has created other – some might say outlandish – gins, including Anty Gin (42% ABV), a collaboration with the Nordic Food Lab, where red wood ants are used as a botanical.
cambridgedistillery.co.uk

ADNAMS
SUFFOLK
One of the east coast of England's most-well known brewers, Adnams of Southwold moved into distillation back in 2010, using nearly 150 years of brewing tradition to build its spirits on. Each spirit is distilled using a base of locally grown, East Anglian malted cereals (rye, wheat, barley and oats) with the "distillery wash" – basically an unhopped beer – fermented in a unique two-strain brewing yeast process that has been in use for more than 70 years. Two main gin styles are produced using the resulting grain spirit: the first, Copper House Dry Gin (40% ABV), bringing together juniper, orris, coriander, cardamom, hibiscus and sweet orange peel, with a First Rate Triple Malt expression (45% ABV) additionally using lemon peel, cassia bark, vanilla pods, angelica root, caraway seeds, fennel seeds, thyme and liquorice root, for a very earthy, powerful aroma and taste.
adnams.co.uk

SILENT POOL GIN
SURREY

Surrey's Silent Pool Distillers, named appropriately after the Silent Pool on the majestic Albury Estate, owned by the Duke of Northumberland, straddle both a historical and forward-thinking approach to making gin. After renovating an original wood-fired boiler, a new custom-built German Arnold Holstein still was installed and a four-stage approach established to make its 24-botanical gin. The more traditional elements – Bosnian juniper berries, liquorice root, cassia bark and orris along with bergamot – are first bruised and then added to the spirit for maceration before being transferred to the still. Then the fresher, more citrus-led botanicals – orange and lime peel, dried pears, Macedonian juniper and Polish angelica – are added to a vapour infusion basket (*see* page 20) in the neck of the still, with rose petals, kaffir lime leaves, linden and elderflower separately macerated to produce a "gin tea infusion", before the spirit is then slowly distilled in a fractional column still (*see* page 24), resulting in a gin that is notably light and floral, with a heady citrusy aroma. It is bottled at 43% ABV.
silentpooldistillers.com

BRIGHTON GIN
SUSSEX

Aptly armed with the moniker "distilled beside the seaside", Brighton Gin's journey began just before the height of the explosion in craft gin in the UK and has almost certainly helped to inspire the wider success of south-coast distilling. Brighton's recipe is simple but well constructed, using juniper, fresh orange and lime peel, locally grown coriander seeds and milk

thistle, which is indigenous to the local South Downs and has long been valued as a liver restorative. It is bottled at 40% ABV.
brightongin.com

ISLE OF WIGHT DISTILLERY
ISLE OF WIGHT

The Isle of Wight Distillery is the first – and currently the only – distillery to be built on the Island, established back in 2014 by lifelong friends Xavier Baker and Conrad Gauntlett, who have a combined expertise in both brewing and winemaking. After laying down the first casks of their whisky in 2015, which is due to mature in 2019, the duo's deep passion for making a locally inspired gin soon came to fruition. Utilizing a modern pot and column still combination (*see* page 24), Mermaid Gin (42% ABV) has a distinct coastal note, with a botanical recipe comprising hand-picked rock samphire and elderflower, Boadicea hops, Sussex-grown coriander seeds, grains of paradise and an earthy mix of liquorice, angelica and orris roots, topped off with

organic lemon zest. Alongside the core expression is HMS Victoria Navy Strength Gin (57% ABV) and an annually released oak-aged wine-cask variant, which broadens the already complex notes of the base spirit.
isleofwightdistillery.com

WHEADON'S GIN
GUERNSEY AND JERSEY

The most westerly of the Channel Islands, Guernsey has a distinct microclimate, which almost certainly helps a would-be distiller to curate the ingredients for a locally influenced gin. The Wheadon family had been producing alcoholic beverages of varying styles since 1865 as brewers when, in 2015, Luke Wheadon, the owner of the Bella Luce Hotel in the parish of St Martin, decided to make a small-batch, coastal-driven gin in the hotel cellars. Since then, the distillery has expanded from a tiny 2.3-litre (5-US-pint) pot still to three 20-litre (5¼-US-gallon) Portuguese alembic stills (*see* page 22) and now a 250-litre (66-US-gallon) German-made Müller still. The first expression

Wheadon released in late 2016 was built around the core notes of juniper, rock samphire and pink grapefruit, followed by more exotic concepts (mandarin, lime and hibiscus, as well as one featuring Japanese yuzu, lemongrass and green tea), all bottled at 46% ABV, with the distiller altering his botanical balance according to the leading top notes. A new Wheadon distillery is now operating in Jersey using some exciting locally derived ingredients, including Jersey Royal potatoes, giving the island the chance to put its very first toe in the spirits pool.
wheadonsgin.co.uk

BLUE BOTTLE GIN
GUERNSEY

Guernsey has another popular locally distilled gin, Blue Bottle, produced by The Three Fingers Distillery in the parish of St Sampson, bottled at 47% ABV.
bluebottlegin.gg

SCOTLAND

As with its contemporaries elsewhere in the British Isles, Scotland's distilleries have contributed an enormously diverse richness to the gin market in the UK, led by the titanic success of the likes of Gordon's and Tanqueray, both historic brands dating back to the mid-1700s and 1800s respectively, whose production was moved to Scotland in 1995. Today, there are more than 70 distilleries producing gin in and around the mainland of Scotland and dotted across its many islands off the west and north coasts.

○ Hendrick's, a game-changing gin

HENDRICK'S GIN
SOUTH AYRSHIRE

Along with Bombay Sapphire (*see* page 69), Hendrick's Gin can rightly be credited with having a major influence in turning the heads of consumers away from other white spirits such as vodka and back to gin.

Created in 1999 and launched into the US market in 2000, Hendrick's was a revolution from a flavour perspective, presented in a unique style of bottle and with a strong tone of voice that gave it a sense of both tradition and innovation. Soon after its debut in the USA, Hendrick's found demand in its home market of the UK, and has become one of the best-selling and admired gin brands.

The extraordinary flavour profile was the brainchild of the distillers at the brand-owner William Grant & Sons (famed for their Scotch whisky distilleries of Glenfiddich and Balvenie, as well as the Grant's blended whisky) and refined at the tail end of the last century by a team of distilling experts, which helped the company develop a gin that was post-flavoured with two delicate botanicals, rose and cucumber (*see* page 20). As such, it is not classed as a London Dry gin, but this modern creation, hyped by vintage marketing, opened up the gin market with its concept of innovation and creativity, underscored by the cucumber garnish in a Hendrick's Gin and Tonic in place of the traditional lemon or lime wedge.

The Girvan distillery in southwest Scotland is a multi-purpose plant that serves as the main volume driver for William Grant's Scotch production as well as neutral grain alcohol and, of course, Hendrick's Gin. The master distiller, Lesley Gracie, has been making the gin for 20 years and in 2018 a new dedicated facility opened up at the Girvan plant for its production. It features two new still houses, bringing the total number to six: four Bennett stills (*see* page 29), including the original antique copper pot hailing from 1860 and three precise replicas, and two Carter-Heads (*see* page 26), one original constructed in 1948 and the other an exact reproduction.

There is also a Hendrick's Gin Palace, with a walled garden and a Victorian-style palm house, flanked by two botanical hothouses used to cultivate botanicals and flora from around the world. It also includes a laboratory, a lecture theatre and bar.

The Hendrick's range consists of two core expressions. The traditional gin (41.4% ABV) uses juniper and ten botanicals including orange peel, yarrow and caraway seeds. But the real point of distinction is the addition of cucumber and Bulgarian rose after the gin has been distilled for a light, delicate result. The second is Orbium (43.4% ABV), where a base of classic Hendrick's Gin is infused with extracts of quinine, wormwood and blue lotus blossom form a more savoury, robust flavour. *hendricksgin.com*

THE BOTANIST
ISLAY, INNER HEBRIDES

Anyone who might be remotely interested in single malt whisky is probably already familiar with the Isle of Islay and its highly distinctive, aromatic, smoky style of whisky that is an experience on the palate like no other. This west coast island, about an hour and a half by ferry from the mainland port of Kennacraig, has fewer than 4,000 residents, but is also home to some of the most well-known and revered whisky distilleries on the planet.

Among the best of these is the Bruichladdich distillery in Port Charlotte, to the northeast of the small island, which, alongside its distinctive whisky, has been producing The Botanist gin since 2011 and was one of the first UK distilleries to embrace the British craft gin revolution. What makes this gin's story so compelling is a combination of its production and botanical make-up. As the name suggests, The Botanist is a heady mix of flavour, with nine core botanicals including cassia bark, coriander seeds, cinnamon, angelica, orris root, liquorice and lemon and orange peel creating the foundation for a colourful palate of 22 locally foraged botanicals harvested seasonally from across the whole island. Floral notes of gorse, elder, hawthorn, chamomile and heather flowers mix with red clover, creeping thistle, mint, wild thyme and wood sage to create a bright but balanced spirit. Alongside traditionally harvested juniper and a small amount of locally grown prostrate *Juniperus communis*, the core botanicals are steeped in spirit overnight, before vapour infusion (*see* page 20) takes place in Ugly Betty, one of a few known working traditional Lomond stills (*see* page 29), which was rescued from potential destruction by the owners of Bruichladdich from

🔊 *The unusual-looking which produces The Botanist gin*

Inverleven, a mainland distillery. After transporting it by boat – a process that was reportedly tracked by the FBI via satellite because of the cargo's unusual shape – and some modification, the first tests began and the initial spirit ran from the stills in 2010, before the recipe was ready for release into the wider world a year later.

A super-high concentrate of around 80% ABV is produced in eight batches per year, with the distillation process lasting 17 hours, around four times the average length of time usually employed in gin making. It is bottled at 46% ABV.

Despite the multitude of botanicals in the recipe, the juniper is very pronounced and upfront, with a delicate floral note developing alongside a well-balanced citrus undertone.
bruichladdich.com/the-botanist

EDEN MILL GIN
FIFE

St Andrews is a location famous for golf and the university, which was founded in 1413. However, for Paul Miller, founder of the Eden Mill distillery, it is hoped that soon it will resonate with all things spirited too.

Established in 2012, Eden Mill is something of a playground for both brewing and distilling, being the first in Scotland to combine both. What grew out of a fervent interest in craft beer led the team to invest in some small Hoga Spanish-made pot stills, on which they began to experiment producing a hop-based gin, which was completely distinctive. A whisky has followed, released in 2018, but the distillery's fascination with gin is still a priority.

A brand-new distillery is being built on the site (a former Victorian paper mill) expanding the capacity from the current 80,000 litres (21,130 US gallons) of spirit (whisky and gin) per year. One dedicated 1,000-litre (264-US-gallon) still is used for gin production, a combination of vapour infusion and direct charge for the botanicals (*see* page 22), which are distilled individually rather than combined and vary greatly. The Original (42% ABV) features tart elements of foraged sea buckthorn, lemon balm and citrus peel, while Love Gin (42% ABV) has a slight pink blush due to a maceration of hibiscus and rose petals. The Hop Gin (46% ABV) delivers a bold aromatic, citrus note from the Australian Galaxy hops, whereas an oak-aged gin (42% ABV) offers pronounced spiced notes. There are also seasonal editions including a Candy Cane Christmas Gin (40% ABV), with head distiller Scott Ferguson continuing to experiment with botanicals including bog myrtle, meadowsweet, pine needles, coffee and cacao.
edenmill.com

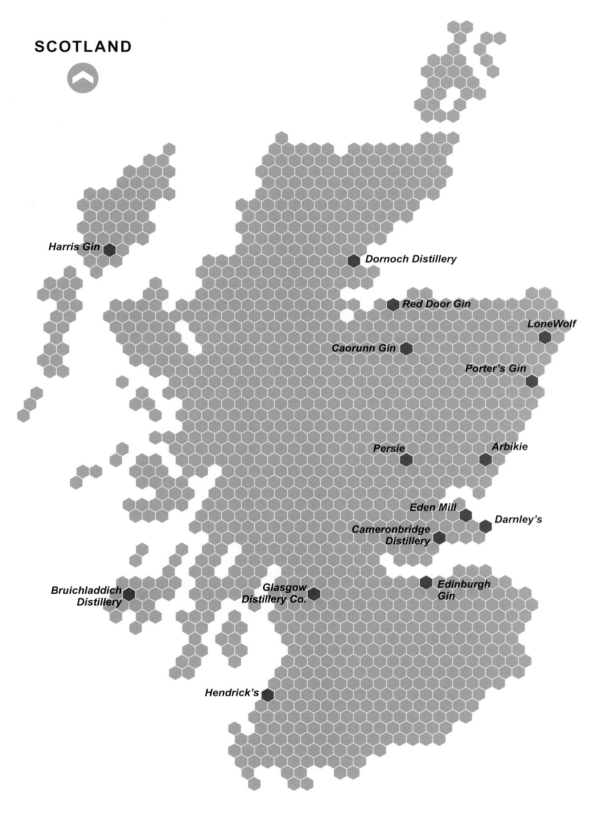

SCOTLAND

Harris Gin

Dornoch Distillery

Red Door Gin

LoneWolf

Caorunn Gin

Porter's Gin

Persie

Arbikie

Eden Mill

Darnley's

Cameronbridge
Distillery

Bruichladdich
Distillery

Glasgow
Distillery Co.

Edinburgh
Gin

Hendrick's

EDINBURGH GIN
EDINBURGH

Rather like London, in the later 1700s Edinburgh was awash with gin distilleries, and by 1777, alongside eight legitimate distilleries, there were said to be around 400 illicit gin distillers operating and making dubious spirit. Today, there are nine working distilleries, the Edinburgh Gin company, owned by Ian McLeod, leading the way since 2010, with two sites, one in the West End of the city and the other in Leith. Their first gin release is a classic London Dry style (43% ABV) featuring 14 botanicals including lavender, pine buds, mulberries and cobnuts, with a hearty citrus burst of orange peel, lime peel and lemongrass. Other editions include the highly original Seaside Gin (also 43% ABV) – a collaboration with Heriot-Watt University that is distilled with some unusual marine plants such as scurvy grass, ground ivy and bladderwrack to create a distinctive minerality.
edinburghgin.com

ISLE OF HARRIS GIN
OUTER HEBRIDES

The islands off the northwest coast are rich in wildlife, despite their barren terrain and brash coastal weather. Harris is no exception and there has been a dedicated gin distillery at Tarbert since autumn 2015, which draws on a strong local community. The gin itself is based around some typically classic botanicals: coriander, cassia bark, bitter orange and grapefruit zest, plus cinnamon, angelica, liquorice root and orris. The inclusion of sugar kelp is where things start to get more interesting. The distillery employs a local diver to forage this maritime botanical during the spring and summer months, after which it is dried and then added to the mix. The gin is bottled at 45% ABV.
harrisdistillery.com

CAMERONBRIDGE DISTILLERY
FIFE

It would be incredibly remiss not to dedicate a notable space in the Atlas to this vast distilling complex near Leven owned by multinational drinks company Diageo, not only claimed to be the largest grain distillery in Europe but also one of the longest standing, having produced grain whisky since 1830, and to this day is the powerhouse behind many global Scotch whisky brands such as Johnnie Walker, Bell's and more recently Haig Club, a partnership with footballer David Beckham. However, since the mid-1990s, Cameronbridge has also been home to the production of Gordon's and Tanqueray, which need no introduction as brands. Despite being respectively the number one and number three biggest-selling brands globally, both carry on inspiring and innovating, particularly Tanqueray, which continues to hold huge sway among the bartending community. Tanquerary No. Ten (47.3% ABV) is still distilled in a tiny pot still (called No. TEN), using a core of juniper, coriander, angelica and liquorice; Rangpur (41.3% ABV), a lime and citrus-led affair; Malacca, a throwback to an old sweetened recipe from Charles Tanqueray in 1830, reminiscent of an Old Tom; and Flor de Sevilla (also 41.3% ABV), a recent step into the orange-flavoured gin market.
gordonsgin.com
tanquery.com

RED DOOR HIGHLAND GIN
MORAY

A newcomer in terms of gin, but for renowned whisky company Gordon & MacPhail, distilling and bottling spirits has been in the family since 1895, operating from Elgin. The Red Door in the name here relates to what actually lies behind: Peggy, the small copper pot still, within the distinctive red warehouse doors at the Benromach Distillery on the outskirts of Forres. London Dry in style (bottled at 45% ABV), the gin is a bold, juniper-forward spirit, with a burst of bitter orange first, some woody juniper notes, floral notes of heather, then tangy sea buckthorn and a subtle, spiced chocolate note on the palate thanks to the inclusion of rowan berries.
reddoorgin.com

CAORUNN GIN
MORAY

Rather like Red Door's connection to the Benromach Distillery, Caorunn is another exceptional gin produced by a whisky distiller – this time the Balmenach Distillery, located in the Cairngorm National Park, which can trace its origins back to 1824. Caorunn may not be able to lay claim to such historical roots, but it is nevertheless one of the longest-established craft gin brands in Scotland, celebrating its tenth anniversary in 2019. What makes it so special is a combination of three important things. First, there is gin master Simon Buley's meticulous eye – and nose – for detail, personally foraging some of the notable botanicals for every batch. Second, the foraged botanicals themselves, which are joined by six classic botanicals: rowan berries, bringing a tart piquancy; bog myrtle, lending an earthy-yet-sweet flavour; plus local heather, Coul Blush apples and finally dandelion leaves. The third element is the unusual addition of what is known as a copper berry chamber in the distillation process: a horizontal copper vessel, built in the 1920s, lined with a series of four porous trays where the botanicals are spread for vapour infusion (*see* page 20). To date, Caorunn have two releases: a standard bottling at 41.8% ABV and a Master's Cut edition at a slightly higher 48% ABV.
caorunngin.com

THOMPSON BROS ORGANIC HIGHLAND GIN
HIGHLAND

The Thompson brothers distil both gin and whisky in the grounds of the Dornoch Castle Hotel on the Dornoch Firth in the Highlands. Their Highland Organic Gin (45.7% ABV) brings together 10% traditionally floor-malted spirit (where barley is malted on a traditional stone malting floor – *see* Essential Terms, page 246) using Plumage Archer barley made at the distillery, which gives a creaminess to the texture, and 90% organic grain spirit. Produced in batches of 3,000 50cl bottles using a 2,000-litre (528-US-gallon) Dutch-made still, it brings together juniper, angelica root, cardamom, aniseed, orange and lemon peel, coriander seeds, meadowsweet, elderflower, black peppercorns and freeze-dried raspberries.
thompsonbrosdistillers.com

PORTER'S GIN
ABERDEEN

Porter's Gin is the result of the coming together of three friends, Ben, Josh and Alex, who happen to be bartenders and gin enthusiasts. After developing the reputation of Orchid, the bar they run in the

city of Aberdeen, the lure of one day developing a house gin in the cellar of the bar was too great and working with a Rotovap vacuum still (*see* page 28) they developed a recipe that includes the more unusual Buddha's hand citrus fruit, typically not as sour and bitter as a lemon, but bringing more fragrant, floral citrus notes. While the gin isn't all made on site (the bulk spirit was developed by G&J Distillers in Warrington – *see* page 75), it is still blended with the team's own distillates before being bottled at 41.5% ABV. It is a punchy Martini gin, with some interesting floral notes.
portersgin.co.uk

LONEWOLF GIN
ABERDEENSHIRE
When a company such as BrewDog decides to enter the world of spirits, you would expect there to be fireworks. Back in 2016, when LoneWolf Spirits began production in Ellon, its Aberdeenshire HQ, the emphasis was on creating everything from scratch: the base alcohol for its whisky, vodka and gin is a 50/50 mix

of malt and wheat beer mash made at the brewery. It is then distilled in a highly unusual, custom-made triple bubble copper still that allows greater copper contact in order to develop a more complex spirit (rather like the Bennett or Florentine style of still – *see* page 29), before being rectified (*see* page 24) into a totally pure spirit. The gins made by head distiller Steven Kersley are relatively conventional by BrewDog's standards, but are complex and bold. The signature release (44% ABV) has lemongrass, pink peppercorns, mace and some floral notes of heather, mingling with Scots pine needles for a fresh aromatic aroma. Gunpowder Gin (bottled at 57% ABV) is a totally different affair: a triple-header of different peppercorns (pink, black and Szechuan), it hits the palate with a hearty zesty note and a warming aniseed spice.
lonewolfspirits.com

ARBIKIE
ARBROATH
A true definition of a single-estate distillery, Arbikie,

owned and run by the Sterling family on the 810-hectare (2,000-acre) Arbikie estate has been making its gin from scratch since the distillery was founded back in 2013. The first of their core gins, Kirsty's Gin (43% ABV), named after master distiller Kirsty Black, uses three different home-grown varieties of potato as the spirit base, Maris Piper, King Edward and Cultra, with the key botanicals of seaweed, carline thistle and Scottish blaeberry macerated before distillation in a 2,400-litre (635-US-gallon) copper pot (the distillery also has a 40-plate column still for making high-strength base spirit – *see* page 24). The second, AK's Gin (also 43% ABV), named after Alexander Kirkwood Sterling, is a different affair altogether, using Viscount wheat grown on the farm and then distilled into spirit, where it meets a different set of botanicals – honey from the farm, cardamom, black pepper and mace. What is also notable is that the farm is recognized by the Slow Food movement and has recently begun a project to grow juniper and many of

its other currently foraged botanicals, which in the long run is a more sustainable way to make gin. Arbikie is a landmark distillery for Scottish gin.
arbikie.com

MAKAR GIN
GLASGOW
Not unlike Edinburgh, Glasgow is going through a distilling renaissance and The Glasgow Distillery Co. occupies the site (Dundashill) of one of Glasgow's original distilleries dating back to 1770. Making both whisky and gin, the company uses a 450-litre (120-US-gallon) German still to produce Makar, a gin that has a number of variants: Makar Original Dry Gin, a juniper-forward style with rosemary, cassia bark, angelica and black pepper as the key botanicals, Makar Old Tom Gin, Makar Oak Aged Gin and most notably a Makar Mulberry Aged Gin, which sees the Original gin rested in bespoke 50-litre (13¼-US-gallon) virgin mulberry wood casks. All are bottled at 43% ABV.
glasgowdistillery.com

PERSIE GIN
PERTHSHIRE
Simon Fairclough, owner of Persie House, a country estate in Bridge of Cally in Perthshire, has taken the novel move of converting some of the former hotel's outbuildings into a small 230-litre (60-US-gallon) distillery. Persie focuses on three distinct botanical flavour styles, the thinking being that it is possible for every gin lover to gravitate toward a specific profile: Zesty Citrus (42% ABV), Herby & Aromatic (40% ABV) and Sweet & Nutty Old Tom (43% ABV).
persiedistillery.com

WALES

With rolling hills and national parks, Wales is the perfect place to forage for unusual botanicals and there are a handful of distilleries exploring that potential to the fullest.

SNOWDONIA DISTILLERY
CONWY

With a surrounding vista as beautiful as the one in which the Snowdonia Distillery sits, producing a gin with a direct relationship to its environment is clearly a no-brainer. Opened in 2015 by the Marshall family, the production is limited to just 5,000 bottles per release and the distillation process focused on a very lengthy initial maceration. Forager's Gin is the core expression, which comes in different batches, depending on the type of botanicals used and time of year they are picked: the first, Yellow Label, was bottled at 44% ABV and was a more floral-led spirit with notes of gorse and heather flowers, while Black Label, bottled at 46% ABV, is a much more warming, spice-led style, using sea buckthorn as a key botanical. *snowdoniadistillery.co.uk*

THE DYFI DISTILLERY
POWYS

Located in the only UNESCO-recognized World Biosphere Reserve in Wales, the Dyfi Distillery has focused on its indisputably stunning surroundings to provide the creative inspiration for its gins. Established by brothers Pete and Danny Cameron in the old slate mining village of Corris, the emphasis is on locality, foraging and a small-batch process, using two 100-litre (26½-US-gallon) stills sourced from Colorado in the USA. Such is the small scale of production that currently just one batch of gin is made per week, each one dated with the vintage and bottled at 45% ABV. Dyfi has three distinctly different gins: Original, which brings together a balance of foraged botanicals including bog myrtle and Scot's pine tips alongside juniper, coriander and grated fresh lemon peel; Pollination, a seasonally made gin using wild flowers and other foraged botanicals collected from within the Biosphere, which covers the Snowdonia foothills, through the Dyfi Forest and down to the estuary marshlands; and Hibernation with a foraged fruit-focused botanical balance that is rested in a white port cask sourced from the Niepoort winery in Portugal's Douro Valley. *dyfidistillery.com*

WALES

Snowdonia Distillery
(Forgaer's Gin)

Dyfi Distillery

Penderyn

BRECON GIN
GLAMORGAN

Predominantly a whisky distillery, Penderyn Distillery has had a foray into the gin world too, releasing a brace of different Brecon gins: Brecon Special Reserve Gin (40% ABV), which follows a comparatively classic path, with ten botanicals in the mix including cassia bark, orris root, coriander seeds and lemon and orange peels; and the more spice-led Brecon Botanicals Gin (43% ABV), which has a heavier emphasis on earthy/spicy tones. Despite the whisky being distilled at the site, the gin is distilled by Thames Distillers in London (*see* page 67), which seems like an opportunity waiting to happen, given the international popularity of the whisky and the large volume of visitors to the distillery.
penderyn.wales

Wales is the perfect place to forage for unusual botanicals.

⌂ *The Welsh countryside is rich in wild botanicals*

IRELAND

Like much of the UK, Ireland – and this includes Northern Ireland – has gone through a complete transformation in terms of the sheer number of distilleries creating craft spirits and notably gin. Historically, Dublin was a thriving scene for whiskey distillation, especially the Liberties area, but over time, with economic challenges and global consolidation, just a handful of major distilling players were left, making a huge variety of own-label and contract products. Today, however, there are more than 30 different Irish gins being produced, with the Irish Spirits Association projecting a target of some five-million-bottle sales of Irish gin globally by 2022. One thing is for sure, the Emerald Isle is shining very brightly indeed when it comes to craft spirits.

DINGLE GIN
COUNTY KERRY

The story behind Dingle Distillery is one of passion and a desire to put one of the most beautiful locations in Europe firmly on the spirits map. Three men, Oliver Hughes, Liam LaHart and Peter Mosley, had tasted success in drinks with their Porterhouse Group – a chain of bars that has spread from their native Ireland to both London and New York. With their appetite whetted in the independent craft beer sector, they set their sights on gin and whiskey, building the distillery on the site of an old sawmill, close to the Dingle Marina, back in 2012. Dingle is the most westerly town in Europe, if you choose to be selective about the location of Reykjavik, so is very much at the mercy of the Atlantic coastal breezes, which almost certainly affects the humidity and temperature of the distillery. At the time of its inception, the Irish craft spirits movement was in its infancy and still very much dominated by four big distillers, but although it was a bold move to set up the first artisan distillery in the region for a hundred years, it has certainly paid off. Fast forward seven years and the spirits being produced have been exceptionally well received by both the industry and consumers alike, winning Ireland Distillery of the Year at the New York International Spirits Competition in 2017 as well as a host of gold medals.

◔ Dingle's award-winning gin

Dingle Original is a vapour-infused gin (*see* page 20), distilled slowly in 500-litre (132-US-gallon) batches in a copper pot still, with a 24-hour maceration period bringing together rowan berries, fuchsia, bog myrtle, heather, chervil, hawthorn, angelica and coriander, giving it an immediate floral note, which balances very well with the juniper. One-shot in style (*see* page 29), the spirit is collected at around 70% ABV, then cut to 42.5% ABV using water drawn from a well 73m (240ft) underneath the distillery. At present there is only one style on offer, but given the strong bond with whiskey making on the same site, it is fair to assume that there are many more innovations to come in the pipeline. *dingledistillery.ie*

IRELAND

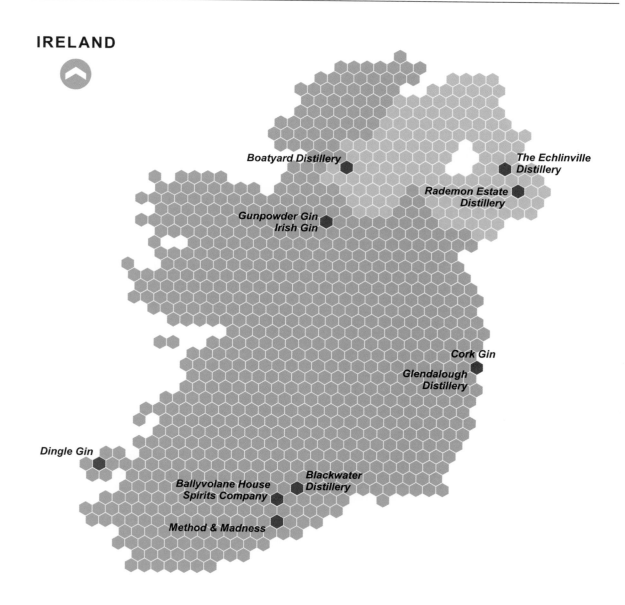

Boatyard Distillery

The Echlinville Distillery

Rademon Estate Distillery

Gunpowder Gin
Irish Gin

Cork Gin

Glendalough Distillery

Dingle Gin

Ballyvolane House Spirits Company

Blackwater Distillery

Method & Madness

THE ECHLINVILLE DISTILLERY
COUNTY DOWN

The Echlinville Estate in the village of Rubane has been an influential part of the area since it was purchased by Charles Echlin in the early 1700s. Today, the imposing house stands as a backdrop for the distillery of the same name, the first to be licensed in Northern Ireland in more than 125 years, when it began distilling whiskey, gin and vodka back in 2013. Like Boatyard (*see* page 90), Echlinville has a committed farm-to-bottle ethos, with barley grown close to the distillery being floor malted at the site (*see* page 82) to be turned into base spirit.

The distillery is the home of the historic whiskey brand Dunville's, but more recently Jawbox Gin, as well as a "house" gin, The Echlinville Irish Pot Still Gin (46% ABV) – a distinctly floral yet complex gin using whin bush (Irish gorse flower) and Strangford Lough seaweed as the local botanicals. Jawbox takes its name from the slang word used for the characteristic boxy ceramic sinks that could be found in most homes around Belfast, often the focal point of some lively kitchen conversations.

Jawbox Gin (43% ABV) is a departure from the Echlinville in style. It veers into a herbaceous, savoury London Dry territory, with most of the 11 botanicals used added directly to the pot still, as well as three being vapour infused (*see* page 20). Traditional cassia, orris root, coriander seeds and liquorice root provide an earthy foundation, with cubeb berries, grains of paradise and black mountain heather bringing out a spicy top note.
echlinville.com/echlinville-irish-pot-still-gin/jawboxgin.com

○ *The column still at the Echlinville Distillery*

BOATYARD GIN
FERMANAGH

Based in an old boatyard on the banks of Lough Erne in Fermanagh, the inspiring Boatyard Distillery is the dream of Joe McGirr, a former manager of the Scotch Malt Whisky Society and partner and distillery manager of The London Distillery Company in Battersea. Returning to Ireland from London gave him the opportunity to apply all the know-how of running a distillery, but in a much more tranquil and arguably less stressful location, applying a genuine farm-to-bottle approach in the process.

Locally grown organic wheat is malted, fermented and then distilled up to 96% ABV in a 500-litre (132-US-gallon) part pot, part column still (*see* page 25) appropriately named Mr Fusion, ready for the production of two key gins. The base alcohol distilled by Boatyard may only account for a minor percentage of the actual spirit used, as it is additionally blended with some organic spirit, but it certainly has an effect on the character and flavour of the overall gin.

The key botanical that links McGirr, the gin and the location is sweet gale, another name for bog myrtle, which is harvested once a year from the family farm, growing wild in the bogs where they also remove peat for fuel. The botanicals are steeped and macerated for 18 hours before distillation in a 250-litre (66-US-gallon) hybrid pot/column still known as Doc Brown commences, which is where another twist in the tale begins. Taking cues from the production of genever, the centre plate in the neck of the still is packed with additional juniper for extra vapour contact in order to highlight the upfront piney/resinous character of the botanical, hence the name Boatyard Double

> "
> The key botanical that links McGirr, the gin and the location is sweet gale, another name for bog myrtle, which is harvested once a year from the family farm.

Gin (which is bottled at 46% ABV). Undoubtedly a bold, full-flavoured gin, it has a very oily, mouth-coating juniper note with a burst of lemon citrus, a warming spiced citrus (coming from the coriander) and a slight floral kick as the juniper notes begin to calm down.

What is also rather extraordinary is that McGirr has no qualms about publishing the exact recipe for the gin on the label of each bottle: 86% juniper, 11% coriander, plus a smattering of liquorice root, angelica, orris root, unwaxed lemon peel, grains of paradise and finally the sweet gale.

Double Gin also has a sibling in the shape of a Boatyard Old Tom Gin (also 46% ABV), which takes the same core botanical percentages but leaves out the orris root and liquorice, substituting them with honey. The resulting sweeter spirit is then matured for four months in a first-fill Pedro Ximenez sherry cask, with no additional ingredients or colour added, giving a wonderfully rich, powerful example.
boatyarddistillery.com

◉ *The picturesque view from Boatyard distillery*

OTHER IRISH GINS TO TRY

SHORTCROSS GIN
COUNTY DOWN
Shortcross is one of Northern Ireland's most well-known craft distilleries, located on the Rademon Estate in Downpatrick. Shortcross Gin's distinctly floral, fruity recipe is based on the ample gardens and woodland that surround the estate, including clover, elderflowers and berries, as well as green apple, the spirit being cut with water drawn from a well on the estate. It is bottled at 46% ABV.
shortcrossgin.com

CORK GIN
DUBLIN
Like the UK's Gordon's (see page 82), Spain's Larios (see page 116) or, more latterly, USA's Seagram's, certain gin brands have come to define a country or a drinking culture. Cork Dry Gin can perhaps be considered as Ireland's stalwart, classic gin, tracing its roots back to 1793, when it was first distilled by the now-defunct Watercourse Distillery. Today, rather confusingly, its production is handled by Irish Distillers at a site in Dublin, which also has a huge distilling complex in Midleton, Cork, producing Jameson blended Irish whiskey and a huge range of single pot still whiskeys. The Midleton distillery is now the home to a brand-new craft gin called Method and Madness Irish Micro Distilled Gin, bottled at 43% ABV, which is distilled on Mickey's Belly, purportedly Ireland's first gin still and named after a Midleton distillery worker called Michael Hurley. The key botanicals are black lemon and Irish gorse flowers, giving a light, floral and zesty aroma and flavour.

The resurgence of Irish craft gin has done little to dent Cork's status as the

number one best-selling gin in Ireland. Cork Dry is not a distilled gin, but is cold compounded, meaning that the base spirit is post-flavoured with botanical essences. The juniper is lighter and more floral in style, with a hint of citrus zest and tangy coriander seeds. It is bottled at 37.5% ABV.
irishdistillers.ie

BERTHA'S REVENGE GIN
COUNTY CORK
The Ballyvolane House Spirits Company is the passion project of Antony Jackson and Justin Green, with the latter taking over the reins at his family home, Ballyvolane House, back in 2004. Both men had a keen interest in gin and a discussion with the great Charles Maxwell (*see* page 67) got them thinking about using whey as a source of the base alcohol for making gin. The duo experimented using whey spirit created from the produce of local dairy farmers in Cork, a handful of different botanicals and a 1-litre (2-US-pint) still until the final recipe was ready, which is now made in a much bigger bespoke pot still. The key botanicals of Bertha's Revenge Small Batch Irish Milk Gin (bottled at 42% ABV) are juniper, coriander, bitter orange, grapefruit, sweet orange,

lemon, lime, liquorice, orris root, angelica, cinnamon, cardamom, cloves, cumin, almond, elderflower and sweet woodruff. The gin's name was inspired by Bertha, a local cow that survived to the age of 49, making it into the *Guinness Book of Records* as the longest-living cow.
ballyvolanespirits.ie

DRUMSHAMBO GUNPOWDER IRISH GIN
COUNTY LEITRIM
Produced by The Shed Distillery, which was founded in 2015 by drinks industry veteran Pat Rigney in Drumshanbo, the gunpowder in Gunpowder Irish Gin (43% ABV) doesn't refer to its flammability, as in many navy-strength gins (*see* page 21), but the inclusion of Chinese gunpowder tea, which is key in this distinct gin. Locally grown meadowsweet, caraway seeds, star anise and a double-header of Chinese citrus fruit (lemon and grapefruit) come together alongside kaffir limes and five classic botanicals. The Shed has a set-up of three Arnold Holstein stills, each with a pot/column combination (*see* page 22), to produce Irish whiskey, vodka and gin.
drumshanbogunpowderirishgin.com

GLENDALOUGH DISTILLERY
COUNTY WICKLOW
One of the first of the new breed of craft distilleries to establish a name for itself, Glendalough was conceived back in 2012 but actually began distilling in 2015, using a 500-litre (132-US-pint) German Arnold Holstein still and an array of foraged botanicals from the Wicklow area, plus some more classic choices, both directly boiled in the still and vapour infused (*see* page 20). The distillery currently produces a Wild Botanical Gin, a four-season set of gins and a sloe gin, all bottled at 41% ABV.
glendalough.ie

BLACKWATER GIN
COUNTY WATERFORD
Peter Mulryan and Kieran Curtin at the Blackwater Distillery have approached their gins in a different way to those who rely so heavily on foraged ingredients. As they point out, they didn't look to the local hedgerows but instead trawled the local archives where they discovered that one of Ireland's biggest historical spice importers, White's of Waterford, was once based about 1km (just over half a mile) away from the distillery, so the duo set about finding unusual, overlooked botanicals to test distil. Blackwater No.5 (41.5% ABV) is a classic London Dry style using 12 botanicals: ten classics and two rather unusual ones, myrtle pepper and bitter almonds, which bring a notable winter spice/marzipan note. The duo has also experimented with ageing in 50-litre (13¼-US-gallon) juniper casks, which rounds out the spirit, adding piney character and a hint of colour.
blackwaterdistillery.ie

WESTERN EUROPE

Western Europe is arguably the true cultural home of gin, given the spirit's foundation in the Netherlands, where the popularity and taste for genever began to spread to surrounding nations and eventually across the Channel. Today, the Netherlands continues to thrive as a producer of both genever and gin, with Germany and Austria sharing a similar appreciation for a more historical approach to gin, known as *Wacholder*, as well as being at the cutting edge of a new breed of craft-orientated modern-styled gins. In Spain, a real "ginaissance" has taken the country by storm and that, in turn, has helped shine a spotlight on the emerging craft spirits movement in France, Italy, Portugal and, more recently, in Greece.

THE NETHERLANDS AND BELGIUM

While for many gin is identified with London, it is historically and spiritually firmly rooted in the Netherlands, which still to this day has a rich and influential reach over global gin production. As gin becomes more regionalized across every continent (excluding Antarctica), utilizing a wide variety of base spirit ingredients and a greater number of locally grown botanicals, it is perhaps easy for consumers to dismiss the often classic, much simpler recipes of some gins produced across Holland and Belgium as lacking complexity. It is also easy for the modern gin drinker to overlook the historical importance and the traditional malt wine flavours of genever (*see* page 18), in addition to the differences in its production style from modern distilled London Dry-style gins. Fortunately, the boom in gin's popularity has also started to bring about a renaissance in these unique products, shining a spotlight back on towns such as Schiedam in Rotterdam, the location of the Herman Jansen and De Kuyper distilleries and once home to 392 distilleries in the boom time of genever in 1880s; Dordrecht in South Holland, home of the Rutte distillery; Deinze in Belgium, where the Filliers family have been producing genever and gin since the 1800s, and of course, Amsterdam, where the Bols company has operated since 1575.

BOLS GENEVER
AMSTERDAM, THE NETHERLANDS

You can't write about the history of gin without talking about Bols (*see* page 15). Bols is the genesis of gin, the world's oldest spirit brand, and the entire category owes a debt of gratitude to Bols and the family who set it up. Beyond that, Bols's innovation in the general world of distilling has seen it become one of the most important and eclectic producers of flavoured liqueurs in the world.

Established in 1575, Bols was set up by the Bulsius family in Amsterdam to produce juniper-flavoured genever. During the 1600s, exporting and importing through companies such as the East India Company and Holland's own version of it, the Vereenigde Oostindische Compagnie (VOC), brought many exotic herbs, spices, fruits and other botanicals from around the world into the country, which were traded in ports such as Amsterdam.

With this ready supply of interesting ingredients to draw on, it is no wonder that Bols became famous not just for its juniper-flavoured spirit but for a whole range of botanical-enhanced drinks. Such was the kaleidoscope of flavours available that by the mid-1600s Bols is recorded as having over two hundred different liqueur recipes, which were exported to more than a hundred different countries via the VOC.

The richness of history at Bols and their pivotal place in the company of distillers globally has enabled them to develop their own museum in Amsterdam, The House of Bols Cocktail and Genever Experience. Here you can explore the history of the company and genever, as well as the key cocktails that have made it such a well-loved spirit.

Today, Lucas Bols is still in private Dutch ownership, and continues to focus heavily on genever and other flavoured liqueurs that they export all over the globe.

The company's genever is built on the classic recipe, starting with malt wine, a distillate of wheat, rye and

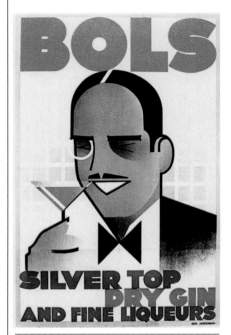

● *Classic vintage Bols advert*

corn with a touch of malted barley to allow for fermentation, that is triple distilled to a low 47% ABV to retain as much flavour from the ingredients as possible – the signature of Bols genever. A distillate of botanicals is then added to the malt wine, which includes coriander, star anise and aniseed. Finally, a malt wine spirit infused with juniper is added, and once these individual components are blended, the final mixture is left to mature in oak casks.

The current range of genever draws on Bols's historic recipe books, and features an unaged genever based on their original 1820 recipe that was used in many cocktails in the 19th century. The ingredients and malt wine base give this a malty, full-bodied taste. Bols Genever Barrel Aged is matured in French oak casks for 18 months. Richer than the unaged edition, the oak gives this a vanilla element with extra woody spices. Both genevers are bottled at 42% ABV.

lucasbols.com

The Netherlands has a rich and influential reach over global gin production.

THE NETHERLANDS AND BELGIUM

Amsterdam Craft Gin Company

Bols

Herman Jansen

Nolet

De Kuyper

Rutte

NETHERLANDS

Zuidam

Filliers

Rubbens Distillery

BELGIUM

FOCUS

GENEVER

The city of Schiedam in the metropolitan area of Rotterdam, the Netherlands, will forever hold a special place in the history of genever production, largely because it was a thriving hotbed of distilleries during the 1800s. Of these, arguably the most enduring have been De Kuyper, Herman Jansen and the Nolet distilleries. Individually, they have created and released many well-known, global brands in their own right as well as continuing to work closely with companies looking to create potential classics of the future.

DE KUYPER, SCHIEDAM
THE NETHERLANDS
The De Kuyper family can trace its distilling roots back to 1695 and today has a diverse portfolio of liqueurs together with several genevers that are bottled under its own name, including Jonge Graanjenever, a simple juniper botanical spirit bottled at 35% ABV. However, they are also the distillers of several contract brands such as Berry Bros. & Rudd's No.3 London Dry Gin.
dekuyper.com

NOLET DISTILLERY
SCHIEDAM, THE NETHERLANDS
One of the city's other enduring distillers is the Nolet family, who recently celebrated 325 years of spirit production. The distillery is famous for producing Ketel One vodka, but alongside this it makes Ketel One Jenever (35% ABV) and also Nolet's Silver (47.6% ABV) and Reserve Dry Gin (52.3% ABV) – a distinctly modern, floral and fruity gin, with peach, Turkish rose and raspberry being the key botanicals.
noletdistillery.com/en/our-brands
noletsgin.com

RUBBENS DISTILLERY
WICHELEN, BELGIUM
Dating back to 1817, the Rubbens distillery is one of Belgium's oldest family producers of genever. It has recently entered the gin market with Poppies Gin (40% ABV) in homage to the servicemen who fought in Flanders Fields during World War One.
rubbens.be

HERMAN JANSEN
SCHIEDAM, THE NETHERLANDS
Herman Jansen, established in 1777 by Pieter Jansen and then developed into a globally distributed company by his great grandson, Herman, is one of the only remaining distillers in Rotterdam to still make malt wine genevers from scratch, using a 100% malt wine and no additional GNS. As such, under the tenure of current generation Dick Jansen, it is one of only two distilleries (the other being the Schiedam Jenever Museum's De Gekroonde Brandersketel distillery) permitted to carry The Seal of Schiedam, dating back to

1902 – a voluntary accreditation for Schiedam pot still distilleries making 100% malt wine genever. Herman Jansen produces a proprietary brand of genever called Notaris, which is a simple juniper-led genever, bottled at 35% ABV.
hermanjansen.com

The distillery has also recently worked with American-based cocktail and spirit expert Philip Duff to produce Old Duff Single Malt Genever (45% ABV), a brand-new product made entirely in the traditional way, using a 100% malt wine (two-thirds rye to one-third malted barley) that is fermented for five days, then distilled three times before being distilled with juniper and Bramling hops.
oldduffgenever.com

It has also worked with gin brand Gin 1689 (42% ABV) to develop a 350-year-old recipe that brand owner Alexander Janssens found after researching for 18 months in the British Library.
gin1689.com

FILLIERS DRY GIN 28
DEINZE, BELGIUM

The Filliers family has been at the forefront of genever production since the early 1800s, and gin more latterly, when Karel Lodewijk Filliers began to explore the concept of distilling some of the grain crop from the family farm. This enterprise was fully realized by his son, Kamiel, who by the late 1800s had revolutionized the family's production of malt wine genever by installing steam power into what was still very much an agricultural business. It was the third generation of Filliers, Firmin, who moved the company into the more modern production of distilled Dry Gin back in 1928, with an initial recipe of 28 botanicals, by today's standards a regular affair but back then quite revolutionary.

In 2012, the company decided to relaunch their Dry Gin 28, the core flavours coming from juniper, Belgian hops, angelica root, allspice and fresh orange, although the finer details of the recipe are still a closely guarded secret known only to the

◉ *Filliers Distillery, Belgium*

current family members running the distillery. The distillation takes place in a pair of small alembic pot/column hybrid stills (*see* page 25) of around 1,000 litres (265 US gallons) in capacity, where one is used primarily to distil the fruity elements of the gin and the other, the more herbaceous, spicy botanicals in different batches, before being blended together and bottled at 46% ABV. In addition to the standard gin, there is a tangerine expression (43.7% ABV) using fruit from Valencia, Spain, a pine blossom edition (42.6% ABV) using *Pinus sylvestris* flowers, a cask-aged version (43.7% ABV) that sees the Gin 28 rested in 300-litre (80-US-gallon) ex-Cognac Limousin oak casks for four months and a tribute limited edition harking back to Filliers's first gin, highlighting

some of the core botanicals in the original recipe including malt, hops, angelica root and lavender.
filliersdrygin28.com

◉ *Filliers Dry Gin*

In 2012, they decided to relaunch their Dry Gin 28, the core flavours coming from juniper, Belgian hops, angelica root, allspice and fresh orange

OTHER DUTCH GINS TO TRY

RUTTE
DORDRECHT, THE NETHERLANDS

Like Filliers, the Rutte story is one of family passion, with distillation skills being passed down from generation to generation. It begins in 1872, when Simon Rutte opened a family café and liquor shop. Developing recipes in the café's small back room, he seized on the popularity of Dutch genever, utilizing his contacts who imported spices and botanicals from the Dutch East Indies. The operation expanded and took over the property as the popularity of Rutte genever and gin grew.

The knowledge and know-how was handed down through five generations of the family until 2003, when the last remaining Rutte (John) passed away. Despite the company coming under the ownership of De Kuyper, another famous Dutch family-run distilling business (*see* page 97), in 2012, the heritage of the distillery is still very much on view. The former living quarters of the shop have been transformed into a museum and tasting room for the Rutte product range and the distillery has resisted the temptation to modernize too far, with master distiller Myriam Hendrick distilling the small-batch gin on Vulkaan (volcano) 4, Rutte's high-tech copper pot still.

The existing Rutte range is both classic and esoteric in its approach. Its standard Dry Gin (43% ABV) is a re-creation of one of Simon Rutte's original recipes, with the distiller looking back through the original archive notebooks for hints on distillation style and botanical recipe, which brings together juniper, coriander, angelica, orris root, cassia,

bitter orange peel, sweet orange peel and fennel. Rutte's Celery Gin (43% ABV) is considered by many connoisseurs and bartenders to be the distillery's crowning achievement, a unique savoury recipe of juniper, celery, coriander, angelica root, sweet orange peel and cardamom. There is also a sloe gin (30% ABV), based on John Rutte's Sleedoorn Likeur recipe from the 1970s, featuring sloes steeped in gin and a touch of malt wine, and is infused with galangal, gentian, blackcurrant and cherries, along with Old Simon Genever (35% ABV), which brings together roasted walnuts and hazelnuts, mace, celery, carob, liquorice and fresh fruit.
rutte.com

ZUIDAM DISTILLERS
BAARLE-NASSAU, THE NETHERLANDS

The van Zuidam family began distilling back in 1975, working on a number of traditional-style liqueurs, genevers, gins and vodkas, before progressing the dark spirits side of the company in 1998 and moving into multi-award-winning rye whiskies and single malts, with the recipe development duties shared between father Fred and son Patrick. The distillery has grown from a 300sq-m (3,230sq-ft) facility with one small copper pot still into a 3,600sq-m (38,750sq-ft) distillery with four stills.

The Zuidam genevers are widely noted for their characterful mix of malt wine flavours and age profiles, including a flagship *korenwijn* style. This is made using a mash of one-third each corn, rye and malted barley that is distilled four times in a copper pot still, then a proportion of the resulting spirit redistilled with three botanicals, juniper, liquorice and aniseed, after which it is blended with the original malt spirit and reduced in strength to 45% ABV. The genever is aged in American oak casks for three separate age statements, one year, three years and five years, each of which are finally bottled at 38% ABV. The older the spirit, the more toffee, vanilla and nutty sweetness it develops alongside the fruity spirit character and herbaceous qualities of the botanicals. There is also a five-year-old 100% rye-based *jonge*-style genever, where the same malt wine recipe is distilled three times and then a proportion of the spirit redistilled with the same three botanicals before being bottled unaged at 35% ABV.

Zuidam also makes a range of three dry gins under the name Dutch Courage. The original recipe uses nine botanicals: juniper berries and orris root from Italy; coriander from Morocco; angelica, sweet oranges and fresh whole lemons from Spain; liquorice root from India; and cardamom and whole vanilla pods from Madagascar. Each botanical is distilled separately in a triple-distilled grain spirit and then blended together before being bottled at 44.5% ABV. A cask-aged version matured in new American oak casks (44% ABV) and an Old Tom (40% ABV) complete the range.
zuidam.eu

GERMANY

German gin has grown immensely in popularity over the past three to four years, largely thanks to the continuing surge in using existing stills that were once the domain of the fruit brandy and schnapps producers and charging them with new juniper-heavy recipes.

MONKEY 47 GIN
BADEN-WÜRTTEMBERG

As stories go, the one behind the development and success of Monkey 47 must rank as among the most fantastical tales in the history of gin. With its roots in the Black Forest, a region with centuries of expertise in the distillation of fruit liqueurs and schnapps, the story begins rather surprisingly with an Englishman in 1951, a certain Wing Commander Montgomery Collins, who after retiring from the Royal Air Force set a completely new course in life. After sponsoring a monkey called Max at Berlin Zoo, he opened a guesthouse in the Black Forest that he named Zum wilden Affen, "The Wild Monkey", after his simian friend. "Monty" then turned his hand to the noble art of distilling, making use of the abundant local juniper (already prized as an ingredient in the production of the famed Black Forest ham) and other plants to create a unique gin recipe, which he titled "Max the Monkey – Schwarzwald Dry Gin" and became the guesthouse's signature spirit for the next couple of decades.

Fast forward to 2006 when Alexander Stein, who has deep-rooted family connections to distilling, was so enthralled to rediscover the story of Montgomery Collins and his Black Forest gin that he decided to leave his job and try to re-create the long-forgotten recipe. After pursuing some old acquaintances of Collins and researching the landscape around the guesthouse, he partnered up with Christoph Keller, a distiller of noted excellence, to develop the concept further. Two years later and 120 trial distillations behind them, the recipe for Monkey 47 was ready, the "47" celebrating the 47 different botanicals that go into the making of the gin.

Until 2015, distillation was carried out in an old Arnold Holstein still at the Stählemühle distillery in Hegau, when it was moved to a new distillery located in Schaberhof just south of Lossburg. Rather than upscaling the operation to work with larger distilling vessels, the team commissioned Arnold Holstein to produce four 100-litre (26½-US-gallon) stills – King Louie, Cheetah, Herr Nilsson and Miss Baker – enabled for both direct pot still and vapour infusion of the botanicals (see page 20) specifically for the project.

The balance between 47 different botanicals is clearly a huge challenge for the distillers, but the core constituent flavours come from both lingonberries and cranberries, alongside spruce, elderflower, blackthorn, bramble leaves and Tuscan and Croatian juniper, in preference to Black Forest juniper because of the sunnier climate that fully ripens the berries.

Before distillation, the more herbaceous botanicals are given a 36-hour maceration in

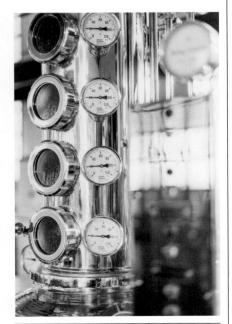

Column still used to make Monkey 47

🜚 *Monkey 47's distinctive bottle*

molasses-based alcohol, while the more delicate floral elements are prepared for vapour infusion. Once the spirit run is complete, each batch is then married for three months in earthenware vessels to develop the overall flavour.

Monkey 47 is bottled at an unsurprising yet clearly inspired 47% ABV, so is a hugely bold gin on the palate. The juniper is restrained at first, delivering a tart, slightly herbal note, but developing into more citrusy, spicy and fruity elements, then a return of a peppery/piney juniper note. In addition to the regular release, along with a Schwarzwald Sloe Gin (29% ABV) there has been an annually released limited-edition Distiller's Cut (47% ABV) since 2011, which brings in different key botanicals each time, ranging from spignel seeds, musk yarrow and, more recently, red mustard cress.
monkey47.com

GERMANY

Gin Sul

Elephant Gin

Doornkaat

Berliner Gin

Siegfried Gin

Ferdinand's Saar

GinStr

Monkey 47

ELEPHANT GIN
SAXONY-ANHALT

The story of Elephant Gin is a compelling one in which German distilling prowess meets African flavour via a touch of philanthropy toward an endangered species, and one of notable success since the brand came into existence back in September 2013.

Elephant Gin is the brainchild of husband and wife team Robin and Tessa Gerlach, who after spending a lot of their time and passion supporting African wildlife causes decided to take the next step in fundraising by creating an African-inspired gin and donating 15% of all profits from sales to two charitable foundations committed to the continuing fight against illegal poaching in Kenya and South Africa. And meeting an apple farmer in Wittenburg, about 80km (50 miles) east of Hamburg, who also happened to own a distillery, proved to be the perfect foundation for building that shared dream.

Each 600-bottle batch of Elephant London Dry Gin is distilled on an Arnold Holstein pot still, using rye-based spirit and a 14-botanical recipe that includes apples from the farm, pine needles, pimento berries and some distinctly African botanicals, such as baobab, devil's claw and African wormwood for additional earthy bitterness. In this regard, it is a one-shot gin (*see* page 29) unlike any other, combining a classic London Dry-style distillation and traditional flavours with some truly unusual elements. It is bottled at 45% ABV.

Besides a navy-strength (57% ABV) version, Elephant Aged Gin (52% ABV) is produced as a limited edition. There is also a sloe gin (35% ABV), where plump sloes are macerated for several months in the original gin before being sweetened and bottled. The result is a very fruity, tart, rich spirit that isn't cloyingly sweet like a few other examples on the market.
elephant-gin.com

15% of all profits goes to two charitable foundations committed to the fight against illegal poaching.

(*see* page 29)

(*see* page 18)

FOCUS

WACHOLDER AND STEINHÄGER STYLES

A domestically distilled juniper spirit, *Wacholder* has historically been especially popular in the Rhineland and Westphalia regions of the country. Of these, Eversbusch is arguably the most prominent brand, the distillery (founded in 1780) producing a heavily juniper-flavoured spirit using the same juniper suppliers since 1817, bottled in traditional earthenware jugs at 46% ABV. A high-strength version, bottled at 56% ABV, was released in 2017 as a tribute to the continued practices of the Eversbusch family, now under the stewardship of Christoph Eversbusch.
eversbusch.de

Steinhäger is another locally distilled juniper spirit from the Westphalia region of Steinhagen, which has been protected under EU Geographical Indication (GI) regulations since 1989. The family-owned Kisker distillery, established in 1732, produces the widely consumed Fürstenhöfer Steinhäger using a recipe that dates back to 1909. Like Eversbusch Wacholder, it is bottled at 38% ABV in *krukes* – ceramic jugs similar to the flagons used for traditional Dutch genever (*see* page 18). As one would expect, the spirit has a very distinct and direct juniper/piney/resinous flavour profile. Kisker also produces Silver Tree (41.5% ABV), a German London Dry gin, the recipe for which the Kisker family developed in 1851 after visiting the Great Exhibition in London.
kisker-brennereien.de

◔ *Apples, one of the key ingredients in Elephant gin*

GINSTR STUTTGART DRY GIN
STUTTGART

GINSTR is the culmination of two years' work by Markus Escher and Alexander Franke, the former, the youngest generation of the German Reisling winemaker Escher Haus; the latter, a well-known radio host, DJ and presenter. Together their plan was to produce a gin that they felt best represented the style of gin they loved and also the city of Stuttgart. Little did they know that practically the first spirit they produced would go on to net one of the biggest prizes at a globally recognized wine and spirits competition.

Launched in December 2016, GINSTR Stuttgart Dry Gin ("STR" being the code for Stuttgart Airport) was consigned to a batch size of just 711 bottles (another playful nod to the duo's love for the city, 0711 being the city's telephone area code) and was the outcome of a carefully thought-out journey through as many locally sourced botanicals as possible, including juniper berries harvested from the Escher Haus vineyards in Remstal on the outskirts of the city along with citrus fruit and rosemary cultivated in local nurseries. Other botanicals were then sourced from the Stuttgart Market Hall supplied by local merchants, such as liquorice root, kaffir lime leaves, hibiscus flowers, pomegranate seeds, cardamom and coriander seeds, the tally of botanicals amounting to 46 different ingredients. The duo can be particularly pleased with themselves, as GINSTR won two highly coveted prizes in 2018: the Gin & Tonic Trophy at the International Wine & Spirit Competition as well as a gold medal at the World Spirits Award.

Distillation takes place at the Escher Haus estate in a 25-year-old hybrid pot/column still (*see* page 25) named Otto after Markus's grandfather, previously used to make fruit spirits and pomace brandy, and which is, incredibly, direct fired using wood from the estate – a relatively rare practice in gin production these days that makes the overall temperature slightly more difficult to control than a steam-heated still, meaning that an entire batch will take the duo a week to distil.

GINSTR has a very vibrant nose, with a punchy citrus aroma arriving first, followed up by some resinous/piney juniper and a broad rooty earthiness. It is bottled at 44% ABV. *en.stuttgartgin.com*

⊙ *Fresh spirit from Otto, the wood-fired still in Stuttgart*

OTHER GERMAN GINS TO TRY

BERLINER DRY GIN
BERLIN
Vincent Honrodt, creator of Berliner Dry Gin in 2013, is from a distilling family that dates back to the 1930s. For his gin, he brings together botanicals grown on the SpeiseGut farm in Berlin and a super-premium grain distillate produced from 100% German-grown wheat, the distiller estimating that over 15,000 grains go into producing a single 70cl bottle of the spirit, bottled at 43.3% ABV.
berlinerbrandstifter.com

GIN SUL
HAMBURG
A gin with an element of wanderlust, GIN SUL is distilled in the centre of Hamburg by Stephan Garbe using a 100-litre (26½-US-gallon) Arnold Holstein still. On the Portuguese coast, specifically the Algarve, several of the key botanicals are sourced including fresh lemons, juniper, coriander seeds, rosemary, allspice, lavender, cinnamon and the final unusual ingredient *Cistus ladanifer* or gum rockrose flowers, which deliver a scent somewhere in between honey and eucalyptus. The result is citrus heavy but with a delicate fresh note, thanks in part to the vapour infusion of the floral botanicals (*see* page 20). It is bottled at 43% ABV.
gin-sul.de

DOORNKAAT GERMAN DRY GIN
LOWER SAXONY
Produced by the Berentzen group based in Haselünne, a distilling company founded in 1758 largely making schnapps, the Doornkaat brand can trace its roots back to 1806. Bottled at 44% ABV, this juniper-heavy, 100% wheat-based spirit gin

is simple yet spice laden, with a tart, dry citrus note on the palate.
berentzengruppe.de

FERDINAND'S SAAR GIN
RHINELAND-PALATINATE
Made on the border where Germany meets France and Luxembourg, Ferdinand's Saar Dry Gin (44% ABV) is arguably one of Germany's most unusual spirits and a truly unique gin. It is distilled by the highly regarded Andreas Vallendar on his estate in Wincheringen-Bilzingen, which can trace its roots back to 1824, where 30 mostly home-grown botanicals are hand-picked, including quince, lavender and thyme, and then combined with sloes, rosehips, angelica, hop blossoms and rose, with further top notes provided by almond shells, coriander seeds and ginger.

The real point of difference is that the resulting gin is then infused with a high-quality Riesling wine produced by winemaker Dorothee Zilliken at the Forstmeister Geltz-Zilliken estate, which contributes a silky texture and fragrant, balanced aroma alongside the botanicals. In addition to the Dry Gin, Ferdinand's Saar also produces a Quince Gin (30% ABV) – "a tribute to British sloe gin", as Vallendar describes it – using fruit from the pair of quince groves next to the distillery. There is also a once-yearly limited Goldcap edition gin (49% ABV), which features dried Riesling grapes, acacia shoots, mirabelles and cocoa beans as botanicals, for a darker, more complex and textured spirit.
saar-gin.com

SIEGFRIED GIN
RHINELAND-PALATINATE
Founded in 2014, Siegfried Gin takes its inspiration from the dragon-slaying Siegfried of German mythology, who, as it is related in the Nibelungen saga, was bathing in dragon's blood when a leaf from the linden tree fell into the bathtub with him. Although Siegfried Rheinland Dry Gin (41% ABV) doesn't contain dragon's blood, the blossom of the linden tree is one of the key botanicals in a list of 18. The distillers Gerald Koenen and Raphael Vollmar also produce Wonderleaf, a non-alcoholic version of the gin, which actually started out as an April Fool's Day joke in 2016, but received such a positive response that the duo spent months developing the recipe.
siegfriedgin.com

AUSTRIA AND SWITZERLAND

Austria is developing its own small scene with a few distillers creating gins using locally sourced botanicals. The Swiss are also intent on making a mark in gin, with some of the key fruit schnapps distillers in the country turning their attention to juniper and botanicals.

RICK GIN
VIENNA, AUSTRIA

Rick Gin was set up in Vienna with the aim of making an Austrian gin for the distiller's own consumption. The key botanicals of juniper berries, coriander, angelica root and lemon and orange peel are combined with many others including ginger, liquorice, lemongrass, kaffir limes and jasmine for the three main expressions that the distillery produces. RICH, bottled at 43%

ABV, uses organic lemons from the country's Zitrusgarten, which boasts a collection of over 280 varieties of citrus; BRAVE, at 47% ABV, features pepper and ginger; and FEEL, at 41% ABV, offers a Mediterranean-inspired version using thyme from Croatia, rosemary from Italy, olives from Spain, home-grown basil and hand-cut orange blossoms.
rick-gin.at

5020 GIN
SALZBURG, AUSTRIA

Taking its name from the postcode of where it is made by Stephan Koudelka, 5020 Gin uses 22 botanicals including lavender, marshmallow, orris root, muscat blossom and rose in addition to juniper, all sourced from organic farming. It is distilled in small copper stills of about 100 litres (26½ US gallons) through the vapour-infusion process (*see* page 20), whereby an aroma basket hangs directly in the still. Once the spirit has been drawn from the distillation, it spends four weeks in glass balloons before being bottled at 43% ABV.
5020-gin.at

AUSTRIA AND SWITZERLAND

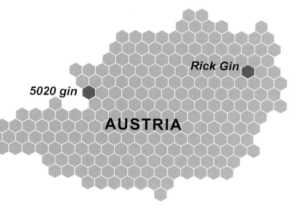

Rick Gin

5020 gin

Xellent gin

AUSTRIA

SWITZERLAND

XELLENT GIN
WILLISAU, SWITZERLAND

Xellent Swiss Edelweiss Gin is made at the DIWISA Distillerie in Willisau using a base of Swiss rye grain (sourced from 18 farmers) spirit, which is also sold as a vodka, and 25 botanicals including edelweiss, woodruff, elderflower, lemon balm and lavender, the latter two grown by the master distiller Franz Huber. All the ingredients are macerated in the base vodka (which is produced in both a pot still and a column still – *see* page 25) for several hours before distillation. It is then diluted down to 40% ABV using pure glacier water from the heart of Switzerland. The distillery also runs gin distillation classes.
xellent.com

FRANCE

France has embraced the gin revolution with a charismatic style and charm of its own, utilizing a grape base for the spirit in several examples (and apples in the case of a few producers in northern France), which brings it closer to the family of French brandies including Cognac, Armagnac and Calvados. One unusual anomaly is what is known as Flanders Genever Artois: a type of juniper-flavoured, genever-style spirit that must be made using a grain base of rye, barley, wheat and oats.

Like German *Steinhäger* (*see* page 103), Slovakian *Borovička* (*see* page 143) or Mahón Gin (*see* page 118), it is a spirit style protected by an EU Geographical Indication (GI) and limited to production in two regions of northern France currently by two distilleries: Houlle (genievredehoulle.com), which is located in the rural countryside about 40km (25 miles) from Dunkirk, and the Claeyssens Wambrechies distillery (distilleriedewambrechies.com), established in 1817, which distils and bottles Loos Genever.

CITADELLE GIN
CHARENTE

Citadelle Gin was conceived in June 1996 at the Château de Bonbonnet in the most French of fashion: over lunch on a sunny terrace. Talk of chateau-to-bottle wines turned to talk of chateau-to-bottle gin, and for founder Alexandre Gabriel, having experience in the world of spirits through Cognac production at the Pierre Ferrand distillery, gin provided a golden opportunity.

The strict rules and regulations imposed by the *appellation d'origine contrôlée* (AOC) means that any Cognac producer is obligated to use their copper pot stills for the Cognac season only, five months of the year, so Gabriel petitioned

◉ *Citadelle's Art Deco bottle*

the AOC for permission to use his stills to produce gin during the remaining months. After five years of negotiations, he finally obtained authorization to distil from April to October, and the foundations for Citadelle Gin were laid.

The next stage was to find a recipe that worked, so he set about researching traditional styles of gin and discovered a recipe from the 18th century developed by a distillery in Dunkirk in 1771, which was housed in the Citadelle within the port town, and later authorized by Louis XVI to produce for the crown.

Today, Citadelle Gin is made in historic French Cognac stills, drawing influence from the 1771 recipe, and now even uses juniper grown on the estate, alongside 18 other botanicals in its Original edition, namely coriander, cardamom, angelica, cumin, nutmeg, almonds, grains of paradise, liquorice, cubeb, savory, cinnamon, star anise, blackcurrant, orris root, violet, fennel, orange zest and lemon. Such is the uniqueness of the production process involved that it has its own patent (No. 17 58092, 01/06/2018), with each botanical being infused in a neutral alcohol made from French wheat for a different length of time (three to four days) and at different strengths to capture its characteristic aroma and flavour.

Once maceration has been completed, distillation takes place over a naked flame in small

Château de Bonbonnet

2,500-litre (660-US-gallon) copper stills. This direct firing of the still heats the spirit hard, creating a natural sweetness. Finally, the gin is bottled at 44% ABV.

Citadelle's classic offering is supported by barrel-aged Citadelle Réserve, which adds yuzu, genepi and bleuet to the same botanical mix before resting the gin in five different types of wood barrels – acacia, mulberry, cherry, chestnut and French oak – for five months. After the ageing period is over, the gin is blended together and refined in an egg-shaped oak barrel 2.45m (8ft) high, then bottled at 45.2% ABV.

Building on this, Citadelle has developed an Old Tom variety where demerara sugar is toasted in copper cauldrons to the first stage of caramelization, then lightly thinned and finally mixed with spirit before being aged for three to four months in casks. This aged sugar is then used to gradually flavour Citadelle Réserve and the resulting gin matured in casks for several months, at the end of which process it is bottled at 46% ABV.

Since 2016, Citadelle have released a series of limited-edition gins under the banner Extrêmes, looking at enhancing individual botanicals within a gin profile, such as wild cherry blossom (42.6% ABV).
citadellegin.com

G'VINE GIN
CHARENTE

Drawing on centuries of grape-growing and grape-distilling expertise in the Charente region of France just north of Bordeaux in the heart of Cognac country, G'Vine was founded by master distiller Jean-Sébastien Robicquet in 2007, who uses local grapes to make a base spirit.

G'Vine Gin is produced in the grounds of Maison Villevert, a family estate that dates back to the 16th century, starting with the distinctive Ugni Blanc grape variety, which is heavily used by France's brandy producers. Harvested mostly in September of each year, depending on the weather during the growing season, a wine is produced from each vintage's harvest before being distilled into the G'Vine base spirit using a column still (*see* page 24).

With the grape spirit providing a neutral-tasting, but smooth backdrop, the next stage in the production of G'Vine is the addition of nine botanicals, split into three

G'vine's still 'Lily Fleur'

groups and distilled separately to preserve their aromatic properties: juniper berries, ginger root, *Quassia amara*, green cardamom, liquorice and lime; and coriander seeds, cubeb berries and nutmeg. A final, signature botanical, the vine flower, is then separately distilled. The flowers bloom for only a few days a year, in June, before maturing into grape berries, so are hand-picked as soon as they appear. In order to capture their aroma and flavour, they are macerated in grape spirit before being distilled in a small copper pot still (formerly used to make perfume). These distillates are then married together and once more distilled in a larger copper pot still, named Lily Fleur.

G'Vine produce two core expressions of their gin: Floraison (meaning "flowering"), bottled at 40% ABV, and Nouaison (meaning "setting"), bottled at a higher 45% ABV and drawing on the additional botanical palette of sandalwood, bergamot, prune, Java pepper and vetiver.

In 2015, G'Vine also revived a gin recipe from 1409, which was discovered in the Netherlands in an out-of-print Dutch language history book about genever. Believed to have been devised by a merchant, the recipe contains a very high percentage of botanicals, including nutmeg, cinnamon, cardamom, ginger, cloves and sage. Two versions of the recipe were produced, Gin 1495 Verbatim (42% ABV), using the original instructions, as well as a modern take, Gin 1495 Interpretatio (45% ABV), using a higher concentration of juniper and citrus notes. Just 100 bottles of Gin 1495 Verbatim were made, packaged alongside Gin 1495 Interpretatio with a copy of the original recipe.
g-vine.com

FRANCE

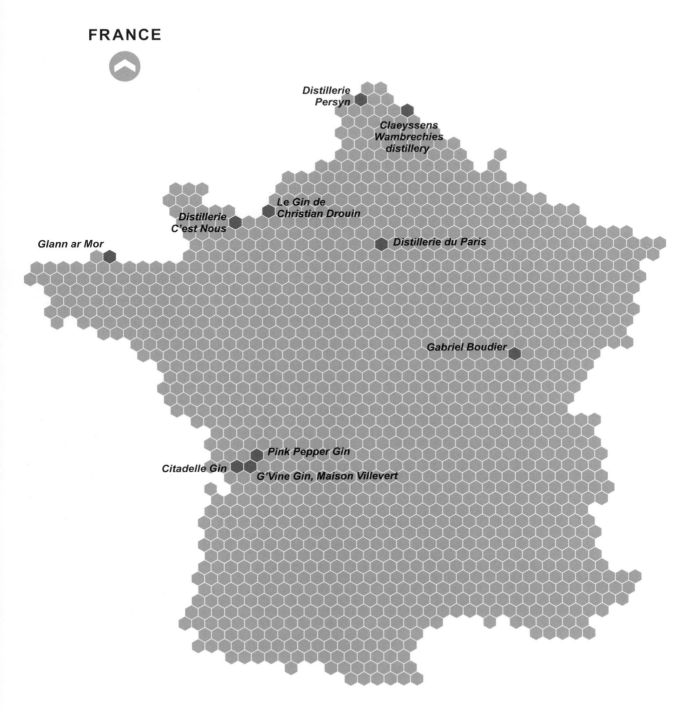

Distillerie
Persyn

Claeyssens
Wambrechies
distillery

Le Gin de
Christian Drouin

Distillerie
C'est Nous

Distillerie du Paris

Glann ar Mor

Gabriel Boudier

Pink Pepper Gin

Citadelle Gin

G'Vine Gin, Maison Villevert

PINK PEPPER GIN
CHARENTE

Founded in 2013, Pink Pepper Gin is made by Miko Abouaf and Ian Spink of Audemus Spirits in the Cognac region of France. Abouaf initially moved to Cognac to take up a role in distilling for Martell and Courvoisier, but subsequently set up his own business making gin, liqueurs and eau-de-vie. Having pursued the aim of helping others create interesting spirits from their own equipment and resources, it was the distillers' own creation, Pink Pepper Gin, that proved the most successful.

Eschewing traditional French distillation methods, Abouaf employed a modern rotary evaporator (*see* page 28) at first, but had to look beyond this small-scale production method as the gin gained in popularity. The company now uses a 25-litre (6½-US-gallon) vacuum still, with each individual botanical element steeped and distilled separately in a neutral wheat spirit base. After distillation it is blended, diluted and bottled at 44% ABV. The botanical selection for Pink Pepper comprises a juniper heart supported by black cardamom, local honey,

> " Comprises a juniper heart supported by black cardamom, local honey, vanilla, tonka beans and of course pink peppercorns.

vanilla, tonka beans and, of course, pink peppercorns.

Alongside Pink Pepper Gin, the duo also produces a series of limited-edition gins. The first, simply called Dive Bar (44% ABV), has a big juniper note accompanied by the smokiness of lapsang souchong tea and cubeb peppers, along with "two secret botanicals, sourced for their sultry, aromatic flare". There is also a port barrel-aged offering (Old Ma's; 47.5% ABV) and a hop-based gin (Hoppy; 41% ABV), created by distilling French brewers Deck & Donohue's Indigo IPA and then infusing it with juniper, angelica and two secret botanicals.
audemus-spirits.com

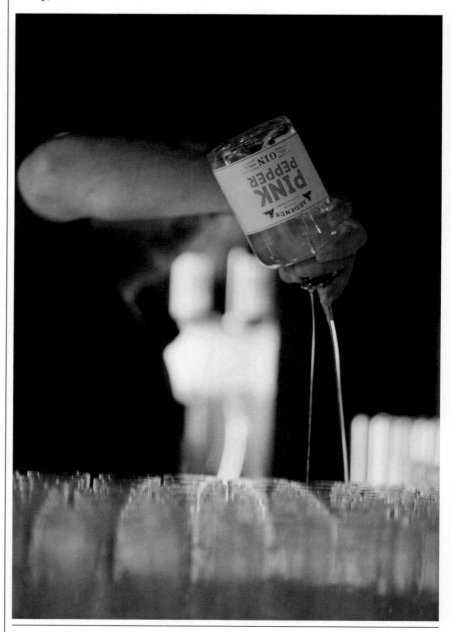

⊙ *Pink Pepper being poured*

OTHER FRENCH GINS TO TRY

DISTILLERIE DE PARIS
PARIS

Brothers Nicolas and Sébastien Julhès set up the Distillerie de Paris in 2015, having grown up in the bakery, grocery and drinks retailing family business and Nicolas having spent some 15 years as a consultant in the spirits industry. It was the first distillery to operate in Paris, producing gin along with a whole host of other spirits in a 400-litre (106-US-gallon) German Arnold Holstein still. Their first release (Gin Batch 1) uses a grape base spirit and botanicals such as fresh coriander and bergamot alongside juniper, jasmine and lavender, while their Gin Bel Air draws on botanicals from the French island of Réunion. Both are bottled at 43% ABV.
distilleriedeparis.com

LE GIN DE CHRISTIAN DROUIN
NORMANDY

In northern France, Calvados producer Christian Drouin has cleverly created his own gin by selecting 30 varieties of apple to make a base spirit. The fruit is picked in the autumn, grated and pressed, the resulting must slowly fermented during the cold winter months and then double distilled in small copper pot stills the following year. To this he adds eight sbotanicals – juniper, ginger, vanilla, lemon, cardamom, cinnamon, almonds and rose – that he believes reflect the flavours within Calvados and which are individually distilled before blending. It is bottled at 42% ABV. The house also produces a limited-edition version of the gin, aged for six months in 225-litre (59-US-gallon) Calvados casks, also bottled at 42% ABV.
le-gin-drouin.com

LE GIN C'EST NOUS
NORMANDY

Founded in 2016, the Distillerie C'est Nous uses French wheat spirit along with eight different botanicals including Croatian juniper, Spanish orange peels and Italian orris root to make their Le Gin C'est Nous (40% ABV). It is distilled in a small alembic copper pot still (*see* page 22) and it is post-flavoured with the essence of Normandy apples.
cestnous-gin.com

SAINT MAUDEZ GIN
BRITTANY

Located in the Tregor region on the northern coast of Brittany, the Glann ar Mor distillery produces Saint Maudez Gin (44.7% ABV), as well as whisky, using a wheat-based spirit and botanicals including juniper, coriander, angelica root, citrus peels and other herbs which are macerated before distillation.
glannarmor.com/

SAFFRON GIN
DIJON

Saffron Gin is produced by French distillery Gabriel Boudier based in the famed city of Dijon in the Burgundy region, which has been making spirits since the late 1800s. Launched in 2008, the gin takes its inspiration from an old recipe the company had in a book from the 19th century. It is created using a wheat spirit distilled in a copper pot still, drawing on nine botanicals, namely juniper, coriander, lemon, orange peel, angelica, orris root, fennel and of course saffron, which gives it a distinct orange colour, and bottled at 40% ABV.
boudier.com

SPAIN AND PORTUGAL

Spain is undoubtedly one of the most important and diverse gin markets in the world and one that the rest of Europe continually looks toward as a virtual barometer of taste. Alongside the popular Gin and Limon, the country's affection for gin has arguably influenced the appreciation and reinvention of the once humble Gin and Tonic into something altogether more sophisticated and adventurous, bringing into play the larger, bulbous, stemmed glass and a multitude of different garnishes, often linked to the botanicals in the chosen gin.

In terms of statistics, in 2018, Spain was the third-largest gin market (behind the Philippines and the USA), and the Spanish out-consumed the rest of Europe with an impressive 1.07 litres (2¼ US pints) per capita – more than the combined thirst of France, Germany and the UK. The increased enjoyment of gin can be attributed to the resonance of well-known brands such as Beefeater (*see* page 63), Gordon's (*see* page 82) and domestic giant Larios (*see* page 116), which continue to perform strongly, as well as the numerous flavoured gins that are entering the market. The craft gin sector has also seen a surge in activity in recent years led by the success of Gin Mare (*see* right), and new brands continue to excite and delight, embracing

a diverse range of botanicals outside the traditional London Dry classics and also exploring different base alcohol sources, such as wine and rye and wheat combinations.

Portugal not only shares a physical border with Spain but also a spiritual bond when it comes to the current popularity of craft gin. While there may not be as many well-known brand names from the country, there is an evident passion to produce distinctly Portuguese gin using a variety of local botanicals.

🅐 *Gin Mare: spearheading savoury*

GIN MARE
CATALONIA, SPAIN

In many respects, Gin Mare can be considered as Spain's most pioneering gin. When it was developed back in 2007, the world had a nascent interest in craft gin, with barely a handful of the recognized names that have come to define the movement but a twinkle in a distiller's eye.

Gin Mare's creators Manuel Jr and Mark Giro, the fourth generation of a Spanish distilling dynasty that dates back to the mid-1830s, have taken the knowledge passed down from their grandfather, Manuel Sr, who successfully launched Gin MG as a brand in the 1940s, which has since gone on to become one of Spain's best-selling gins. However, while this more classically styled London Dry gin (think big, juniper-forward notes and a sharp burst of lemon citrus) may have acted as the jumping-off point for the brothers, it was by no means to act as a benchmark recipe.

In fact, Gin Mare has set out on an altogether different flavour path and it can probably be credited as one of if not *the* first distinctly "savoury" gins to hit the market. The brothers trialled a range of individual botanical distillates, rounding on a combination of Arbequina olives, which are grown and harvested locally to the distillery in Vilanova (a beautiful countryside property with its own chapel that houses the still), along with basil, thyme and rosemary to bolster the herbaceous heart. Add to this Valencian orange peel, the peels of lemons from Seville, coriander, cardamom and, of course, juniper, and a highly complex recipe begins to be revealed. Using Arbequina olives has proved to be a challenge in itself, given that the variety is on the diminutive side, so around 15kg (33lb) are needed for each batch of gin and every year the acidity will vary depending on the success of the harvest.

Each botanical is macerated separately for around 36–40 hours, except the citrus elements, which are brought together and married in spirit for up to a year in advance of the final distillation, which takes place in a 250-litre (66-US-gallon) Florentine pot still (*see* page 29), a remarkably unusual shape with a distinct copper boil ball to aid reflux of the spirit back into the pot (also used at G'Vine in France – *see* page 110). Once distilled, the finished gin is diluted with neutral spirit (making a multi-shot in style – *see* page 29) and bottled at 42.7% ABV.

Gin Mare really is unmistakable on the nose and palate: the citrus is surprisingly dominant, but given its initial maceration time, the clarity of the tart lemon and sweeter, fresh floral notes of the orange peel shine through brightly before anything else. Then comes the savoury element, almost saline at first, but with a fragrant woody/forest floor note. The juniper is still evident, but perhaps driven in a more piney/menthol direction. A truly original and distinctive gin indeed.
ginmare.com

LARIOS GIN
MÁLAGA, SPAIN

The concept of a truly national spirit is alive and kicking with Larios, unquestionably Spain's most enduring and popular gin brand. Larios can trace its roots back to 1866, when French wine entrepreneur Charles Lamothe, and his Spanish associate Fernando Jiménez founded the Jiménez Lamothe company. Their distilleries in Malaga and Manzanares began to revolutionize the style of spirits in Spain, and by 1916, the third marquis, José Aurelio Larios, who provided the financial backing to the duo, eventually took over the company, changing its name to Larios & Cía, with Larios Dry Gin becoming a mainstay brand in 1932.

The brand rose to prominence during the 1980s due to the growing popularity of the Gin and Tonic across Spain, and passed into the hands of French drinks giant Pernod Ricard in the late 1990s, and is now under the ownership of American/Japanese company Beam Suntory that also owns Gilbey's London Dry,

Spain's enduring Larios gin brand

Japanese Roku Gin (*see* page 231) and recently acquired London-based craft gin pioneers Sipsmith (*see* page 64).

Since the rise of gin culture in Spain, which has unquestionably led to the rise in popularity of craft gins right across Europe and now North America, the original Larios London Dry hasn't found favour in a growing market of gin connoisseurs, who are largely driven by the transparent process of craft and small-batch gin distilling. However, renamed and repackaged as Larios Ginebra Mediterránea (37.5% ABV), it remains one of the world's most popular gins, and is still Spain's best-selling gin thanks to its simple botanical recipe, with a prominent focus on juniper, coriander and orange peel, and mixability.

To compete with the new gin revolution, the company has released a more contemporary – and more distinctly flavoured – version, Larios 12 (40% ABV), which is distilled five times and has a much more citrus-led palate. The "12" relates to the number of botanicals used, namely Mediterranean lemon, orange, tangerine, mandarin, clementine, grapefruit and lime, providing tangy bursts of character, alongside juniper, nutmeg, angelica root and coriander. The final element is orange blossom, which is added during the final pass of distillation; a subtle addition, but it helps to round out a broad-shouldered expression with a touch of floral finesse. A post-strawberry-flavoured pink-hued Rosé and a Citrus version flavoured with Mediterranean oranges have recently hit the shelves in response to the growing demand for more fragrant-flavoured gins, both bottled at 37.5% ABV.
lariosgin.es

SPAIN AND PORTUGAL

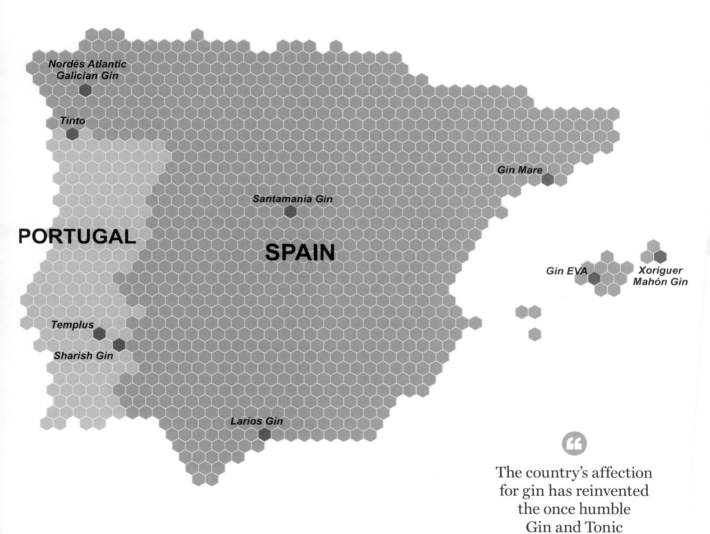

Nordés Atlantic
Galician Gin

Tinto

Gin Mare

Santamanía Gin

PORTUGAL

SPAIN

Gin EVA

Xoriguer
Mahón Gin

Templus

Sharish Gin

Larios Gin

The country's affection
for gin has reinvented
the once humble
Gin and Tonic
into something more
sophisticated
and adventurous.

XORIGUER MAHÓN GIN
MENORCA, SPAIN

The port of Mahón in Menorca, the most easterly of the Balearic Islands, has in many ways been strongly associated with gin for centuries. While it was under sporadic British occupation up to 1802, when it was finally assigned to Spain under the Treaty of Amiens, it was a valuable naval outpost, overflowing with British sailors, who, having acquired a thirst for gin, found themselves without a readily available supply other than what was imported. The locals of the island took matters into their own hands, bringing in juniper berries from other parts of the Mediterranean and starting to distil with it using a wine-based spirit.

This practice fortunately continued long after the British withdrew, and the Pons family are still the proud producers of Xoriguer (pronounced *Sho-ri-gair*), named after one of the traditional old windmills the family used to own, a brand that was established in the late 1930s. Today, the gin is still manufactured in the same way: using wood-fired alembic stills (*see* page 22) and a wine-based spirit that is cut with local water before being added to the stills. Vapour infusion of the botanicals occurs in a copper basket in the neck of the still, where, apart from the given juniper, the exact recipe remains a closely guarded secret known only to a few of the Pons family. What is surprising here is that the process produces a distillate that runs off the stills at 38% ABV before being bottled at the same strength, rather than a high-strength concentrate. The result is a distinctive fruity, juniper-forward style of gin.

Xoriguer now has an EU Protected Geographical Indication (PGI) in recognition and protection of the unique Mahón gin style.
xoriguer.co.uk

OTHER SPANISH AND PORTUGUESE GINS TO TRY

NORDÉS ATLANTIC GALICIAN GIN
GALICIA, SPAIN

The story of Nordés starts with the meeting of three friends: one with distilling experience and two with a fine understanding of wine, one from the perspective of an award-winning sommelier and the other an entrepreneur in the wine trade. Based in the small town of San Pedro de Sarandón, about 20km (12 miles) from Santiago de Compostela in the very northwest of Spain, they produced the first gin in the region, influenced by the weather and winds brought in by the Atlantic Ocean, which lies roughly 60km (37 miles) to the west. One of the key USPs here is that Nordés is made using a base spirit that contains a proportion of Galician Albariño grape wine, which, once distilled, is balanced out with a grain-based spirit. The wine is known for its hugely aromatic, almost Gewürztraminer style, and this is carried over into the resulting gin, which features 11 distinct botanicals: six that grow wild in Galicia, including sage, laurel, verbena, eucalyptus, peppermint and glasswort seaweed from the coast, alongside juniper, black tea, hibiscus flower, ginger and cardamom. The effect is a highly perfumed gin, with the fragrance of the wine and herbaceous botanicals producing a heady aromatic top note that surrounds the juniper. It is bottled at 40% ABV.
nordesgin.com

SANTAMANÍA GIN
MADRID, SPAIN

Santamanía is the project of Javier Domínguez, Ramón Morillo and Victor Fraile, together with their pair of Christian Carl stills. The trio established their Destilería Urbana ("Urban Distillery") to produce a small range of their own craft-distilled spirits including a number of gins, but also to act as the alchemists for those looking for collaboration and experimentation on a very small batch. So far, four gins are on offer, using grape-based spirit as the starting point and a surprisingly classic range of botanicals such as juniper, orris root, coriander and the more exotic Spanish *azafrán* (saffron), as well as batches aged in French oak casks and a collaborative edition with Australian gin pioneers Four Pillars (*see* page 217), bottled at 40% ABV.
destileriaurbana.com

GIN EVA
MALLORCA, SPAIN

Gin EVA was founded in 2011 by husband and wife team Stefan Winterling of German descent and Barcelona-born Eva Maier, who not only have a love for distilled spirits but also a background in winemaking and vinification. The two met when they were working at the same winery in Geisenheim and subsequently moved to Mallorca where they began working in the vineyards and also developing the concept of bringing gin distillation to the island. Winterling discovered that Mallorca was rich in wild juniper, growing around the dunes of the local beaches, so they began to experiment using this as the base of a recipe alongside fennel, rosemary, lavender, coriander, liquorice, hibiscus flower, angelica, nutmeg, cardamom, ginger and citrus peels (orange, grapefruit and lemon). The result is a surprisingly fatty, oily, juniper-led Dry Gin (bottled at 45% ABV), high in complexity. Winterling has also been developing small batches of experimental gins (all 45% ABV): La Mallorquina, an olive-based gin supported by just juniper and coriander, which is deceptively complex and very savoury, as well as *Citrus bergamia*, using bergamot as the standout botanical, and Green Spice, which takes its inspiration from exclusively green herbs and botanicals, including sencha tea, bay leaves, green pepper and fig and orange leaves alongside unripened juniper berries and green oranges.
gin-eva.com

GIN TEMPLUS
ALENTEJO, PORTUGAL

The city of Évora, some 110km (70 miles) east of Lisbon, is the capital of the Alentjo region and renowned for its Roman remains, including the Temple of Diana, the ruined columns of which still survive from the first century AD building and form the centrepiece of what was designated a UNESCO World Heritage Site back in 1986. Those same ancient columns adorn the bottle of Templus, arguably Portugal's first organically certified gin, produced in the historic city. All the botanicals and grain spirit used fall under the organic category and are biologically certified, with the resulting gin (bottled at 37.5% ABV) displaying a surprisingly light, citrus-forward character, with a hint of peppermint/menthol on the palate alongside a piney juniper note.

SHARISH GIN
ALENTEJO, PORTUGAL

Teacher turned distiller Antonio Cuco launched Sharish in 2013. He produces his gin in the beautiful Alentejo region in south-central Portugal with its abundant supply of botanicals, including citrus fruit and apples, notably the wonderfully light-coloured and fragrant Bravo Esmolfe variety, which features as one of the key botanicals together with juniper, lemon verbena and vanilla. Each botanical is individually macerated in a spirit that is made with a mixture of molasses, wheat and a small proportion of rice, then distilled in one of two 300-litre (79-US-gallon) copper pot stills. Alongside the Sharish Original, which has a distinct floral fruitiness before the juniper arrives, Cuco also produces what he calls his Blue Magic gin, which, as the name suggests, is a vibrant blue colour until the addition of tonic, when it changes to a light pink, thanks to the addition of an essence of blue butterfly pea flower. Both expressions are bottled at 40% ABV.
sharishgin.com

TINTO GIN
VALENÇA, PORTUGAL

In one respect, Tinto is about as close to a borderline gin as you could probably get, in that the town where it is produced sits quite literally on the border between northern Portugal and southern Spain. Walk roughly half a kilometre (third of a mile) north and you would be in Galicia. In fact, the gin itself was inspired by a walk along the bank of the River Minho, which, according to its creator Joao Guterres, has an abundance of wild flora to enjoy. Using a wheat- and rye-based spirit, Guterres macerates poppy, lavender, laurel, elderflower, willow leaf, rosemary, eucalyptus and a few other locally collected herbs, along with blackberries, lemon and orange peels and one final unique ingredient, the pear-like perico fruit, which gives the eventual gin its deep red colour. After a 90-day maceration period comes the blending and triple distillation. The result (bottled at 40% ABV) is undoubtedly a fruity affair, but the gin base has some unique, herbaceous notes alongside a characterfully sweet, tart and fresh taste.
gintinto.com

ITALY

Italy is home to the world-famous grape distillate grappa, and using this expertise and often a grape base, the country is producing a number of excellent gins that draw on both local botanicals and water sources. It is also one of the major suppliers in the world of high-quality juniper berries, harvested especially around Tuscany, Umbria, Arezzo and the high altitudes and microclimates that surround pockets in the Apennine Mountains.

MALFY GIN
TURIN

The Vergnano family, who launched Malfy in 2016, has been producing spirits in Moncalieri near Turin for more than a century. Today, the Torino Distillati is run by Carlo Vergnano, his wife Piera and their children Rita and Valter. Turin is famous for both its wines (the Barolo region is close by) and its distilleries, and both combine in the production of the region's renowned vermouth. It is also home to many leading Italian companies, such as Fiat and Lavazza coffee.

The gin is made by master distillers Beppe Ronco, a trained oenology and distillation expert who studied at Alba University, and Denis Muni, an engineer, using a unique stainless-steel vacuum still (*see* page 28) not often seen in gin production, which enables the fresh aromas of the local botanicals to be retained, producing a gin that is intrinsically linked to the terroir.

Five native botanicals are used in Malfy Originale including coriander, angelica and cassia bark, in addition to the premium-quality native juniper. Italian citrus is equally highly sought after both as a botanical and the ultimate garnish in a Martini cocktail (*see* page 54). So it seems only natural that Malfy Gin should draw on lemon as one of its main ingredients, using both Amalfi Coast lemons and Sicilian lemons, which are steeped in a wheat-based alcohol before the oils are pressed from the peels. The result is an intense citrus extract that is then

◍ *Malfy's Denis Muni*

distilled with the local juniper and other botanicals, including two more types of citrus: grapefruit and orange. After distillation, the spirit is cut with spring water from the highest water source in Italy, atop the Monte Viso, and bottled at 41% ABV.

There are three other main expressions, all drawing on exclusively Italian ingredients and all bottled at 41% ABV. Malfy con Limone is distilled with Sfusato lemon peel from the Amalfi Coast, classic Italian juniper and five other botanicals, as well as using Italian coastal oranges and Sicilian grapefruits, while Malfy con Arancia features the peels of Sicilian blood oranges, harvested in November, and four other botanicals besides Italian juniper. Malfy Gin Rosa majors on the peel of Sicilian pink grapefruits, grown in citrus groves on the Mediterranean coast, rhubarb and five other botanicals including local juniper.

The entire Malfy range carries the stamp G.Q.D.I. (*gin di qualità distillato in Italia*) on the bottle, which signifies that the product was distilled in Italy.
malfygin.com

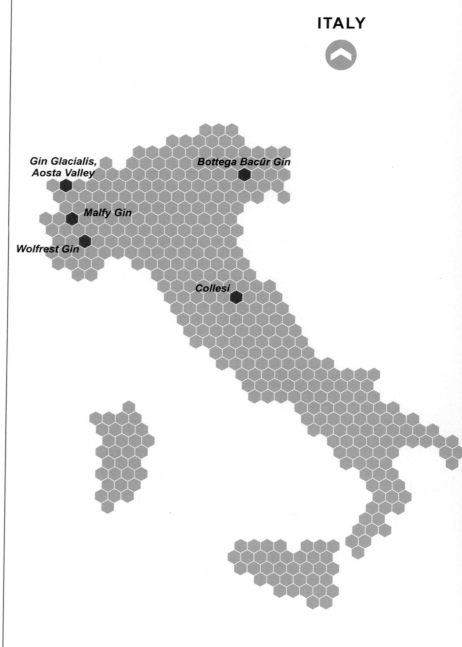

ITALY

Gin Glacialis, Aosta Valley

Bottega Bacûr Gin

Malfy Gin

Wolfrest Gin

Collesi

> Often with a grape base, the country is producing a number of excellent gins that draw on both local botanicals and water sources.

BOTTEGA BACÛR GIN
VENETO

A natural intuition for making great drinks at third-generation family-run Bottega, producers of top-quality prosecco for almost a century, has been turned toward gin, drawing on their other expertise of distilling honed through the production of grappa since 1967. Best-known for their Gold Prosecco, which is as much prized for its shiny gold bottle as its light, delicate flavour, Bottega launched their Bacûr Gin in 2017. It is crafted by infusing spirit with locally grown juniper berries, sage leaves and lemon zest, along with a range of other botanicals, then double distilled, with only 24,000 bottles being produced each year. The result is a gin with a bouquet that, like prosecco, is fine and fresh, designed to be simply served with a couple of ice cubes and sipped (bottled at 40% ABV). Bacûr means copper in Ancient Greek, and this is seen in the continuation of the company's theme of mirrored packaging, with the gin housed in an eye-catching copper bottle.
bottegaspa.com

⊙ *Fresh lemon peel*

OTHER ITALIAN GINS TO TRY

GIN GLACIALIS
VALLE D'AOSTA
Guglielmo Levi, the son of a famous grappa producer, moved to the Valle d'Aosta in northwestern Italy at the foot of Mont Blanc where he built his Levi Distillery. To make Gin Glacialis, he infuses wild juniper growing in the region's high mountains, with no other added botanicals, before distilling in an alembic pot still (*see* page 22) and bottling at 42% ABV.
grappalevi.it

COLLESI GIN
MARCHE
Giuseppe Collesi first set up his distillery at the end of 2001 in Apecchio (on the border between Marche and Umbria) to make grappa, which is traditionally produced in Friuli, Veneto and Trentino, but soon successfully expanded the business into craft beer brewing and other spirit distilling. Collesi Gin is made with a base distilled from barley grown on the Collesi estates to which he adds seven different botanicals: juniper from the Apennine Mountains, Visciole sour cherries from the Marche region, hops, wild roses, walnut shells and peels of Italian oranges and lemons. These botanicals are macerated in the pure grain alcohol base before being diluted with pure water from the Monte Nerone reservoir, chilled at -15°C (5°F) for at least 30 hours, filtered, bottled and then left to age in the dark for four months. It is bottled at 42.8% ABV.
collesi.com

WOLFREST GIN
PIEDMONT
Wolfrest is located in Montelupo Albese, a small village in the Langhe, near the heart of the Barolo wine region in Piedmont, which is also famous for the production of hazelnuts and herbs. Founders Valentina and Giovanni use Umbrian juniper and Pernambuco sweet orange from the Liguria region as their key flavour drivers. Five additional botanicals are locally sourced, including elder that grows wild in the woods, as well as roasted hazelnuts, bay leaf, thyme and wild rosemary. It is bottled at 43% ABV.
wolfrestgin.com

GREECE

Greece is a country steeped in an illustrious heritage of fine alcoholic drinks: from sweet wines hailing from the islands, to the national spirit Metaxa growing in popularity as the current wave of bartenders look to their roots for inspiration. It now has a locally produced gin too, no doubt the first of many if the explosion of interest in distilling gin continues to spread across Europe.

GRACE GIN
EVIA (EUBOEA)

Vassileios Katsos and his brother Spyros set up their AVANTES Distillery in 1963 in the town of Chalkida on the island of Evia (Euboea), about 80km (50 miles) north of Athens, where they produced ouzo, wine, brandy and vermouth. It later moved to Drosia outside of the town, and in 2005, the distillery passed into the hands of Chara Katsou, Katsos's daughter, an oenologist. It is here that Grace Gin was launched in 2016, conceived by three friends, Hara and Katerina Katsou and Lila Dimopoulou, the name taking its inspiration from the Three Graces of Greek mythology, the goddesses of youth, beauty and mirth. The recipe in terms of both the style of the distillation process and the botanical make-up took more than a year to develop, the team finally settling on 13 different botanicals including rock samphire, myrtle, Greek cedar and orange blossom. Using a neutral grain base, the gin is 100% distilled and bottled at 45.7% ABV.

avantesdistillery.gr
lkc-drinks.com

The Founders of Grace Gin

SCANDINAVIA

Scandinavia has a rich heritage of distilling that has stemmed from the distinctly herbaceous akvavit, which is based around the flavours of fennel, dill and caraway. Alongside a hugely popular craft single malt and rye whisky scene that is rapidly expanding, distillers are now turning their attention to gin across the whole Scandinavian region.

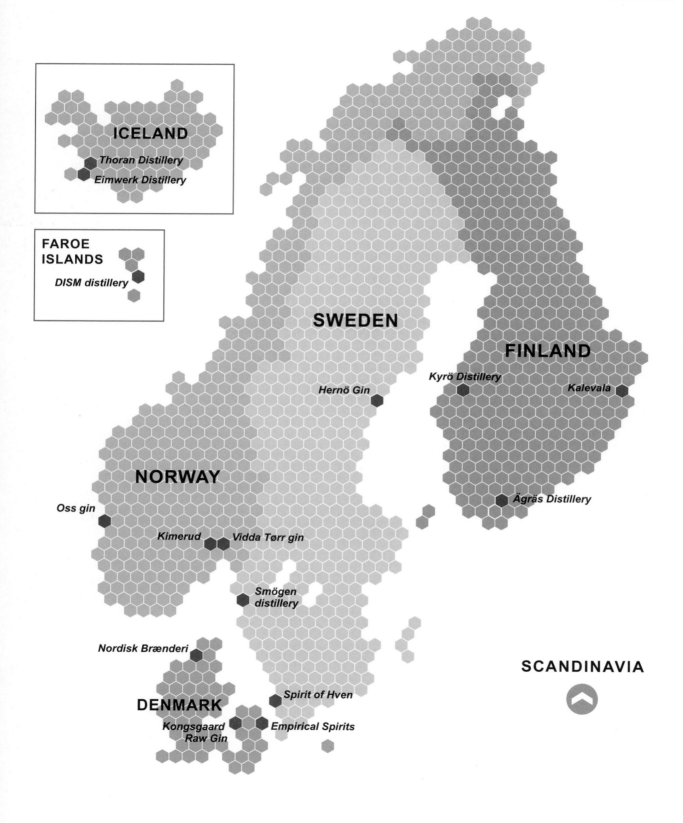

ICELAND

Thoran Distillery
Eimwerk Distillery

FAROE ISLANDS

DISM distillery

SWEDEN

FINLAND

Kyrö Distillery

Kalevala

Hernö Gin

Ägräs Distillery

NORWAY

Oss gin

Kimerud   Vidda Tørr gin

Smögen distillery

Nordisk Brænderi

Spirit of Hven

DENMARK

Kongsgaard Raw Gin

Empirical Spirits

SCANDINAVIA

SWEDEN

A new wave of distillers coming through means that Sweden's renowned dedication to spirits, traditionally vodka and more recently whisky too, is extending to the world of gin. Swedish tastes lend toward producing gins with a savoury, earthy, herbal note as the key element of terroir.

HERNÖ GIN
DALARNA

Jon Hillgren was working as a bartender in London when he fell in love with gin. He returned to Sweden with the idea of starting the country's first dedicated gin distillery, travelling the world for inspiration and knowledge whilst employed for the Swedish government. In 2011, Hillgren and his wife bought an 19th-century farm in Dala, 420km (260 miles) north of Stockholm, and created an organic gin only using water from their own well.

Hernö is distilled with eight botanicals, all of them organic, namely juniper, cassia, lemon peel, vanilla, coriander, lingonberries, black pepper and meadowsweet, with the production done by hand and each bottle numbered. Their two copper pot stills, Kierstin, a 250-litre (66-US-gallon) small-batch German version, and Marit, a larger 1,000-litre (264-US-gallon) still, are filled with a wheat-based spirit before a maceration period of 18 hours for the juniper and coriander, then the other botanicals are added and distilled.

The core range consists of a classic London Dry, bottled at 40.5% ABV, and a navy strength, made from the same distilled gin but diluted to 57% ABV. Hernö also produces an innovative Juniper Cask Gin, the first to be matured in juniper wood casks, using the same distilled gin but diluted to 47% ABV and matured in cask for 30 days, adding an intense juniper note. Hernö Old Tom Gin, diluted to 43% ABV, sees the meadowsweet increased and a touch of sugar added.

Hernö also releases an annual High Coast Terroir Gin limited edition, which uses a malt base spirit from the nearby Lockeby Brewery, distilled to 75% ABV and then blended with a regular wheat base alcohol of 96% ABV. The 2018 edition was redistilled with botanicals from around the distillery, all hand-picked by Jon's mother Yvonne: juniper berries, spruce shoots, elderflower and rowan berries. Hernö Sipping Gin is an annual limited edition (ABV variable), whereby their classic London Dry gin is aged in casks previously used by other producers, from ex-Laphroaig whisky casks, Swedish whisky, American bourbon and sherry casks. All Hernö gins are not chill filtered (*see* page 29). *hernogin.com*

HVEN ORGANIC GIN
SKÅNE
Located on the island of Hven (Ven) between Denmark and Sweden, Spirit of Hven Distillery began production in 2008, and operates a conference centre and hotel with restaurant and pub. Using a wheat base, the team take a sideways look at gin making, drawn from their experience in whisky production, by macerating their botanical mix, including local juniper, grains of paradise and Guinea pepper along with citrus, and then resting the flavoured spirit in oak casks for 18 months. Once distilled, it is rested in stainless steel for three months before being distilled again, reduced to 40% ABV and bottled on site. *hven.com*

STRANE GIN
BOHUSLÄN
The small distillery of Smögen was established in the Swedish town of Hunnebostrand, about 130km (80 miles) north of Gothenburg, in 2009, but it wasn't until 2014 that the distillery turned its hand from whisky to gin. Using a tiny wood-fired, 100-litre (26½-US-gallon) pot still, they called their gin Strane, after a local harbour. Distiller Pär Caldenby uses a mix of 12 botanicals including sage, lemon peel, basil, mint and sweet almond to create 3 distillates, which he then blends. These are adjusted in volume according to the style of gin, including Merchant Strength at 47.4% ABV, Navy Strength at 57.1% ABV, Uncut Strength at a whopping 76% ABV, which is matured for 18 months in a former sherry cask, and even an Ultra Uncut at a mighty 82.5% ABV. *strane.se*

DENMARK

Danish distilling has hitherto focused on its native spirit of akvavit, yet there are now plenty of distillers who are taking inspiration from the world-class restaurant scene in the country, both in the cities and in the deepest countryside, to produce some imaginative gins.

KONGSGAARD RAW GIN
EAST ZEALAND

This Danish gin draws inspiration from the forest, using botanicals such as charred oak, resin and cinnamon bark, combined with ginger, tiger nuts, galangal and liquorice root. Locally sourced and hand-picked Danish apples are also used in the recipe, to make for a truly unusual gin. To add to its unique nature, the gin is distilled in an open-flame copper Cognac still, using a wheat-based spirit to build the flavours on. It is bottled at 44% ABV.
kongsgaardgin.com

NORDISK GIN
NORTHERN JUTLAND

Engineer and adventurer Anders Bilgram, leader of various expeditions in the Arctic region and a member of the Adventure Club in Copenhagen, decided to start his own distillery Nordisk Bænderi in Northern Jutland, having been inspired by his experience of several illegal microdistilleries producing their own version of vodka along the coast of the Arctic Ocean. His series of gins comprises Edition Northstar (44.8% ABV), using Danish apples, sea buckthorn, Icelandic angelica seeds, Swedish cloudberries, Greenlandic *qajaasat* or Labrador tea and wild rose petals from northwestern Denmark; Edition Sarek (43.7% ABV), featuring birch leaves, pine needles, lingonberries, blueberries and angelica root; and Edition Sloe (29.2% ABV). The gins are distilled in hand-made German copper pots, diluted with the water from the distillery's own borehole and all are bottled by hand before being numbered and signed.
nordiskbraenderi.dk

EMPIRICAL SPIRITS
COPENHAGEN

Drawing on their time working at world-class restaurants such as Noma in Copenhagen, the team of chefs behind Empirical Spirits runs an experimental distillation laboratory that encompasses all sorts of different styles of whacky and wonderful distillates. To list their offerings would be akin to nailing jelly to a wall, with releases that have included simply "smoked juniper" and others containing chilli and pearl barley. Needless to say, this art-house distillery, with exceptionally unusual stills, will constantly twist and turn in the production of some of the most interesting and extraordinary gins (and other styles of spirit) available anywhere in the world.
empiricalspirits.co

BARALDUR TURT GINN
FAROE ISLANDS

Founded in 2008, the DISM distillery was initially established to produce a local *akvavitt*, but has also begun production of the Faroe Islands' first gin called Baraldur, Faroese for "juniper", which uses local spring water to dilute the spirit, bottled at 37.5% ABV.
dism.fo

Denmark's Nordisk Gin

FINLAND

The Finns have long had an affinity with gin, stretching back to their iconic "gin long drink" developed for the Helsinki Olympic Games of 1952, but now they have a gin distilling scene to truly call their own.

KYRÖ DISTILLERY COMPANY
OSTROBOTHNIA

The Finns consume six times more rye spirit than the world average, so the idea of distilling a rye-based gin as well as a rye whisky came to a group of friends while chatting in a sauna. The concept grew and before long the team were serving their first rye spirits at a Helsinki speakeasy called *Kyrön Matkailun Edistämiskeskus* ("Kyrö Tourism Board"). True to their declared motto "In Rye We Trust", after a few months the team moved their distilling operation to a permanent site, in an old dairy in the village of Isokyrö, making it one of the world's most northerly distilleries.

The five friends who founded the distillery now run an extraordinary team of professionals dedicated to making their rye gin and whisky along with a range of products such as bitters and a "gin long drink". Having very strict laws regarding the sale of alcohol, Finland was in need of a product it could sell alongside beer at the 1952 Olympics, so the Hartwall brewery came up with an innovation: a cocktail in a can comprising gin and grapefruit. Suddenly the country had a national drink, and today you will find a dedicated section for "gin long drinks" alongside beers and wines in stores throughout Finland. Kyrö's take on this tradition is a sparkling cranberry and gin mix called Longkyrö (5.5% ABV), which uses one of their core gins: Napue (46.3% ABV), as a base, topped off with fresh cranberry juice and botanicals such as rosemary.

Kyrö's other main gin is Koskue (42.6% ABV), a barrel-aged gin made using a Kothe still with a capacity of 1,200 litres (317 US gallons). Both Napue and Koskue use a 95%-ABV rye spirit that is produced using Finnish wholewheat rye. Ten foraged local botanicals including sea buckthorn, cranberries and birch leaves are macerated in the spirit for 16 hours. When the distillation process starts, another two botanicals, hibiscus and elderflower, are added to a basket in the still to add more flavour through vapour infusion (*see* page 20). Koskue is rested in American white oak casks for about three months and fine-tuned with freshly distilled orange peel and black pepper, to add to the vanilla flavours that are drawn from the barrel-ageing process.

Alongside its core gins, they also produce a range of experiments under the banner of Study Series. *kyrodistillery.com*

Checking the still at Kyrö

OTHER FINNISH GINS TO TRY

KALEVALA GIN
NORTH KARELIA
German chemical engineer Moritz Wüstenberg begin distilling in 2010 as a hobby, but by 2014 he was distilling for commercial purposes, bottling and distributing his range of Kalevala gins. Instead of drawing on a rye base as with Kryö (*see* left), the distillery uses an organic wheat spirit that is filled into their small copper still named Sampo. For their classic Dry distilled gin, juniper is added and left to macerate in the 80% ABV spirit for 24 hours, after which only four other botanicals – mint, rosebuds, raspberry leaves and rosemary – are added and placed in a vapour basket (*see* page 28). The final result is bottled at 46.3% ABV. They also produce a Navy Strength version at an unconventionally low ABV of 50.9%. *kalevalagin.com*

ÄGRÄS GIN
UUSIMAA
The Ägräs Distillery is based in an old ironworks in the village of Fiskars, 88km (55 miles) west of Helsinki. Master distiller Tomi Purhonen uses just four botanicals to produce Ägräs Gin: juniper, wild angelica, red clover and lemon peel. Ägräs Abloom Gin has the same botanical base but with the addition of hibiscus flowers and local honey in the distillation process. Both gins are bottled at 43.7% ABV. *agrasdistillery.com*

ICELAND

With its clear glacial waters, Iceland is a natural choice for building a distillery, although the gin craze has only really just begun in the country, with several small craft operations grabbing the reins of the botanical bandwagon and taking it to some very unusual places indeed.

VOR GIN
GREATER REYKJAVÍK

Established in Reykjavík a decade ago, Eimverk Distillery first intended to primarily produce a small-batch Icelandic whisky, using barley grown on the southern shore of the country. After 4 years and 163 trial distillations, the family-based distillery cracked a recipe that they were truly happy with and Flóki was born. The distillers certainly aren't shy about experimenting with flavour, and one of the first releases to achieve global recognition was a variant of the original whisky smoked using sheep dung, which is, bizarrely, quite a thing to the native Icelandic population. The experimentation has also extended into the distillery's gin production, with VOR Icelandic using the same base spirit of malted barley as for the whisky, which is redistilled in pot stills with a singular botanical recipe: wild Icelandic juniper berries, local rhubarb, crowberries, Icelandic angelica root, foraged birch leaves, creeping thyme, kale, Iceland moss and sweet kelp. The flavour is highly distinctive and surprisingly herbaceous, with an underlying malty note, which, given the base spirit, makes a lot of sense. It is bottled at 47% ABV.

A barrel-aged version of VOR (also 47% ABV) is aged in new American oak casks for two months, giving a hint of vanilla and coconut to the already flavoursome gin.

◉ *Icelandic gin*

There is also a "sloe-style" variant that mixes the barrel-aged gin with the juice of blueberries and locally grown crowberries.
vorgin.is

MARBERG GIN
GREATER REYKJAVÍK

A new craft distillery established by distiller Birgir Már Sigurðsson, Thoran Distillery has explored the classic London Dry playbook as the inspiration of its very first gin, Marberg Icelandic London Dry Gin. Bottled at 43% ABV, it is both juniper and citrus heavy, also bringing in a combination of coriander, orris root, angelica, black pepper and grapefruit. However, the twist comes from using red seaweed, locally known as söl or dulse, giving a slightly saline, umami aspect to the flavour, which is more noticeable over ice.
marberg.is

NORWAY

In the middle of the constant tussle over which Nordic country is entitled to call akvavit their own, a handful of Norwegian distillers have put their distilleries to good use in making gins that draw on the country's rich flora, which varies significantly from coast to coast.

OHD
OSLO

Located in the Bryn neighbourhood of Norway's capital city Oslo housed in an historic red-brick industrial building dating back to the 1880s, Oslo Håndverksdestilleri, or OHD as it is generally known, was commissioned in 2015 by founders Marius Vestnes, Marcin Miller and Martin Krajewski, drawing on the expertise of Dave Gardonio, a graduate of Edinburgh's Heriot-Watt University and a trained biochemist, brewer and distiller.

Eighty-eight years earlier in 1927, the government-run State Wine Monopoly acquired Norway's last operational distillery, which signified the end of proud local and independent distilling traditions. However, recently there has been a handful of small, independent distilleries starting to produce different spirits across Norway, of which OHD is one.

Putting its energy into making a series of spirits, the distillery produces *akevitt*, drawing on a blend of native herbs and spices, a digestive bitter that features 16 botanicals including bog myrtle, yarrow and juniper berries and, of course, gin.

VIDDA Tørr Gin (*vidda* translating from the Norwegian as "plateau") draws inspiration from traditional British Dry gins but is infused with Nordic botanicals, notably a selection of herbs and spices from the Norwegian mountains, which makes it lean more in the direction of a traditional Norse *akevitt*. A total of 11 botanicals are used, namely heather, meadowsweet, elderflower, chamomile flower, yarrow, bilberry, sorrel, angelica and calamus roots and pine shoots, in addition to juniper. These are left to macerate for at least 12 hours in a German 650-litre (172-US-gallon) Carl still. It is bottled at 43% ABV.
oslohd.com

Bottling line at OHD in Oslo

OTHER NORWEGIAN GINS TO TRY

BAREKSTEN GIN
BERGEN
The Oss Craft Distillery, not far from Norway's second-largest city Bergen, is where former bartender Stig Bareksten produces Bareksten Gin, bottled at 46% ABV, using a base spirit made from potatoes. Drawing mostly on Norwegian wild berries, the gin is made in five 600-litre (159-US-gallon) stills, and was awarded the coveted Double Gold at the San Francisco World Spirits Competition in 2017.
barekstenspirits.com

KIMERUD GIN
BUSKERUD
Master distiller Ståle Håvaldsen Johnsen makes Kimerud Gin at his family farm distillery in the Lier valley in the Norwegian village of Tranby, 32km (20 miles) southwest of Oslo. Using 22 botanicals including walnut, coriander, lemon peel, angelica and ginger root, mint, orange peel and the Scandinavian herb *Rhodiola rosea*, picked from the cliffs of the Arctic's Norwegian Sea coast, the spirit is distilled five times, then diluted using pure mountain water and bottled at 40% ABV. Playing on its Nordic heritage, the distillery also offers an aged gin (42% ABV), matured for a total of six months in old sherry and French oak barrels, all having been previously used for their own akvavit.
kimerud.no

THE BALTIC STATES

The Baltic States have traditionally been noted for their vodka, fruit liqueurs and balsams –
a highly distinctive, strongly flavoured herbaceous spirit drink. But gin has begun to catch up,
with a variety of examples now being produced domestically in Latvia, Estonia and Lithuania.
It is interesting to note that the latter has secured EU Geographical Protected Status for its gin.

ESTONIA, LATVIA AND LITHUANIA

CRAFTER'S GIN
TALLINN

At the Liviko distillery, established in 1898, Crafter's London Dry Gin is produced using Estonian grain and botanicals in its "recipe no. 23", in a copper pot affectionately called Mamma Ilse. The key botanicals are veronica, hand-picked from Kubja Ürditalu, and fennel seeds, and it is bottled at 43% ABV.

Crafter's Aromatic Flower Gin (44.3% ABV) uses a wild rose flower extract containing a natural copper colour pigment, but when tonic is added it turns light pink. Other botanicals include meadowsweet, lavender, chamomile, elderflower, yuzu and lemon and orange peels. *craftersgin.com*

LAHHENTAGGE ÖSEL DRY GIN
ÖSEL

The Lahhentagge Distillery uses juniper from the island of Ösel, alongside lilac, cowslip, elfin thyme and Nordic ginger, to make Ösel Dry Gin, bottled at 45% ABV. *lahhentagge.com*

CROSS KEYS GIN
RIGA

Produced in Latvia's capital by Latvijas Balzams, a company that also produces two other brands of gin, Kristofors and LB Gin, Cross Keys (which takes its name from the crossed keys emblem – a historical symbol of urban hospitality) is a simple, very contemporary gin, made by the same distillery team that creates Riga Black Balsam, a complex dry bitter spirit dating back to 1752 that contains 17 botanicals. In contrast, Cross Keys Gin (bottled at 41% ABV) features only four botanicals, namely juniper, chamomile, rosemary and linden blossoms, which gives the gin a very floral, delicate style that doesn't shroud the juniper at its heart. *crosskeysgin.com*

THE BALTIC STATES

Crafter's London Dry Gin

Flavorwood

ESTONIA

Lahhentagge

Cross Keys Gin

LATVIA

LITHUANIA

Vilniaus Degtiné distillery

FLAVORWOOD SMOKY GIN
TALLINN

This unusual gin is made by first drawing oak and juniper wood smoke through the botanicals before distillation. It is bottled at 42.5% ABV.
smokygin.com

VILNIAUS DEGTINÉ
VILNIUS

In the world of gin, there are but few geographical areas protected under Regulation (EC) No 110/2008 of the European Parliament, among which is Lithuania's capital city Vilnius, where the Vilniaus Degtiné distillery makes the only example currently in production, as it has for the past 30 years or so. Today, the distillery is one of the largest producers of high-strength neutral base spirit, which they use for a variety of brands, and one of the leading producers of alcoholic beverages in the Baltic States, making three different gins. The first is a mix of gin and bitters called Frankenstein, bottled at 41.5% ABV. The second, Thorn Gin, is a more contemporary style of gin distilled in small batches using dill and orange zest as the key botanicals, bottled at 40% ABV. Finally, Vilnius Gin, bottled at 45% ABV, includes botanicals such as juniper, dill seeds, coriander and orange, and due to its production process qualifies as a London Dry gin.
degtine.lt/lt/dzinas/dzinas-vilniaus-500

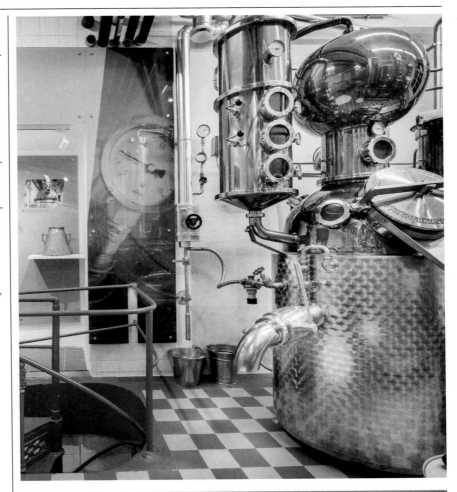

◉ *Labelling Crafter's Gin*

EASTERN EUROPE AND RUSSIA

For many gin producers around the globe, Eastern Europe is a vital part of the true fabric and lifeblood of the spirit, thanks to the abundant supply of high-quality juniper that predominantly grows across the southern Slavic countries. Indeed, some of the choicest berries are harvested in the hilly terrain of Macedonia's Skopje region, all the way down to the more tranquil shores of Lake Ohrid. While there may not be any fervent craft distillation scene to be found, its importance cannot be overlooked. With regards to Russia, for a country that is so vast and with such a voracious culture of socializing and drinking, it is surprising how little an impact gin has had. However, with its strong interest in classic drinks and a hotly developing world-class bar scene, it is surely only a matter of time.

EASTERN EUROPE AND RUSSIA

Barrister,
Ladoga Distillery

Veresk Dry Gin

RUSSIA

Green Man Gin

POLAND

BELARUS

Lubuski

Rodionov
& Sons

Stock Spirits

Stock Spirits

CZECH
REP.

Rudolf Jelinek

Distillery Žufánek

St. Nicolaus Distillery

Zwack & Co

Agárdi Distillery

HUNGARY

CZECH REPUBLIC AND SLOVAKIA

Herbal, bitter-led spirits such as absinthe and *Becherovka* have been the dominant domestically produced spirits across the Czech Republic, with the latter beginning to find fans across Eastern Europe. The country ranks 41st in the world in annual consumption of gin according to International Wine and Spirits Record (IWSR) statistics (one behind Russia – *see* page 147), with 80,000 nine-litre (2½-US-gallon) cases sold per year.

Slovakia is an interesting producer of gin in that it has its own Protected Geographical Indication (PGI) in the shape of *Borovička*. This single botanical spirit must, by law, use a grain spirit as its base and contains a sweetener.

STOCK SPIRITS
LIBEREC

A national producer that also operates across Poland, Slovenia and Croatia, Stock Spirits manufactures the three best-selling mainstream domestic gins: Dynybyl Special Gin (37.5% ABV), Stock (40% ABV) and Stock Prestige London Gin (40% ABV).
stockspirits.com

RUDOLF JELÍNEK
ZLÍN

The other major Czech producer, Rudolf Jelínek in the town of Vizovice, produces Slovácká gin (technically a *Borovička* or juniper brandy – *see* right), a simple spirit featuring juniper as the only botanical, aged for six months before it is bottled at 45% ABV.
rudolfjelinek.com

OH MY GIN
ZLÍN

Marcela and Josef Žufánek with their three sons established the small Žufánek Distillery in 2000 in the village of Boršice u Blatnice near the border with Slovakia and Austria, which has since bucked the trend by creating the Czech Republic's first recognized craft gin. Having been making fruit liqueurs, brandies and absinthe, back in 2013 they decided to produce a test run small batch of a gin called OMG (Oh My Gin) – to critical acclaim. At its heart are 16 botanicals, including juniper, coriander, cubeb, grains of paradise, angelica, almond, lavender, fresh orange peel and flowers from the Czech national tree, the small-leaved linden, which are macerated for 36 hours in neutral alcohol before being distilled in 1,200-litre (317-US-gallon) batches. Following the gin's success, in 2015 the distillery invested in a pair of 300-litre (80-US-gallon) copper pot stills

from German manufacturer Arnold Holstein. A limited edition, OMFG, uses wild bourbon or voatsiperifery pepper (*Piper borbonense*) from Madagascar and frankincense as key botanicals. Both are bottled at 45.5% ABV.
ohmygin.com

ST. NICOLAUS DISTILLERY
BRATISLAVA

Arguably one of the most popular producers of *Borovička*, St. Nicolaus reduces its juniper-flavoured distillate to 37.5% ABV using water from the Liptov mountain region to create Liptovium Borovička. The company also makes The London No.1 gin (47% ABV), which has a blue colour added post-distillation for effect.
stn-trade.sk

◉ *OMFG Gin*

HUNGARY AND CROATIA

More widely known for fruit-based liqueurs, and spirits – especially *pálinka*, one of Hungary's national delicacies, a handful of distillers have been exploring the subtleties of gin production too, with some interesting results.

AGÁRDI GIN
CENTRAL TRANSDANUBIA

Steiner Manor, the location of the Agárdi Distillery for nearly two decades, lies on the outskirts of the city of Székesfehérvár, and a stone's throw from Agárd, home of the popular Lake Velence holiday resort. Under the control of Tibor Vértes, the distillery is arguably the most awarded in Hungary, collecting over 300 prizes for its range of *pálinka*, which includes apricot, plum, apple, pear and black cherry, using fruit harvested from the abundant orchards that grow across the Lake Velence region. However, Vértes has also made his first foray into gin distillation, using the distillery's Christian Carl copper pot and stainless steel column stills. Agárdi Hungarian Dry Gin is a simple, traditional juniper-forward style, with lavender and citrus notes emerging in addition to the central more herbaceous elements, bottled at 43% ABV.
agardi.hu

ZWACK & CO.
BUDAPEST

One of Hungary's oldest and most famous drinks companies, Zwack & Co. (established in 1790), which produces the bold and very distinct Unicum, a bittersweet digestive herb liqueur, has reintroduced its Marine Dry Gin, which was popular between the World Wars and bottled at 37.5% ABV. Marine is one of the most commonly drunk gins in Hungary, and in addition to the original recipe, the company has released Kalumba Madagascar Spiced Gin (also 37.5% ABV), distilled using botanicals mainly from Madagascar and the African continent, including calumba root, lemon balm, cubeb peppers, clove, cinnamon leaves, pink peppercorns, turmeric, aniseed, lime peel, nutmeg flower, cardamom, nutmeg, ginger, vanilla, coriander seed, Curaçao peel and, of course, juniper berries, before being aged in oak casks with dried figs to give a dark, sweet fruity flavour.
zwackunicum.hu

OLD PILOT'S GIN
ZAGREB

The Distillery Duh u Boci, which translates into English as "The Spirit in the Bottle", was set up in Croatia's capital Zagreb by two pilots, distilling Old Pilot's Gin using hand-picked Croatian botanicals of juniper, orange, lavender, sage, olive leaves and angelica. Their use of an iStill (*see* page 27) allows them to suspend their chosen botanicals in alcohol in order to slowly release their oils, while a vapour lifts the oils into the upper parts of the still to be condensed again. Once distilled, the gin is bottled at 45% ABV.
duh-u-boci.com/en

◉ *Hand labelling Old Pilot*

POLAND

With a neutral base spirit being the starting point for any gin, the Poles surely have a head start with their history and heritage in the world of vodka production, and there are some trailblazing gin producers that are taking the idea of infusing high-quality spirit with sophisticated flavour seriously.

LUBUSKI GIN
POMERANIA

The country's best-selling gin, made by the Henkell & Co. distillers, has been in existence since 1987, taking its base grain and juniper from Lubusz Land, the area that surrounds both sides of the Oder River. Three versions exist in the range: the regular Lubuski (37.5% ABV), which is surprisingly complex and features juniper, coriander, cumin, bitter almonds, bay leaf and angelica root as the core botanicals among others; a lime flavour-infused edition (37.5% ABV) and a seven-year-old aged version (40% ABV), matured in both oak and chestnut casks.
henkell-polska.pl

POLUGAR NO.10
(VIA RUSSIA)

Polugar, the Russian term for half-burned bread wine, is the long-term project of Boris Rodionov of Rodionov & Sons, who has been conducting research studies into the old spirit recipes of the Russian nobility, after many of the products and techniques were lost when distilling was monopolized by the state at the end of the 19th century. No.10 is an extraordinary spirit that uses a base mash of rye and wheat, which is first double distilled in a copper alembic still (*see* page 22), then finally triple distilled with a whole range of botanicals: wild juniper, coriander, cumin, fennel, thyme, black cardamom, lemon peel, angelica, liquorice and orris root, fennel seeds, cinnamon, calamus, cloves, almonds, young pine cones, basil, cranberry, lingonberry and cloudberry, alongside another 12 Siberian herbs that are only known to Rodionov. The spirit is produced in Poland (bottled at 38.5% ABV), but it is hoped that eventually the recipes and craft can return to their native Russia to be truly authentic.
rusvin.ru

The best-selling gin, Lubuski

Polugar imaginative No.10 gin

RUSSIA AND BELARUS

Aside from the more well-known western gin brands, Russia's domestic craft gin scene has yet to really develop anywhere like it has on other continents. According to recent IWSR statistics (*see* page 143), Russia was ranked the 40th country in the world in terms of gin consumption by market. Vodka remains the dominant force, however; so too does home distillation for personal consumption. *Samogon*, meaning "self-distilled", is the name for spirits made for personal use, which has been an entirely legal practice since 1997 across most of the country, often using sugar, potatoes and other vegetables, fruit or bread as the base ingredient.

Russia's Barrister Gin

VERESK, TVER
RUSSIA

Founded in the late 19th century, the history of this major Russian distiller, once known as the Kashin Distillery, mirrors the turbulent times faced by the country over the past century. When the state monopolized vodka production at the turn of the 20th century, the distillery was one of the key producers of spirit, which it transported via the local railway. The business managed to survive both Russian revolutions, a partial closure during World War Two and more turbulence throughout the 1980s and 1990s. Today, it produces three gins of varying quality, which are almost exclusively for consumption across Russia and a few other Baltic countries: Galoway, Veresk Dry and Veresk Premium Quality, all bottled at 40% ABV. *veresk.com*

GREEN MAN GIN
MINSK, BELARUS

Minsk-based distillery group Minsk Grape Wines produces a number of wines, vodkas, liqueurs and ciders alongside Green Man Gin, a rudimentary, juniper-flavoured spirit, bottled at 40% ABV. *luding.ru*

BARRISTER GIN
ST PETERSBURG, RUSSIA

Arguably Russia's most contemporary gin, Barrister hit the market in 2017, produced by the Ladoga Group of distillers in St Petersburg, which also produces the Drevniy brand of gin for the domestic market. Barrister has been designed to capture the attention of the younger domestic consumer and beyond by playing on a very English aesthetic and history of gin and the English legal system. The core release, Barrister Dry Gin, is a six-botanical recipe comprising juniper berries, fresh lemon peel, coriander, anise, cardamom and cinnamon, all of which are distilled separately and blended together before being bottled at 40% ABV. An Old Tom version also includes allspice, nutmeg, angelica, almond and cubeb berries, again bottled at 40% ABV. In 2018 they expanded their range to include naturally flavoured gins. A single botanical dominates each, such as Barrister Orange, bottled at 43% ABV. *barrister-gin.com*

NORTH AMERICA

USA

Today, the US gin scene has exploded, with Canada beginning to follow suit (*see* page 180), helping to make the USA the second-largest nation of gin consumers in the world (losing out to the Philippines – *see* page 243). The craft gin movement sees no sign of slowing down, with hundreds of small distilleries now producing gin across the country. And the move away from the traditional juniper-heavy style of London Dry toward the so-called New Western gin style – characterized by a focus on other botanicals such as lavender, citrus and coriander as the dominant element – is now pushing the boundaries of gin flavours further. This is coupled with an exploration into sourcing more unusual local species of juniper (*see* page 34), as well as bringing the concept of barrel-aged gins (*see* page 21) to a new generation of savvy, curious gin drinkers.

EAST COAST USA

Since the eastern seaboard was the point of arrival for the early settlers from Europe, most significantly the Dutch landing in what is now the New York area, it is no surprise to see gin-related activity so heavily concentrated in this part of America.

NEW YORK DISTILLING COMPANY
NEW YORK

It is said that during Prohibition there were more than 50,000 illicit stills in New York City, with a distilling heritage dating back as far as the 1700s. But since the early 1930s, there had been no new distilleries in the New York area until the turn of this century, when Allen Katz found himself in the now ultra-cool Willamsburg district in Brooklyn and decided he wanted to make honest gin that reflected the outlawed Prohibition-era product. He was able to secure a farm distiller's licence from New York State to get the distillery up and running in 2011 because all the grains for his rye whiskey were to be sourced from local farmers.

Included in the company's portfolio alongside the rye whiskey is a selection of gins that showcases the broad nature of flavour and styles within the gin category. The production set-up is built around a 1,000-litre (264-US-gallon) Carl still in which all the botanicals are directly placed, with no maceration or vapour infusion – *see* page 22. The first gin to be produced was named Dorothy Parker American Gin after the famed New York writer and socialite, her quote about the Martini being a lasting memoir of anyone who has visited iconic cocktail establishments such as Dukes Hotel in London (*see* page 54). Using a blend of traditional and modern botanicals including juniper, elderberries, citrus, cinnamon and hibiscus petals, this is very much a contemporary gin in the way it draws from those elements and delivers its flavour. It is bottled at 44% ABV.

The second gin in the distillery's canon is navy-strength Perry's Tot, in this case honouring the legacy of Matthew Calbraith Perry, Commandant of the Brooklyn Navy Yard from 1841–3, who as early as 1833 was "instrumental in founding its Naval Lyceum to promote the diffusion of useful knowledge – and cement the link which unite professional bretheren", according

◉ *Tribute to a great: Dorothy Parker Gin*

◉ *New York Distilling Company*

to the distillery. It goes on to explain that the gin was designed to "celebrate the attitude and approach that connects the ingenuity and grit of 19th-century Brooklyn with contemporary enthusiasts who continue to revive an American cocktail culture". Bottled at 57% ABV, it draws on a juniper heart, with cinnamon, cardamom, star anise and three citrus peels – lemon, orange and grapefruit – in support. The unusual addition is wild flower honey, collected from hives in upstate New York, around 2.5 litres (5¼ US pints) to every 1,000-litre (264-US-gallon) batch of gin – not to add sweetness, but to give greater viscosity to the spirit.

The New York Distilling Company team has developed its own take on a genever (*see* page 18) called Chief Gowanus, based on an 1809

It is said that during Prohibition there were more than 50,000 illicit stills in New York City.

American recipe for making a version of "Holland gin" from American rye whiskey, Brooklyn having been a Dutch colony in the 17th-century, and using grains grown in New York State. It is created by returning unaged, double-distilled rye whiskey spirit to a pot still with juniper berries and Cluster hops (thought by the team to have been the variety most likely in use in the early 19th-century) and distilling it through a third time. Once rested for three months in an oak barrel, it is bottled at 44% ABV. *nydistilling.com*

BLUECOAT GIN
PHILADELPHIDA

Bluecoat Gin is inspired by the ordinary folk who signed up to fight in the Revolutionary War (1775–83) against their British rulers, who were known as "bluecoats" in reference to the uniforms worn by the American militia, in turn celebrating the American spirit of rebellion and independence. Launched in May 2006, it is produced by Philadelphia Distilling, the first craft distillery to be established in Pennsylvania since the Prohibition era. Having expanded its operation, it is now based at a site that formerly housed the Ajax Metal Company, smelters and founders from the late 1800s to the mid-1940s, which was abandoned decades ago, so it took the Philadelphia Distilling team a year to prepare the 1,200sq m (13,000sq ft) of warehouse for its new life. Opened in December 2015, it also houses their offices, a tasting room, a bar and a retail store.

The process of making the gin is to start with a high-proof neutral grain spirit in which the organic botanicals are macerated in the distillery's hand-hammered copper stills from the fifth-generation Forsyth family in Scotland. The infused spirit is then boiled to a vapour and condensed back into a liquid, before being blended down with water to 47% ABV and bottled in the one-shot method (*see* page 29).

The classic American Dry Gin is the first of three main expressions (all bottled at 47% ABV), made with 100% organic botanicals. The recipe is a secret, but it does contain juniper, angelica, coriander seeds and a blend of US-sourced citrus peels. An oak-aged version, first released in November 2014, utilizes a barrel-finishing process from the 18th century, whereby the gin spends a minimum of three months in cask. There is also a limited-edition elderflower-infused version, which is only available at the distillery. *bluecoatgin.com*

◉ *Bluecoat Gin Distillery*

FLEISCHMANN'S GIN
KENTUCKY

Charles Fleischmann was Czech by birth, the son of Alois (or Abraham) Fleischmann, a Jewish distiller and yeast maker, and his wife Babette. Educated across Hungary, Vienna and Prague, he spoke various languages and eventually married a Russian, Henriette Robertson, in New York. Having managed a distillery in Vienna, Fleischmann came to the USA in 1865. In 1868, Charles and his brother Maximillian, together with distiller James Gaff, set up a company with the aim of producing two related yet very different products – compressed yeast and distilled spirits. In succeeding with the former, the brothers revolutionized baking and enabled the commercial production of bread. The original Fleischmann plant was built in 1870 in Ohio to produce both gin and vodka, along with some early examples of bourbon whiskey. Post-Prohibition, Fleischmann acquired a distillery in Kentucky, the home of US whiskey making, to which all the company's spirits production was moved. Fleischmann went on to own 14 manufacturing facilities and the family became so wealthy that they often commuted to New York from Santa Barbara, California, in their own private railcar.

In the latter part of the 20th century, the Fleischmann distillation business was passed between various drinks companies before settling in the hands of Barton Brands in 1995, which is now owned by the Sazerac Company of New Orleans.

The legacy of the Fleischmann yeast production served as a patron for the company's distilling ambitions during Prohibition and today allows the gin to lay claim to being – the Prohibition era aside – the oldest continually produced gin in the USA or "America's First

Gin", as the label proudly states. Fleischmann's Extra Dry Gin (bottled at 40% ABV) remains one of the biggest selling in the USA, a basic gin that offers little talk of its botanical make-up or indeed the process by which it is made. This, however, should not take away from the true American Dream story on which the product is built, and the historical significance of the gin's place in US distilling history. *sazerac.com*

IRON FISH DISTILLERY
MICHIGAN

Iron Fish Distillery is Michigan's first working farm solely dedicated to the practice of distilling small-batch craft spirits located on a reclaimed abandoned 1890s farmstead. Heidi Bolger and David Wallace together with Sarah and Richard Anderson purchased the farmland on which the distillery sits in 2011, but it wasn't until 2013, after a trip to Scotland and the Isle of Islay, that the team decided to establish a distillery.

○ *The American Classic, Fleischmann's*

They produce their spirits from the ground up, growing their own grain as well as sourcing grain from other Michigan farms that are respectful of the health of nearby watersheds in their farming practices. This "soil-to-spirit" distilling, as they call it, is the basis on which the family-operated distillery runs, and their use of non-GMO grain along with native yeast is at the heart of this. Practising their own milling, mashing, fermenting and distilling, the distillery takes its name from the Steelhead fish that run the nearby Betsie River. On their estate, they grow 25 hectares (60 acres) of grain, the team working with Michigan State University to help protect the environment, with the aim of cultivating and harvesting using sustainable and natural practices. Their Michigan Woodland Gin, bottled at 45% ABV, is built on a base of winter wheat using native botanicals including sprigs of Concolor fir, and is cut with water from their own aquifer well. They also produce a barrel-aged version, again bottled at 45% ABV. *ironfishdistillery.com*

EAST COAST USA

MAINE

Barr Hill Distillery
VERMONT

Maine Distilleries' Cold River

Bullyboy Distillers

NEW YORK

Berkshire Mountain Distillery
MASSACHUSETTS

Son's of Liberty
RHODE ISLAND

Iron Fish
MICHIGAN

Long Road Distillery

New York Distilling Co

Brooklyn Gin
Breuckelen Gin

Detroit City Distillery

PENNSYLVANIA

Bluecoat Gin

The District Distilling Co.
WASHINGTON DC

Castle & Key

Fleischmann's Gin
KENTUCKY

Durham Distillery
NORTH CAROLINA

Corsair Distillery
TENNESSEE

Southern Artisan Spirits

Dark Corner Distillery
SOUTH CAROLINA

FLORIDA

St. Petersburg Distillery

BREUCKELEN GIN
NEW YORK

Taking its name from the borough of Brooklyn, which Dutch settlers in the 17th-century called Breuckelen after the town of their homeland, Breuckelen Gin was founded in 2010 by Brad Estabrooke to produce both whiskey and gin. The operation, housed in a garage in Sunset Park, takes a nose-to-tail approach to making its spirits from scratch, producing a neutral wheat spirit base using local grains to New York in a 400-litre (106-US-gallon) Kothe still. Retaining some of the flavour of the wheat in the base spirit is part of the favour profile of the core release Glorious Gin, which features juniper, rosemary, ginger and fresh lemon peel and grapefruit peels. Each botanical is individually macerated and distilled before being blended, diluted and bottled at 45% ABV. The distillery also has an oak-aged version first released in 2011, again bottled at 45% ABV.
brkdistilling.com

BROOKLYN GIN
NEW YORK

Emil Jättne and Joe Santos founded Brooklyn Gin in 2010 in their bid to make

a high-quality small-batch US gin by hand. The Warwick Valley Winery and Distillery in Warwick, New York, distils the gin in a Christian Carl copper pot still using a base spirit made from 100% US corn sourced from small farms and fresh citrus peels that are all cut by hand along with the juniper. The production process from maceration through to bottling (at 40% ABV) takes three days, with each batch producing 300 bottles of gin.
brooklyngin.com

DISTRICT DISTILLING CO.
WASHINGTON, DC

This distillery takes a decidedly different approach to its gin and distilling, which is the centrepiece of its restaurant and bar. Working with Molly Cummings, Professor of Biology at the University of Texas and an expert in foraging wild juniper, the company has released two gin expressions, each centred around an individual species of juniper: WildJune Western Style Gin (45% ABV), which has wild redberry juniper (*Juniperus pinchotii*) at the core of its recipe, and Checkerbark American Dry Style Gin (47% ABV), using checkerbark or alligator juniper (*Juniperus deppeana*).
district-distilling.com

COLD RIVER GIN
MAINE

Maine Distilleries' Cold River was founded in 2003 by potato farmer Donnie Thibodeau who along with his brother Lee, finding himself with a surplus of stock that year, approached brewer Chris Dowe, now master distiller, about a venture into spirits. Based in Freeport, the distillery employs what it calls a "ground-to-glass" spirits production, starting with a potato spirit base. Cold River

Gin is made using a German Carl still, building on the potato spirit with a mixture of juniper along with orris root, coriander, angelica, cardamom and lemon and orange peels. All its spirits are cut with water from the Cold River aquifer, the gin is bottled at 47% ABV.
coldrivervodka.com/gin/

BERKSHIRE MOUNTAIN DISTILLERS
MASSACHUSETTS

Having purchased an apple orchard in 2004, Chris Weld and his wife started to experiment in the world of distilling with the aim of producing apple brandy. They established Berkshire Mountain Distillers on the farm in 2007, and eventually ended up with two versions of gin, Greylock (40% ABV) and Ethereal (around 43% ABV), the latter having a movable recipe that evolves with each batch. At the farm distillery, Weld has planted juniper as well as other botanicals essential for gin production such as angelica and orris root, together with liquorice. They opened a new distillery on Main Street in Sheffield in 2018.
berkshiremountaindistillers.com

BULLY BOY DISTILLERS
MASSACHUSETTS

Set up by Dave and Will Willis, Bully Boy Distillers began on a farm outside Boston, where the brothers made cider from the local apples, which led them to experiment with producing apple brandy on a tiny 4.5-litre (1¼-US-gallon) still. It was the science of fermentation, distillation and ageing that attracted Dave, a skill set he further honed by working alongside experienced distillers in Missouri and Chicago, while Will has gone on to head up the sales side of the business. They use a near 700-litre (185-US-gallon) Kothe still to produce

two main types of gin (and interestingly a 3,500-litre/925-US-gallon Christian Carl still for everything else). Their London Dry-style, called simply Gin (bottled at 45% ABV), uses a sugar-cane spirit base, which the brothers say gives them a more robust foundation to build on, with flavours that include Italian juniper, Californian coriander, grapefruit, cardamon, chamomile and blueberry among other botanicals. Their Estate Gin (bottled at 47% ABV), on the other hand, starts life with a base of neutral grain spirit and apple brandy, which they distil from high-strength cider fermented at Stormalong Cidery in Sherborn just outside Boston. The botanicals used are also very different, beginning with the types of juniper, Albanian as well as local juniper (*Juniperus virginiana*), along with coriander, lemon, hibiscus, pink peppercorns and a few others that are kept secret.
bullyboydistillers.com

TRUE BORN GIN
RHODE ISLAND

After spending time working at Maker's Mark Bourbon in Kentucky, Mike Reppucci set up the Sons of Liberty Spirits Company to produce a variety of different spirits, all of which start life as a Belgian-style beer, made from a mixed mash bill of wheat, oats and barley. The company's True Born Gin (bottled at 45% ABV) is described as being genever in profile (*see* page 13), featuring juniper, coriander, orange peel, lemongrass and hops, and using the vapour-infusion method (*see* page 20) for extracting the flavours of the botanicals and hops. Any residual liquid is bottled as a sour beer.
solspirits.com

CALEDONIA SPIRITS
VERMONT

Inspired by the views from the Barr Hill Nature Preserve, Ryan Christiansen and Todd Hardie set up Caledonia Spirits in 2011, named after its location in Caledonia County in Vermont, with a vision to support local agriculture by making craft spirits from the region's raw materials. Initially using a unique 68-litre (18-US-gallon) direct-fired still (see page 29), they produced a honey-inspired Bar Hill Gin (45% ABV) and vodka, making nearly 450 gin distillations in a year in an attempt to keep up with demand. In 2013, they upgraded to a larger 1,500-litre (396-US-gallon) still and a year later the distillery launched Tom Cat, a barrel-aged gin, and then set out on a mission to build their own barrels. Over the course of six months, the Caledonia team worked with local foresters, sawyers and truckers to find sustainably harvested lumber and employed Bob Hockert as their master cooper. The first edition of 100% Vermont-grown white oak barrel-matured Tom Cat was released in 2016 (bottled at 43% ABV). Back in 2015, head distiller Christiansen

purchased the company from Hardie, who subsequently bought a local farm that now supplies the distillery with rye.
caledoniaspirits.com

CARDINAL GIN
NORTH CAROLINA

Located in the foothills of the Blue Ridge Mountains in the town of Kings Mountain, the family-run distillery of Southern Artisan Spirits (SAS), founded in 2012, produces Cardinal Gin using only organic ingredients. Among the key fresh botanicals, some of which are grown locally, are apricot stones, cloves, frankincense, mint and spearmint. They also produce a barrel-aged version, both bottled at 42% ABV.
southernartisanspirits.com

CONNIPTION GIN
NORTH CAROLINA

The Durham Distillery was set up in Durham by Melissa and Lee Katrincic, who have taken classic gin-making traditions and combined them with "techniques borrowed from modern chemistry". The small-batch gin distillation starts with a 230-litre (61-US-gallon) custom-designed German copper pot still and a vacuum distillation (see page 28) of the more robust botanicals – Indian coriander, angelica root and cardamom, along with juniper. The more delicate botanicals – cucumber, citrus and honeysuckle flowers – are individually vacuum distilled at room temperature in a 20-litre (5¼-US-gallon) Rotovap (see page 28) before being blended into the gin base. Their two expressions are Conniption American Dry (bottled at 44% ABV) and Conniption Navy Strength (57% ABV), which uses botanicals such as Indian coriander, caraway, rosemary, cardamom and cassia with Rotovap-distilled fig and citrus.
durhamdistillery.com

JŌCASSEE GIN
SOUTH CAROLINA

The Dark Corner Distillery, a craft microdistillery set up in Greenville in 2011, uses a system that was designed by its founder Joe Fenten to pot distil Jōcassee Gin using citrus, honeysuckle and magnolia blossoms as their key botanicals. These botanicals are harvested in the spring and summer months before being macerated in spirit and then filtered. The resulting spirit is then distilled in a 1,325-litre (350-US-gallon) Scottish copper pot still for a final time (bottled at 42% ABV). A barrel-aged version is also available, rested in American charred white oak barrels before being diluted with fresh local water and bottled at 42% ABV.
darkcornerdistillery.com

OLD ST. PETE TROPICAL GIN
FLORIDA

Henry Kasprow, a fourth-generation distiller, set up the St. Petersburg Distillery together with the Lafrate family in 2014. They use copper pot stills to produce their Tropical Gin (bottled at 45% ABV), drawing on the Florida quintessentials of sunshine and citrus fruits in balancing juniper with citrus peels among a mix of 14 different botanicals.
stpetersburgdistillery.com

CASTLE & KEY RESTORATION RELEASE GIN
KENTUCKY

Will Arvin and Wes Murry took over and revived a former distillery in Millville founded in 1887 by legendary distiller Colonel Edmund Haynes Taylor Jr. The site was ground-breaking for the era, featuring unique architectural elements including a castle, a classical springhouse and sunken gardens, which, by the end of the last century, had been left in ruins. With the

establishment of the Castle & Key Distillery, it lives once more in a state famed for distilling. Castle & Key source their ingredients locally and distil from selected grains rather than using bulk vodka to create their spirits. Restoration Release Gin is made on local Vendome copper stills using a base spirit of 17% yellow corn, 63% rye and 20% malted barley along with chamomile, ginger, rosemary, lemon verbena, liquorice and angelica roots, coriander and, of course, juniper. Bottled at 53% ABV, each bottle details the make-up and botanicals on the label.
castleandkey.com

CORSAIR GIN
KENTUCKY/TENNESSEE

Founded in 2008 by childhood friends Darek Bell and Andrew Webber, Corsair Distillery was first established in Bowling Green, Kentucky, before setting up another site in 2010 in Nashville, Tennessee, becoming the first craft distillery in the city since Prohibition. Corsair can truly be called one of the most innovative and eclectic distillers in the USA, with their spirits winning over 800 medals at national and international spirits competitions. Corsair Artisan Gin is made in small batches in a hand-hammered pot still, and takes its flavour from orange, lemon and coriander (bottled at 44% ABV). Corsair has pushed the boundaries of the spirits category and its barrel-aged gin is no exception. It is matured in ex-rum barrels, which brings an unusual sweet, fruity/spicy note, with vanilla and tropical fruit aroma and flavour, alongside woody undertones of cinnamon, clove and ginger and a distinct botanical balance (bottled at 46% ABV).
corsairdistillery.com

CENTRAL USA

As the craft distilling scene has swept through the USA, producers making a variety of aged spirits such as whiskey have also turned their attention to white spirits including gin to help them build toward a complete spirits portfolio. But so great has the market for their gin become that many of these producers have made it their main focus of production.

F.E.W SPIRITS
ILLINOIS

Established in 2011 by former brewer and spirits fanatic Paul Hletko, whose grandfather ran a very successful brewery during World War Two in the former Czech Republic, F.E.W is one of the founding partners of the renaissance in US craft distilling. What makes the distillery's story so compelling is that it proudly resides in the moderately sized city of Evanston on the north side of Chicago, which was a thriving hotbed for the Women's Christian Temperance Union of America more than 80 years ago, at a time when the nation was locked within the crushing grip of Prohibition. This ironic connection is further underscored by the correspondence of the titular F.E.W with the initials of Frances Elizabeth Willard, widely considered to be the matriarchal driving force behind the movement back in the 1890s, and the fact that Evanston was still a dry city until the late 1990s.

Today, F.E.W is one of the more remarkable gin distilling operations in that it creates all its base alcohol from scratch rather than buying in neutral spirit from a third party and redistilling it with botanicals to produce a gin. The base is essentially the same spirit, which is then filled into casks to create F.E.W's bourbon, made from a mash bill of corn grown in Indiana, rye and wheat, plus a small amount of malt to help start the fermentation process. As a result, the gin has a distinctly malty, sweet cereal flavour.

A total of 11 botanicals are used in the core American Gin recipe, which

The line up at F.E.W distillery

F.E.W distillery, Chicago

include orange and lemon peels, hops, vanilla, cassia bark and grains of paradise, alongside a healthy amount of juniper. These are steeped in a large tea bag inside the gin still before distillation begins. It is then bottled at 40% ABV.

There are also several variants of the core gin on offer, including a Breakfast edition, which also incorporates Earl Grey tea for an aromatic bergamot note, a higher-strength (57% ABV) version as well as a barrel-aged version, which brings a creamy, oaky note to the flavour, with gingerbread spice on the finish. This gin is aged for four months in small, brand-new American oak barrels and uses a botanical mix that includes a greater emphasis on spice, providing a more robust spirit to interact with the oak. After maturation it is bottled at 46% ABV.

Each of Hletko's gins has a unique recipe and he is always experimenting and adding (or subtracting!) from his range.
fewspirits.com

DEATH'S DOOR GIN
WISCONSIN

A true spirits producer, Death's Door Distilling started as an experiment to see if agriculture could be restored, promoted and conserved on Washington Island, and has since blossomed into a fully fledged business with the construction of the company's state-of-the art distillery in Middleton. Founded by Brian Ellison and opened on 4 June 2012, it is the largest craft distillery in the state and one of the largest in the region with an annual capacity in excess of 250,000 cases of finished product, including a range of whiskey, gin, vodka and something called Wondermint, an artisan-crafted peppermint schnapps.

The distillery takes their base spirit very seriously, and in conjunction with the local Michael Fields Institute, which works toward sustainable agriculture, two specific varieties of hard, red winter wheat Harvard and Carlisle (generally used for making flour) that grow well in the unique maritime conditions on the Island were selected to provide the basis for their gins, along with corn and malted barley, also the recipe for their vodka. The barley used in the production of the gin, vodka and whiskey is also grown in Wisconsin in partnership with other farmers. First, the barley and wheat are fermented and subsequently passed through their stripping column still (*see* page 249) to bring the spirit to over 80% ABV before a second distillation through their vodka stills pumps up the ABV to above 96%. The corn is then fermented and distilled separately using the same process.

The watchword at Death's Door is sustainability, with the botanicals for the gin being sourced within the state where possible. In fact, the company holds an annual juniper harvest festival on Washington Island where guests pick wild juniper berries (*Juniperus virginiana*) for the gin.

Death's Door Gin uses a simple yet effective mix of these wild juniper berries and local coriander and fennel seeds in a vapour-extraction process (*see* page 22), fewer botanicals being required to create the impact of flavour in the bottle because of the depth of flavour in the base spirit itself. It is bottled at 47% ABV.

At the end of 2018, Death's Door Spirits was acquired by another local distiller, Dancing Goat, and production of the gin has moved about 50km (31 miles) east to the town of Cambridge.'
deathsdoorspirits.com

Simple but brilliant: Death's Door Gin

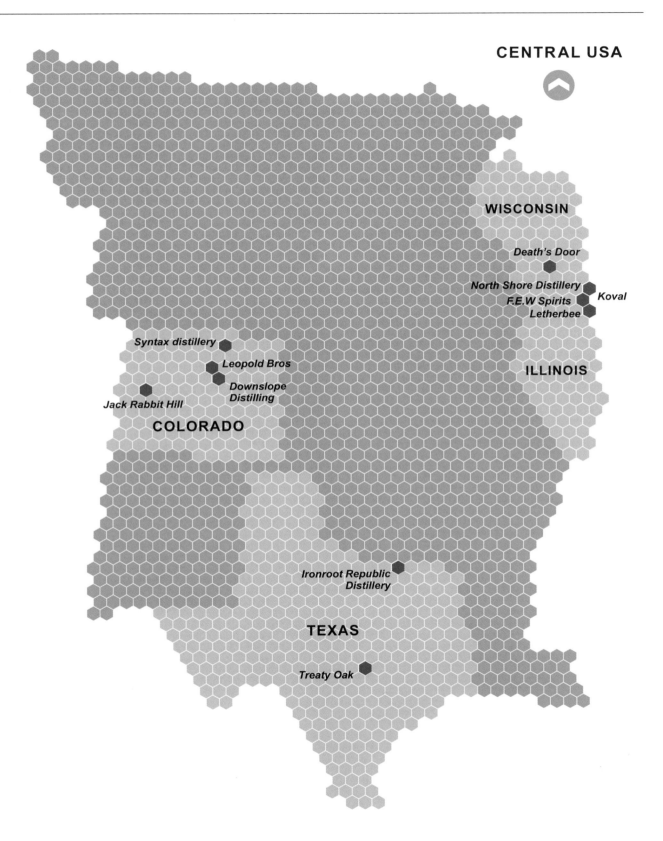

CENTRAL USA

WISCONSIN

Death's Door

North Shore Distillery

F.E.W Spirits   Koval

Letherbee

Syntax distillery

Leopold Bros

Downslope
Distilling

ILLINOIS

Jack Rabbit Hill

COLORADO

Ironroot Republic
Distillery

TEXAS

Treaty Oak

WATERLOO GIN
TEXAS

Texas has become a serious player in the world of craft distilling, and when it comes to gin there is a decent heritage for the state to call upon. One of the earliest adopters was Daniel Barnes who, in 2005, started Graham Barnes Distilling, now called Treaty Oak Distilling, named after a 500-year-old tree in Austin under which Stephen F Austin signed agreements defining the borders of Texas.

Their original range consisted of just one spirit, a rum, which was followed six years later in 2011 by a gin somewhat curiously called Waterloo Gin, until you learn that Waterloo was the original name for Austin. In 2016, the distillery moved to a bigger production site, a 12-hectare (28-acre) property in Dripping Springs around 40km (25 miles) from Austin, where they have a strong focus on sustainability, employing a specialist in the field, Jamie Biel, to monitor water quality and expand their sustainability initiatives. The company calls itself "a collective of distillers, sommeliers, botanists and architects", drawing inspiration from the state of Texas.

Treaty Oak use a spirit made from a mixed mash bill of corn and wheat for their gins. Their flagship gin, Waterloo No.9, features a core of juniper, coriander and aniseed, with additional flavours coming from pecans, lavender and grapefruit zest, all harvested in Texas and vapour infused (*see* page 20). It is bottled at 47% ABV, cut with limestone-filtered Texan spring water. Waterloo Antique Gin is aged in medium-char white oak barrels to mirror the Dutch genever style (*see* page 18) and is left to mature for 18–24 months before being bottled at 47% ABV. An Old Tom-style gin (*see* page 21), Waterloo Old Yaupon features honey that is produced exclusively from wild Yaupon holly (*Ilex vomitoria*) flowers, which adds sweetness and viscosity. It also draws on additional flavours of makrut (kaffir) lime, aniseed and orris root, and is bottled at 45% ABV.

All the gins are distilled using Treaty Oak's proprietary distillation process and their unique stills, comprising a column-style rectifier atop a pot still (*see* page 25), produced by Vendome in Kentucky. Their citrus fruits are sourced from the Texas Valley in partnership with a grower called US Citrus, the largest producers of limes in the country. In developing their gins, the distillery and US Citrus found that younger, immature citrus fruits hold more essential oils in their skins than older, more mature fruit. waterloogin.com

◉ *Treaty Oak, the home of Waterloo Gin*

They have a strong focus on sustainability, employing a specialist in the field, Jamie Biel, to monitor water quality and expand their sustainability initiatives.

KOVAL
CHICAGO

Established in 2008, KOVAL can claim the honour of being the city's first distillery to be opened since the mid-1800s, when it was founded by husband and wife team Dr Robert and Dr Sonat Birnecker, with Robert bringing with him a wealth of distilling expertise from his native Austria, where he helped establish his grandparents' distillery to great success. Today, KOVAL produces organic whiskey, liqueurs and gin following the grain-to-glass concept rather than buying in neutral spirit to redistill, with a 5,000-litre (1,320-US-gallon) German Kothe-made still lying at the heart of the operation. KOVAL Dry Gin (bottled at 47% ABV) is reminiscent of a juniper-forward London Dry style, but backdropped with a fresh, floral botanical balance, made with a unique variety of woodland spices. Juniper and wildflowers develop first, followed by grassy notes and vanilla aromas. A barrel-aged version (also 47% ABV) is left to rest in KOVAL whiskey casks, lending a viscosity, spice and creaminess to the gin.
koval-distillery.com

LETHERBEE GIN
CHICAGO

Main man Brenton Engel is something of an industry legend among the bartending community of Chicago and Letherbee is his playground where, along with his cohorts, he creates everything from gin to barrel-aged absinthe and Bësk, a somewhat forgotten, bitter wormwood-based Swedish spirit that bartenders like to treat each other to as a comforting (yet fiery) handshake. Engel's distillation skills originated a little over

12 years ago when he cooked up batches of moonshine in his basement, which got everyone from bartenders to local chefs talking about what might be possible. The punchy 48% ABV gin is Letherbee's flagship spirit, bringing together 11 botanicals. Juniper heavy, it includes a classic mix of coriander, cardamom, angelica root and cinnamon, with cubeb berries bringing a peppery spice, along with lemon and orange peel in the citrus department, plus a hint of

liquorice, fennel and a smooth almond nuttiness. A radical Autumnal edition, alongside a Vernal edition, released each year brings roasted hazelnuts, cocoa nibs and black walnuts into the botanical mix.
letherbee.com

NORTH SHORE DISTILLERY
ILLINOIS

A story not dissimilar to KOVAL (*see* left) in that what we find here is a pioneering husband and wife team, this time laying claim to helping kick-start the entire craft distilling scene in Illinois. Derek and Sonja Kassebaum opened the doors of North Shore Distillery in 2004, and have now moved from their original site to an entirely purpose-built development, which still houses Ethel, the original 250-litre (66-US-gallon) German-made still, named after Sonja's grandmother. At the heart of a wide portfolio of spirits (including vodka, rum and akvavit) are four varieties of gin: Distiller's No. 6, Distiller's No. 11 (both bottled at 45% ABV), which has a

juniper-heavy London Dry feel, Mighty Gin, a high-strength 55% ABV version of the No. 6, and a Scofflaw Old Tom (45% ABV), which also brings in fresh orange peel to the citrus-forward profile, plus aniseed and osmanthus blossoms, giving a fresh, peach/apricot floral aroma. Using a core selection of lemon peel (hand-grated fresh rather than dried), cardamom and cinnamon, alongside delicate floral notes, the botanicals are infused into the base spirit for several hours before being distilled.
northshoredistillery.com

DETROIT CITY DISTILLERY
DETROIT

Eight childhood friends set up Detroit City Distillery in the heart of Detroit with the aim of making alcohol the old-fashioned way using local Michigan barley. The distillery creates small-batch artisanal whiskey and vodka as well as gin using local ingredients sourced directly from farms nearby, and for some of their experimental gins they source the botanicals just two blocks from the distillery's front door. Railroad Gin, bottled at 44% ABV, uses juniper, cardamom, coriander, star anise, orris root, fresh orange peel and cinnamon all from one supplier, Germack Co. in historic Eastern Market. Peacemaker Gin, also bottled at 44% ABV, features just five botanicals, namely juniper, coriander, orange peel, white pine and blue spruce, the latter two having been planted by the distillery founders over 20 years ago on Forsyth Farm in Bath, Michigan.
detroitcitydistillery.com

LONG ROAD GIN
MICHIGAN

From their home in the Grand Rapids, the Long Road Distillers (so named as they didn't want to take any shortcuts) make their entire range of spirits, which includes gin, whiskey, vodka and apple brandy, from scratch. Drawing on local farms for their selection of cereals, their gin is built on a base of 100% red winter wheat grown at the nearby Heffron Farms in Belding, established in 1921 and run by the fourth generation of farmers from the same family. The wheat is milled from whole grain and fermented on site, then the six botanicals that go to make up Long Road Gin are each distilled individually and blended together, before being bottled at 45% ABV. Long Road use Vendome stills from Kentucky and Müller pot stills from Germany.
longroaddistillers.com

CAPROCK GIN
COLORADO

Jack Rabbit Hill Farm near Hotchkiss in western Colorado's North Fork Valley began as a diversified organic farm in 2000 but then moved into biodynamic farming in 2006, rearing sheep and cattle and growing some 7 hectares (18 acres) of grapes. As well as producing wine and some cider, they make brandy, vodka and gin, all their spirits being farm fermented and distilled in a German copper pot still. Their CapRock gin (bottled at 41% ABV) is certified organic, made using a base spirit distilled from Jonathon and Braeburn apples grown at Ela Family Farms and organic winter wheat.
jackrabbithill.com

DOWNSLOPE DISTILLING
COLORADO

Founded in 2009, this experimental distillery based in Centennial is a deliberately small-scale affair, producing a range of truly individual rums, vodkas, gins and whiskeys, currently amounting to ten regular items. Their still is also remarkably unusual, custom designed with a Double Diamond head, resembling two diamonds resting on top of one another. Downslope Ould Tom Gin is made using a base of cane sugar, first pot distilled (and described by the distillery as "anything but neutral") and then 11 botanicals infused into the cane spirit in a small hybrid still (*see* page 25). It is bottled at 40% ABV.
downslopedistilling.com

LEOPOLD BROS.
COLORADO

Founder of Leopold Bros., a family owned and operated distillery in Denver, Todd Leopold studied malting and brewing at the Siebel Institute of Technology in Chicago. After graduating in 1996, he trained at the Doemens Academy in Munich, focusing on the production of lager beers, before apprenticing at several breweries and distilleries throughout Europe. Brother and co-founder Scott Leopold studied economics and industrial and environmental engineering before, in 1999, joining forces with Todd in opening a microbrewery in Ann Arbor, Michigan, called Leopold Bros., which soon expanded into distilling, releasing its first spirits in 2001. Having built a strong following for their eco-brewing techniques using organic ingredients, in 2008 they relocated their operations to Scott and Todd's home state of Colorado.

Leopold Bros. produce a range of whiskeys, gins, vodka, liqueurs and, unusually, fernet, absinthe and aperitivo products. They malt and mill their own barley as well as ferment their own mash, and everything is distilled on site. For their American Small Batch Gin, the brothers distill each botanical individually, including coriander, pomelos, orris root and Valencia oranges, before blending them together and bottling at 40% ABV. Their Navy Strength gin comes in at 57% ABV and uses bergamot as a lead botanical, while Summer Gin, at 47% ABV, features coriander, blood orange, lemon myrtle leaf and *Helichrysum angustifolium*, the "immortal flower".
leopoldbros.com

SYNTAX SPIRITS
COLORADO

Located in historic downtown Greeley, Syntax Distillery was founded by distiller Heather Bean in 2010, producing what they term Precision Spirits according to a grain-to-glass philosophy using local raw ingredients and pure Colorado water, and rooted in sustainable production practices such as the use of recycled bottles and packaging. They make whiskey, vodka, rum and gin using handmade stills, holding true to their ideal of never using neutral grain spirits or blending Syntax products with base spirits from other distillers. They source all their grain from farmers within 160 km (100 miles) of the distillery and their sugar cane molasses from Florida. Rose Gin is built on their base vodka spirit with a botanical recipe of juniper, red rose petals, lavender flowers, sweet orange peel, lemon and lime zest, angelica and liquorice roots, cardamom and coriander seeds and Indonesian cinnamon, using both direct distillation and vapour infusion (*see* page 20). It is bottled at 40% ABV.
syntaxspirits.com

IRONROOT TEXAS DROUGHT GIN
TEXAS

Established by the Likarish Brothers Robert and Jonathan in Denison, Ironroot Republic has embraced the field-to-glass approach, milling, mashing, fermenting and distilling their spirits on site. The Texas Drought Gin they produce is a distinctly citrus-forward spirit with hints of bergamot and vanilla, bottled at 40% ABV.
ironrootrepublic.com

WEST COAST USA

From as far north as Seattle in Washington, which has a hugely vibrant distillation scene of its own with just under 30 craft distilleries, all the way down to California's San Diego, the West Coast is arguably responsible for the beginnings of the craft gin movement in the USA, which has spread out eastwards over the last decade. In fact, it is hard to comprehend just how far the scene would have developed had it not been for the ingenuity and passion of a few distillers. These innovators have moved the category away from simply replicating the classic London Dry style popular in Europe, looking beyond the traditional flavour profile and bringing in an altogether different set of botanicals – notably juniper native to the West Coast – to create a style that is proudly North American.

Changes in legislation – especially in Washington State – have meant that there are fewer hurdles for the would-be distiller to jump through when building a new distillery, and it is now easier for consumers to sample and purchase craft spirits on the sites where they are made, rather than strictly through licensed third-party outlets. There is also a huge diversity in base spirit, with wheat-, rye- and grape-based spirits all being distilled in-house, giving additional character to the structure of each gin.

ST. GEORGE GIN
CALIFORNIA

Alameda's St. George Spirits can proudly proclaim that they undoubtedly pre-empted the explosion of US craft distillers, enjoying three decades of success distilling eau-de-vie, vodka, gin and more recently a fine malt whiskey. Under the mission statement of "we don't distil to meet your expectations, we distil to exceed your imagination", the St. George team, led by original founder Jörg Rupf along with new owner Lance Winters and master distiller Dave Smith, has been making pioneering spirits since 1982. Notably, it was the first legal small distillery to be opened in the USA since the repeal of Prohibition in 1933. Despite the capacious surroundings of their distillery

building – a converted naval hangar – the focus on attention to every small detail is what makes the spirits from St. George so interesting.

There are five production stills on site, which are all hybrid pot/column (*see* page 25), ranging from a pair of 250-litre (66-US-gallon) vessels, one 500-litre (132-US-gallon) and another pair of large 1,500-litre (396-US-gallon) stills. However, the initial exploratory work is conducted using 10-litre (2¾-US-gallon) and 30-litre (8-US-gallon) mini development stills.

St. George has three gins in its repertoire, Terroir, Botanivore and Dye Rye Gin, each with its own unique story and botanical make-up. Terroir was Winters' and Smith's concept of effectively distilling the aromas of the Californian forest landscape, which overlooks the

St. George Distillery's Lance Winters

St. George Distillery

bay near the distillery. Much of the recipe is made up of foraged botanicals including a key note of Douglas fir, alongside coastal sage, fresh bay laurel and juniper, balanced out with some classical botanicals such as cardamom, orris root, coriander seeds and citrus peels. The distillers employ the relatively unusual technique of roasting the coriander in a wok to release more aroma compounds, which they say captures the "intoxicating earthy bouquet of the region's chaparral". From here, the fir and sage are distilled individually in the 250-litre (66-US-gallon) still to minimize the effects of seasonal variation. The fresh bay laurel leaves and juniper are then vapour infused in a botanical basket in the same still, with the rest of the botanicals placed directly in the pot of the 1,500 (396-US-gallon) still (*see* page 22). The result is a hugely aromatic, distinctively fresh, pine-led gin – complex and unique.

Botanivore introduces the likes of Citra hops, caraway, dill seeds, the earthy notes of star anise, Malabar black peppercorns and angelica root for a much more spice-laden flavour. The Dry Rye Gin, while a much simpler affair, brings into play the distillery's unaged rye spirit as the base and uses 50% more juniper than the other recipes, alongside black peppercorns, grapefruit and lime peels, caraway and coriander seeds, creating a broader, peppery, herbaceous flavour. All three expressions are bottled at 45% ABV.
stgeorgespirits.com

JUNÍPERO GIN/ HOTALING & CO
SAN FRANCISCO

Celebrating a 21st birthday is something of a rite of passage to many in the USA, and in a number of respects, the same applies to Junípero, the first gin created by Anchor Distilling Company back in 1998 (once part of the Anchor Brewing Company, now under different ownership and renamed Hotaling & Co.), which hit this landmark age last year. Like Anchor's original owner Fritz Maytag, who first bought the brewing company in 1965 and retired from the business completely in 2010, Junípero is something of a pioneer, appearing on the scene before craft distilling was even remotely the widely used phrase it is today and paving the way for

San Fran's original craft gin, Junípero

other distillers on the West Coast to explore this rapidly emerging category-in-waiting. Today, it feels that it has truly earned the right to be known as "America's original craft gin".

That said, from a flavour perspective, Junípero didn't try to stand out too far from the more ubiquitous brands at the time. It followed a classic London Dry recipe, boldly juniper forward, as the name suggests, with a solid citrus backbone and hints of coriander, cardamom, cassia bark and angelica root, although the exact formula is still a closely guarded secret. It is also notably bottled at a much higher strength compared to that of other "regular" gin expressions, 49.3% ABV, which to the casual, non-navy-strength gin drinker might be a stretch on the palate. However, Junípero was designed to be the gin of choice in the resurgence of the Gin and Tonic and classic cocktail culture, and its broad-shouldered juniper notes remain as distinct as ever even when doused with a mixer.

Junípero has two spiritual siblings that are also made by Hotaling & Co. One is Anchor Old Tom Gin (bottled at 45% ABV), which is also pot distilled with juniper and other classic botanicals, but sweetened by the addition of star anise, liquorice root and, rather unconventionally, stevia, sourced from Paraguay where it has been used as a culinary ingredient for centuries. The second is Genevieve Gin, a genever-style spirit (*see* page 18) using a mash bill of wheat, barley and rye malt, redistilled in copper pot stills with the same botanicals used in Junípero and bottled at a slightly lower ABV of 47.3%.
hotalingandco.com

GIN NO. 209
SAN FRANSISCO

Gin No. 209 may indeed never have existed if it hadn't been for the detective work of Leslie Rudd, the proprietor of the prestigious winery Edge Hill Estate in St Helena, Napa Valley. Noticing some faint writing on an old barn that was being used for hay at the property, Rudd discovered that it was signage from the late 1800s, which read "Registered Distillery No. 209". Some further digging around revealed that it referred to the winery's founder, William Scheffler, who not only created some of the most impressive wines of his era but was also something of a distiller at heart. The titular "209" refers to the licence number given to Scheffler by the Federal Government back in 1882. The distillery was subsequently re-established by Rudd, but constraints on space meant it was eventually relocated to Pier 50 in San Francisco, and is said to be the only distillery in the world to effectively be built over water.

The exact botanical recipe for Gin

> Ingredients include Calabrian juniper, bergamot orange peel, lemon peel, cardamom pods, cassia bark, angelica root, coriander seeds and bitter orange.

No. 209 remains under wraps, but the distillery does reveal that the ingredients are sourced from four continents and include Calabrian juniper, bergamot orange peel, lemon peel, cardamom pods, cassia bark, angelica root, coriander seeds and bitter orange. After the botanicals are macerated for 11 hours in a spirit made from a base of Midwestern corn, distillation takes place by batch in 11-hour cycles in a 7.6m (25ft)-tall pot still, which was commissioned by Scottish coppersmiths Forsyths, who have served the Scotch whisky industry since the 1890s. The design was based on the tall, slender-necked stills used by Highland single malt Glenmorangie, which, rather ironically, were reputedly gin stills before they were repurposed in order to make whisky.

The Original No. 209 gin is citrus led, with distinct floral notes, leading into an emerging spiciness with cardamom and coriander (bottled at 46% ABV). In addition to this expression, the distillers have been experimenting with several barrel-aged editions, including Sauvignon Blanc and Chardonnay casks, both of which give additional structure and a distinct colour to the gin.
distillery209.com

Martini time with No. 209 gin

WEST COAST USA

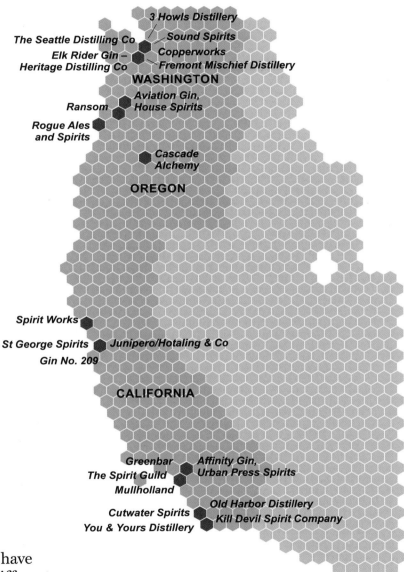

3 Howls Distillery

Sound Spirits

The Seattle Distilling Co

Copperworks

Elk Rider Gin –
Heritage Distilling Co

Fremont Mischief Distillery

WASHINGTON

Aviation Gin,
House Spirits

Ransom

Rogue Ales
and Spirits

Cascade
Alchemy

OREGON

Spirit Works

St George Spirits

Junipero/Hotaling & Co

Gin No. 209

CALIFORNIA

Greenbar

Affinity Gin,
Urban Press Spirits

The Spirit Guild

Mullholland

Old Harbor Distillery

Cutwater Spirits

Kill Devil Spirit Company

You & Yours Distillery

> Innovators have
> brought in a different
> set of botanicals –
> notably juniper native
> to the West Coast –
> to create a style that
> is proudly
> North American.

AVIATION GIN
HOUSE SPIRITS, OREGON

The story behind Aviation began back in 2005, when Seattle-based bartender Ryan Magarian came across what he described as a "subtle, summer gin", which immediately piqued his interest, especially in relation to the world of pre-Prohibition cocktails, one of his major passions. The reason for this subtlety was that the juniper, although still present in the recipe, wasn't overpowering the other botanicals. Recognizing the opportunity to develop something different for a potential new generation of gin drinkers, Magarian met the Portland distiller Christian Krogstad and after much experimentation with seven different botanicals they hit on the recipe for Aviation.

While the idea of a gin not centred around juniper may feel slightly blasphemous to the purist consumers of traditional juniper-heavy brands, Aviation sees the other botanicals providing a stage for the juniper to be appreciated as more of a member of the cast rather than as a bold, brash solo act.

The production process to make Aviation, a single-shot gin (*see* page 29), takes place in 100-case batches and begins with an 18-hour maceration period, where the botanicals – cardamom, coriander, French lavender, aniseed, juniper, two kinds of orange peel and sarsaparilla root (a hugely popular ingredient in pre-Prohibition times but relatively uncommon today) – are placed in nylon bags for steeping. The macerated spirit is then mixed with water and distilled for about seven hours, with the cut running from the still at around 72% ABV, before being further diluted with water to 42% ABV.

The result is a slightly rooty, earthy note, with hints of vanilla, almost

> Aviation sees the other botanicals providing a stage for the juniper to be appreciated as more of a member of the cast rather than as a bold, brash solo act.

medicinal notes and then some sweeter spices. In many respects, Aviation is atypical of the New Western style of gins (*see* page 249) that the US craft distilling movement has embraced over the last decade.
aviationgin.com

⊙ *Actor Ryan Reynolds, stakeholder in Aviation gin*

OTHER WEST COAST USA GINS TO TRY

COPPERWORKS GIN
WASHINGTON
Founded in 2013 by Jason Parker and Micah Nutt, both with backgrounds in brewing, the Copperworks Distilling Co. had cause for celebration at the end of 2018 when it was crowned Distillery of the Year by the American Distilling Institute. The distillery's USP is its traditional-style copper pot stills, one very tall, slender-necked example (similar in design to the Gin No. 209 still in San Francisco – *see page 172*) being specifically designed for producing gin. The base spirit for its Small Batch Gin is made from malted barley grown in Washington State, and nine botanicals are used in addition to the essential juniper (bottled at 47% ABV). *copperworksdistilling.com*

ELK RIDER GIN/ HERITAGE DISTILLING CO.
WASHINGTON
Founded in 2011 by Justin Stiefel, his wife and a few friends while sitting around a campfire, Heritage Distilling Co. (HDC) is now the fastest-growing spirits brand in the Pacific Northwest and the largest independently owned distillery in Washington. It runs six distilleries, with a variety of different still types and sizes, the smallest being a collection of 120-litre (32-US-gallon) "hillbilly" pot stills with adjustable plate columns and the largest a 3,000-litre (793-US-gallon) pot that is used for producing vodka, whiskey, rum and gin. HDC produce two distinct gins, Elk Rider Crisp Gin and Batch No. 12 Gin, which both have a core botanical recipe of juniper, coriander and sweet orange peel and are bottled at 47% ABV. *heritagedistilling.com*

EBB + FLOW GIN
WASHINGTON
Sound Spirits can claim the lofty title of being Seattle's first legal distillery since Prohibition was lifted, founded by owner and distiller Steve Stone back in 2010. Since then, Stone has taken an esoteric approach, producing a handful of liqueurs, an akvavit in homage to the local Norwegian neighbourhood and two, 100-bottle-batch Ebb + Flow gins: a traditional version and an Old Tom, bottled at 47% and 44% ABV respectively. Both are designed around a spirit base of malted barley spirit made by the distillery and neutral grain spirit, which brings additional floral, fruity character to the botanicals of juniper, coriander, cardamom, elderflower, orange peel and angelica and orris roots. The Old Tom is a similar recipe but sweetened with cane sugar and rested for two months in the distillery's old single malt whiskey casks. *drinksoundspirits.com*

SEATTLE DISTILLING GIN
WASHINGTON
Paco Joyce and Ishan Dillon founded Seattle Distilling in 2011 to produce a gin from scratch using a base spirit made from hard red winter wheat, cultivated by a growers collective and a local farm in Moses Lake, Washington. The botanical recipe is made up of 11 ingredients, including Vashon Island-grown lavender, elderberry, coriander seeds, whole hazelnuts and juniper, and distilled by vapour infusion (*see page 20*) in a 1,325-litre (350-US-gallon) pot still with a dedicated column and stainless-steel base (*see page 24*). Joyce reclaimed the old still, built back in 1955, from its duties as a steam kettle in a Texas high school. The gin is bottled at 40% ABV. *seattledistilling.com*

FREMONT MISCHIEF GIN
SEATTLE
Mike Sherlock founded his mischievously named distillery in Seattle a decade ago with the emphasis firmly on "agri-distilling" as he describes it: essentially working closely with the local community of farmers who cultivate the grains used in each spirit, particularly rye and soft winter wheat, which is sustainably grown in the Skagit and Willamette Valleys west of the Cascade Mountains. Sherlock currently distils his gin using his house-made vodka as the base, which is distilled to around 96% ABV before being rested for three months. The spirit gives a soft, toasted marshmallow/nuttiness to the gin, along with coriander, juniper, citrus peels and floral peppers. It is bottled at 42.5% ABV. A barrel-aged version is also available, bottled at 45% ABV, which is matured in Mischief Rye casks, resulting in additional caramel, vanilla and soft pepper herbaceous notes. *fremontmischief.com*

3 HOWLS GIN
SEATTLE
Founded in 2013 by Will Maschmeier, 3 Howls Distillery is based in the heart of Seattle's SoDo neighbourhood, the inspiration for the name coming from a trip to the Isle of Islay in Scotland, where Maschmeier learned of the legend of the Cù-Sìth, which howls three times before taking the soul of its next victim. The distillery produces two gins: a Classic, bottled at 45% ABV, and a Navy Strength, bottled at 57%, made using a 1,140-litre (301-US-gallon) hybrid pot still with a stainless-steel pot and a copper column element (*see page 25*). *3howls.com*

CASCADE ALCHEMY OREGON GIN
OREGON
This distillery is one of only a handful across the whole USA to explore the use of local juniper, in this case *Juniperus occidentalis,* which is hand-picked from the Badlands area to the east of the city of Bend where the distillery is located. The gin (bottled at 45% ABV) has a distinctly pine/resinous note and is very juniper forward in style, as one would expect. *cascadealchemy.com*

RANSOM GIN
OREGON

One of the most remarkable things about Ransom Spirits, based in McMinnville, is the simplicity employed in each area of the production process of its wines and spirits in terms of doing as much by hand as humanly possible, which has been the ethos of founder Tad Seestedt since it opened back in 1997. The making of Ransom Dry Gin begins with a base wort of malted barley and rye mashed and fermented on site – essentially a malt wine not dissimilar to Holland's genever (see page 18). Alongside this, the botanicals, namely Oregon marionberry and local hops, as well as organically certified juniper, lemon and orange peel, coriander seeds, caraway, cardamom, star anise and angelica root, are infused in a corn-based spirit before distillation. The gin is then distilled using a direct-fired (see page 29), hand-beaten, 1,000-litre (264-US-gallon) Prulho alembic pot still (see page 22), before being bottled at 44% ABV. Ransom Old Tom Gin is aged in ex-wine barrels for a more robust, oak-forward flavour, also bottled at 44% ABV. *ransomspirits.com*

ROGUE SPIRITS SPRUCE GIN
OREGON

Rogue's heritage can be traced back to the late 1980s when founder Jack Joyce established a series of very successful brewpubs and restaurants around Oregon, which two decades later diversified into distilled spirits, setting up a distillery in Newport. Alongside a number of whiskeys, Rogue distills Spruce Gin using ingredients grown on Rogue Farms in Tygh Valley

and Independence, Oregon, including freshly picked cucumbers that are hand-peeled – in fact, it takes 45kg (100lb) of cucumber flesh to produce each batch of gin. Distilled by Jake Holshue in a 2,080-litre (550-US-gallon) copper still made by Kentucky's Vendome coppersmiths, the gin brings together fresh Oregon spruce alongside the cucumbers and nine other botanicals – juniper, ginger, orris root, orange, lemon and tangerine peels, grains of paradise, angelica root and coriander seeds – macerated in a mixture of GNS (grain neutral spirit) and local coastal water. Rogue also produces an aged version, Pinot Spruce Gin, which is matured for four to six months in Oregon Pinot Noir barrels for a spicy, vanilla-led flavour. Both editions are bottled at 45% ABV. *rogue.com*

GREENBAR DISTILLERY
LOS ANGELES

Founded in 2004 by partners Melkon Khosrovian and Litty Mathew, Greenbar Distillery is LA's first new distillery since Prohibition ended in 1933 and promotes a strong organic ethos when it comes to the spirits it makes, with the distillery gaining United States Department of Agriculture (USDA) organic certification across its diverse range. The

most recent of these is City Bright Gin, a spirit that the founders hoped would represent the diversity of flavours within the cuisine of the city. Using a base of wheat GNS (grain neutral spirit), the botanical recipe includes juniper, ancho chillies, angelica, basil, Californian bay, cardamom, cassia bark, coriander seeds, cubeb, black cumin, fennel, grapefruit, lemon balm, lemon, lemongrass, kaffir lime, lime, pink and Sichuan peppercorns, peppermint, spearmint and star anise, for a very spice-laden, complex aroma and taste. Greenbar's City Amber Gin delivers an even more sophisticated result, thanks to the spirit being distilled and then macerated with the botanicals, which intensifies the flavour and gives the gin its amber colour. Both expressions are bottled at 42% ABV. *greenbardistillery.com*

THE SPIRIT GUILD ASTRAL PACIFIC GIN
LOS ANGELES

Miller Duvall, whose family has been farming in California for six generations, and Morgan McLachlan of Scottish–Canadian descent with a passion for all things Anglo including gin, founded The Spirit Guild Distillery in 2012, with McLachlan as master distiller. Their proprietary

Astral Pacific Gin (bottled at 43% ABV) rather unusually has a base spirit made from fermented clementines, giving it a distinctly sweet fruitiness. The botanical recipe brings together juniper, coriander, angelica, cinnamon, grapefruit and clementine peels, orange tree leaves, pink peppercorns, pistachios, sage and orris root. *thespiritguild.com*

AFFINITY GIN
CALIFORNIA

Part of the Urban Press Winery, Urban Press Spirits, set up in 1995, is the oldest craft distillery in LA County, and under the tenure of head distiller John Broker, it produces Affinity Gin (44% ABV), which is distilled using a 180-litre (48-US-gallon) Christian Carl copper pot still. The core botanicals – organic juniper, fresh oranges and fresh lemon – are given a 24-hour maceration in a US neutral grain spirit before distillation. Affinity is a very citrus-forward gin with delicate spice and a slight pine freshness from the juniper. *urbanpressspirits.com*

CUTWATER GIN
CALIFORNIA

Formerly part of the Ballast Point Brewing Company, Cutwater emerged as a new company in 2016, building one of the West Coast's largest – and arguably most impressive – new distilleries. The facility in San Diego is a 4,650sq m (50,000sq ft) complex comprising a distillery-cum-restaurant that houses a number of copper pot stills and a 12m (40ft) column still, all made by Kentucky's Vendome coppersmiths. Cutwater's Old Grove Gin is a bold, juniper-led spirit, with a touch of cardamom spice and some resinous pine notes, bottled at 44% ABV.
cutwaterspirits.com

SPIRIT WORKS DISTILLERY
CALIFORNIA

The brainchild of Timo and Ashby Marshall, the Spirit Works Distillery was founded in 2012, based in Sebastopol. With Timo hailing from the southwest of England and Ashby the West Coast of the USA, both have brought

different approaches to the art of distilling. The mostly female team of distillers and brewers, including head distiller Lauren Patz, control the entire process of distillation. For their core gin (bottled at 43% ABV), the base spirit made from organic Californian red winter wheat is mixed with juniper, orris, angelica root, cardamom and coriander, with citrus notes provided by hand-zested orange and lemon, as well as a floral top note from hibiscus flowers.
spiritworksdistillery.com

MULLHOLLAND NEW WORLD GIN
CALIFORNIA

Matthew Alper, an acclaimed cinematographer working on a number of high-profile Hollywood films, assisted by Emmy-nominated actor Walton Goggins founded Mulholland Distilling, based in Downey, which produces New World Gin using juniper, coriander, angelica, French lavender, Japanese cucumber and Persian lime using a base of non-GMO corn spirit, bottled at 48% ABV.
mulhollanddistilling.com

OLD HARBOR DISTILLING CO. SAN MIGUEL SOUTHWESTERN GIN
CALIFORNIA

Founded by Michael Skubic, who is also the co-founder of the Hess Brewing Co, Old Harbor is the first licensed distillery in the East Village area of San Diego. Skubic currently produces San Miguel Southwestern Gin (not to be confused with the Filipino San Miguel gin, *see* page 243), which is herbaceously styled, using locally grown lime, cucumber, fresh coriander and sage as the key botanicals. It is bottled at 47% ABV.
oldharbordistilling.com

VALOR WEST COAST GIN
CALIFORNIA

Effectively San Diego's first distillery since Prohibition was repealed in 1933, Kill Devil Spirit Co. (the name comes from an old association with rum production) started life in 2011 and its first major spirit was Valor West Coast Gin, which focuses broadly on the terrain and climate of San Diego. Using an organic base spirit, the key botanicals are grown locally, including grapefruit and Chinook hops, with the final spirit being cut to 47% ABV using pH-balanced water drawn from a local well.
killdevilspirits.com

YOU & YOURS DISTILLING CO.
CALIFORNIA

Launched in 2017, You & Yours was San Diego's first urban distillery and craft cocktail bar, producing a very citrus-led Sunday Gin using a grape-based spirit. A seasonally available Winter Gin has a much more spice-led recipe. Both are bottled at 40% ABV.
youandyours.com

FID STREET HAWAIIAN GIN
HAWAII

Located in the Island's pineapple-growing region of Upcountry Makawao, Hali'imaile Distilling started life when the LeVecke family, who had already helped to build the brand fame of the likes of local Hana Bay and Whaler's rums, were looking for a change in pace and to create a distillery of their own. They met Colorado-based distiller Mark Nigbur, who was using pharmaceutical glass distillation equipment to great success, and the same technique was brought over to Maui.

The base ingredient for their spirit is pineapple. High in sugar content, it takes around 18 months to grow, but only a few days to become overripe, so it needs to be picked and processed quickly. Hali'imaile's Fid Street Hawaiian Gin (bottled at 45% ABV) uses a quantity of the pineapple-based spirit supplemented with a base of grain spirit, while the botanical recipe includes lavender, orris, cedar leaf, angelica, lemon and orange peels and extra pineapple.
fidstreetgin.com

CANADA

Canada is a thriving outpost of small distillers seeking to stake their claim on a nation of curious, thirsty consumers. Historically, Canada's production of a national gin has been limited, but largely thanks to the Prohibition era (1920–33) in the USA, the country was relied upon by those wanting to sip a Gin Sling or a Martini as a producer of alcohol – and as a route for importing liquor into the USA. Today, the Canadian gin scene has spread across at least nine of its provinces but has especially taken off in the western province of British Columbia, where there are just under 80 independent distilleries, with at least 35 making a gin, supported by two bodies: the Craft Distillers Guild of British Columbia and the BC Independent Distillers Association (BCIDA). Like the West Coast of the USA, many of these have explored the farm-to-bottle approach, or are looking to their local surroundings for inspiration.

CANADA

With ten provinces and three territories across a landscape which stretches over 5,500km (3,417m), Canada is a country of extremes in both climate and also flavour. From a gin perspective, it is starting to explore its diverse flora in greater detail, seeking out unusual flavours for botanical recipes. From the wilds of the eastern Yukon to the urban chic of the major cities in Ontario and Quebec and beyond to Nova Scotia in the west, distillers are finally putting Canada on the global gin map.

> " Canada is starting to explore its diverse flora in greater detail, seeking out unusual flavours for botanical recipes.

OKANAGAN SPIRITS
BRITISH COLUMBIA

Western Canada's oldest craft distillery is now celebrating a decade and a half of production and still very much focusing on the concept of being a flagship harvest-to-flask company, using only locally grown fruits and grains as the base ingredients for the spirits it creates. Since 2004, when father Tony Dyck and his son Tyler founded the distillery, it has developed a wide portfolio of

The Okanagan Spirits gin bottle

products, from fruit liqueurs and brandies, through to vodka, gin and akvavit, and on to dark spirits including British Columbia's first single malt whisky. Today, it operates from two locations, a smaller distillery based in Kelowna and a flagship site in Vernon, BC, which contains what the owners claim to be North America's tallest still, with a 7.6m (25ft)-high, 50-plate column sitting alongside a 2,000-litre (528-US-gallon) copper pot still (*see* page 24). Two gins are distilled here, using radically different base spirits. The first, Essential Gin, uses a spirit made from locally grown grains, while for the second, Family Reserve Okanagan Gin, Okanagan apples grown in local orchards are crushed and fermented on site as the foundation for the base spirit. Both are distilled to 96.4% ABV in the column still, before being redistilled in a copper flavour still with the botanicals and bottled at 40% ABV. The key botanicals in the recipe are juniper, spruce tips, coriander, rhubarb, orris, violet flower and rose, alongside tarragon and lemon balm in the Family Reserve.
okanaganspirits.com

ST. LAURENT GIN
QUEBEC

Among the very first Canadian microdistillers to pioneer the craft gin scene that is currently flourishing, St. Laurent's Jean Francois Cloutier and Joel Pelletier cite the ever-changing climatic conditions in the city of Rimouski (located at the mouth of the St Lawrence River, a body of water that turns into the North Atlantic) as the main influence for their flavours, with its harsh, blustery winters and saline-heavy air. The gins have a coastal note, thanks in part to one key botanical, laminaria seaweed (kombu), which the team harvest from locations along the Bas-St-Laurent region surrounding the city. Distillation takes place in Papa Wong, a 1,000-litre (264-US-gallon) copper and stainless-steel pot still designed by the founders, with an unusual, custom-made copper sphere at the top of it, which is used to hold the rectangular botanical infusion basket (*see* page 22) and resembles a deep-sea diver's helmet.

The gin (bottled at 43% ABV) comprises a recipe of juniper, coriander seeds, angelica root, cassia bark, liquorice root, lemon peel, bitter orange peel, cubeb berries and grains of paradise, which is vapour distilled before being left to macerate with the laminaria seaweed, giving a slight saltiness to the flavour. An aged Vieux version (47% ABV) sees the gin being transferred from the maceration tanks into ex-whisky oak casks for a year in order to round out the piney/resinous notes, adding a creaminess. *distilleriedustlaurent.com*

> "
> The gins have a coastal note, thanks in part to one key botanical, laminaria seaweed (kombu).

◉ *Cocktail time with St. Laurent*

CANADA

YUKON
*Yukonshine
Distillery*

BRITISH
COLUMBIA

ALBERTA

*Ampersand
Distilling Co*

*Strathcona
Spirits*

SASKATCHEWAN

MANITOBA

QUEBEC

*Okangangan
Spirits*

*Victoria
Spirits*

*Lucky Bastard
Distillers*

*St Laurent
Spirits*

*Sheringham
Distillery*

*Eau Claire
Distillery*

ONTARIO

NOVA
SCOTIA

*Phillips
Fermentorium
Stump Gin*

*Capital K Tall
Grass Gin*

*Ironworks
distillery*

*Spirit of York
Distillery*

Dillon's

AMPERSAND GIN
BRITISH COLUMBIA

The Schacht family launched the Ampersand Distilling Co. in October 2014 on an organic farm in the Cowichan Valley on Vancouver Island, after spending roughly three years building their stills completely from scratch. The gin is produced via vapour infusion (see page 20) in a 1,000-litre (264-US-gallon) pot still, called Dot, and the base spirit used is also distilled by the distillery from 100% British Columbia-grown wheat in a 500-litre (132-US-gallon) column still, fondly referred to as Dash. The column, unlike any other still in the world, is packed with tiny copper coils to create a maximum surface area for rectifying the base spirit up to 97% ABV (see page 249). The recipe comprises eight botanicals, which include angelica, cardamom and orris root, alongside a burst of citrus peel and juniper. The gin is bottled at 43.8% ABV. *ampersanddistilling.com*

PHILLIPS FERMENTORIUM STUMP COASTAL FORAGE GIN
BRITISH COLUMBIA

Produced by Phillips Brewing Company's Fermentorium distilling house, STUMP Coastal Forest Gin seeks to encapsulate the distinct flavours found in the forests that surround its location in Victoria, using hand-foraged botanicals including Cascade hops, grand fir, bay laurel, coriander and lavender, alongside the juniper. The spirit is created in-house, first being distilled on a British-made pot still that dates back to the 1920s before it is rectified in a new German-built still (see page 249). It is bottled at 42% ABV. *fermentorium.ca*

SHERINGHAM SEASIDE GIN
BRITISH COLUMBIA

Had the co-founder Jason MacIsaac not moved to a rustic cabin located to the west of Sheringham Point on Vancouver Island back in 2003, he may never have had the impetus to develop a gin. It was there that he unearthed old moonshine bottles supposedly from the Jordan River Hotel, rumoured to have had a still in the cellar. The name Sheringham, to which the distillery pays homage, was given to the area in 1846, which was shortened to Shirley in 1893 after the first post office was built, so that the name would fit on the local postage stamp. The gin (bottled at 43% ABV) has a citrusy character with briny notes and is made from a base spirit distilled using British Columbia-grown white wheat and malted barley, with the key botanical being winged kelp (*Alaria marginata*), hand-harvested from the coastline. *sheringhamdistillery.com*

VICTORIA GIN
BRITISH COLUMBIA

One of the oldest craft distilleries in Canada, Victoria Distillers has ridden the crest of the boom in craft spirits by building a firm relationship with the bartending community and describes its spirits as essentially "liquid bar tools". Back in 2016, the distillery outgrew its location and moved to the Seaport Place waterfront of Sidney, where it houses two copper pot stills, producing three gins. Victoria Cocktail Gin was arguably the first premium craft gin to make a major impression across the country, featuring a ten-botanical recipe. An oak-aged version, Oaken Gin, helps to round off the spirit and create a more buttery complexity. Empress 1908 Original Indigo Gin is a collaboration with bartenders at the renowned Q at the Empress Bar restaurant in the city, which has a higher proportion of juniper than the proprietary gin, alongside grapefruit peel, rose, ginger, coriander, cinnamon and Fairmont Empress Blend tea, and a pronounced blue hue thanks to an infusion of the butterfly pea flower. All three gins are bottled at 42.5% ABV. *victoriagin.com* *empress1908gin.com*

BADLAND SEABERRY GIN/STRATHCONA SPIRITS
ALBERTA

Strathcona can lay claim to a genuine first in being the first-ever distillery to be built in Edmonton, the capital city of Alberta. The base spirit at the heart of its distilling operation is made on site from hard red wheat grown 23km (14 miles) from Edmonton. Its Badland Seaberry Gin is a London Dry style using ten botanicals including wild juniper foraged from along the Red Deer River and seaberry that grows in abundance around Edmonton. It is bottled at 44% ABV. *strathconaspirits.ca*

EAU CLAIRE DISTILLERY
ALBERTA
This farm-to-bottle distillery is housed in a building that once served as Turner Valley's movie theatre and dance hall in the late 1920s. The distillery sources specific grain varietals locally to make its own spirits from scratch. Its Parlour Gin (bottled at 40% ABV) is pot distilled using juniper, rosehips, Saskatoon berries (which resemble blueberries, but are more closely related to the apple family, with a sweet, almondy flavour), lemon, orange, mint, coriander and other spices that deliver a drier flavour.
eauclairedistillery.ca

CAPITAL K TALL GRASS GIN
MANITOBA
The province's very first craft distillery based in Winnipeg, Capital K launched its inaugural product, a vodka, back in 2016 and produces the base spirit from grains – predominantly wheat and rye grown across Manitoba, distilled using an 5.5m (18ft), 20-plate column still. Its Tall Grass Gin (bottled at 45% ABV) was launched in 2017 and uses a mixture of grains for the base spirit, with the botanicals in the recipe including juniper, coriander seeds, rosehips, orange peel, cardamom, chamomile and lemongrass.
capitalkdistillery.com

IRONWORKS GIN
NOVA SCOTIA
Pierre Guevremont and partner Lynne Mackay set up their Ironworks Distillery, named after a once-thriving maritime blacksmiths, in the old port of Lunenburg on Nova Scotia's South Shore in 2009. The duo create everything from scratch, using locally grown juniper berries and other Nova Scotia-sourced botanicals, including rosehips and a small quantity of balsam fir bud eau-de-vie to make their London Dry-style gin (42% ABV).
ironworksdistillery.com

DILLON'S
ONTARIO
Geoff Dillon and his father Peter, a botanical expert, along with business partner Gary Huggins decided to base their distillery in Beamsville, right in the heart of the Niagara wine region, to give them an abundance of raw materials on which to draw for their base spirits (when creating gin and other products). Dillon's range includes Dry Gin 7, which brings together seven botanicals, vapour infused (*see* page 20) in a 100% Ontario rye spirit and bottled at 44.8% ABV, along with Unfiltered Gin 22, an altogether different beast, made from a base of Niagara grapes and 22 vapour-infused botanicals, bottled at 40% ABV.
dillons.ca

SPIRIT OF YORK GIN
ONTARIO
Occupying the former malting room of what was one of the city's largest distilleries, Gooderham & Worts, which closed in 1959, the Spirit of York Distillery Co. is once again aiming to bring local flavours to Toronto. Using Ontario-grown rye as the base, rectified in two huge 44-plate German column stills (*see* page 249), Spirit of York Gin (bottled at 40% ABV) brings together 15 botanicals including juniper, cinnamon, coriander seeds, angelica root, fennel seeds, cubeb pepper and star anise.
spiritofyork.com

UNGAVA GIN
QUEBEC
Arguably the most well known of all Canadian gins, Ungava was created back in 2010 by Charles Crawford and Susan Reid, owners of cider and ice wine producers Domaines Pinnacle, located not far from the town of Cowansville in Quebec. Its notoriety comes from its distinct colour, a vivid yellow that it develops through the production process and its six core botanicals. Ungava is not a distilled gin in the traditional sense. Instead, the gin is made in two parts: firstly, an initial distillation using a base corn spirit with several of the botanicals, then a secondary compounding process (*see* page 18) that creates a more intense flavour and colour in the finished product, which is bottled at 43.1% ABV. The unusual botanicals are harvested in the summer from the North of Canada near the Arctic, namely wild rosehips, crowberries (an evergreen that grows across the Arctic tundra), Labrador tea (a white-flowering evergreen), cloudberries, Arctic blend (a plant similar to Labrador tea) and wild Nordic juniper, which grows in abundance across the Ungava region that inspired the gin's name.
ungava-gin.com

LUCKY BASTARD DISTILLERS
SASKATCHEWAN
Since it was founded in 2012 in Saskatoon, Lucky Bastard has had to endure temperatures ranging from -40°C (-40°F) in the winter to around 35°C (95°F) during the summer. Given the extremes, the local landscape has partly inspired the recipe for the distillery's Gambit Gin (bottled at 40% ABV), which uses Saskatchewan wheat spirit as the base, alongside locally grown Saskatoon berries (*see* above left) and coriander from the Saskatchewan province, combined with a handful of more traditional, internationally grown botanicals: juniper from northern Italy, Turkish star anise, chamomile flowers from the UK, lemon peel from Florida and cloves and angelica from Asia.
luckybastard.ca

YUKON AURAGIN
YUKON
Yukonshine Distillery owner and distiller Karlo Krauzig certainly has plenty of time to produce spirits in a province where the sun can shine for up to 20 hours a day. Krauzig has an unusual recipe for his base spirit: a combination of locally grown rye and wheat, to which he adds a distillate made from the Yukon Gold potato, highly prized in the province and low in starch, giving the spirit a particular butteriness. AuraGin is a citrus-forward gin, bringing in grapefruit, lemon and lime peel, which is first macerated and then redistilled with around a dozen other botanicals in a vapour-infusion basket (*see* page 20). It is bottled at 40% ABV.
yukonshine.com

CENTRAL AND SOUTH AMERICA

While drinkers are mostly content with their local spirits of mezcal in Mexico, pisco in Peru and cachaça in Brazil, gin is nevertheless starting to make inroads into parts of Central and South America that have not been traditionally linked with gin. Driven mainly by the Iberian heritage of these countries, demand for the spirit is rising and some local gin producers are making an appearance.

MEXICO

Famous for the spirit mezcal, made in small stills across the country, Mexico has been slow to embrace the global gin revolution, especially given the wonderful array of local botanicals from which distillers can take their inspiration and flavour profiles. Thankfully, this situation has changed recently with a host of new craft and artisanal producers drawing on the local terroir with an eye on export potential.

GIN KATÚN
YUCATÁN

Katún is the first gin to be produced in Mexico's Yucatán peninsula. Made at Destilados y Licores Meridanos in Conkal just outside of Mérida, it was developed by four friends from Mexico, Roberto, Augusto, Cristian and Raúl, plus Javier from Spain. It took over a year for the team to research the best combination of local botanicals from Yucatán, their key objective being to reflect the region's rich raw materials. Gin production began at the Conkal distillery in August 2017, using 17 botanical ingredients including four different varieties of chilli as well as other spices, fruits and highly aromatic flowers, all sourced from Yucatán and elsewhere in the country, with the exception of juniper, the only imported ingredient. The botanical blend is macerated in a neutral alcohol made from corn, a staple grain in Mexico, for at least ten days. This infused spirit is then distilled in a 250-litre (66-US-gallon) copper alembic still (*see* page 22) handmade in Portugal. After a period of settling, it is mixed with water from the underground caves, or cenotes, before being bottled at 42% ABV.
facebook.com/ginkatun/

"

The key objective being to reflect the region's rich raw materials.

A classic Negroni with Katún gin

DIEGA GIN
MEXICO CITY

This premium Mexican gin is handmade by a family business with more than a hundred years of history in the south of Mexico City. A 100% organic product, a precise selection of botanicals is used including lemon peels, lemon verbena and chamomile, and double distilled at the low temperature of 65°C (149°F) before being rested in French oak barrels for two months and then filtered through charcoal, a process that removes some of the colour and rounds off the flavour of the gin. Bottled at 38% ABV, it was created by Grupo Nus in 2016, in conjunction with the Flor de la Paz foundation of Valle de Bravo, to support organic farming in Mexico. instagram.com/diega_gin/

PIERDE ALMAS
OAXACA

Mexico is also home to some gins that draw on the concept of using a mezcal or agave distillate base. Produced in Oaxaca from 100% naturally fermented agave, with a strong focus on social, cultural and environmental awareness, the Pierde Almas distillery produces Botanica +9, which starts with a mezcal spirit that is distilled twice before a selection of classic gin botanicals are macerated in the spirit and then distilled once again. The nine botanicals are star anise, angelica and orris roots, cassia bark, coriander seeds, fennel seeds, nutmeg, orange peel and, of course, juniper. The rather simply named Mezcal Gin is made using a base distilled from the Cenizo agave and a mix of traditional botanicals including juniper, angelica, coriander seeds and orange peel, with some native

and unusual ingredients such as ancho chilli peppers, hibiscus and avocado leaves making an appearance too. Both expressions are bottled at 45% ABV. pierdealmas.com

ARMÓNICO GIN
QUERÉTARO

Located in San Juan del Río, Andrés Valverde produces Armónico Gin at La Insoportable Brewery and Distillery, which he founded in 2016, where his desire and passion to develop the culture and art of making high-quality alcoholic beverages in Mexico was realized. The gin was launched in 2017, with Valverde creating a recipe that builds a complex character of citrus, floral and spicy notes on a base of corn alcohol. The distillation takes place in a tiny gas-fired

300-litre (80-US-gallon) copper pot still using 32 botanicals; 12 traditional ones usually found in London Dry gin production and 20 local botanicals, such as Mexican cinnamon, Mexican jasmine

and damiana (Turnera diffusa), to name just a few. Depending on the flavours, some of the botanicals are macerated while others are vapour infused (see page 20). The gin is bottled at 50% ABV and presented in 500ml (17 fl oz) bottles, which are hand-filled and labelled at the distillery. armonicogin.com

CENTRAL AND
SOUTH AMERICA

MEXICO

Armónico

Diega

Katún Gin

Pierde
Almas

Dictador

COLUMBIA

London To
Lima Gin

PERU

BRAZIL

La Republica 'Andina'
Bolivian Dry Gin

BOLIVIA

YVY Distillery

Amázzoni
Gin

Weber
Haus

Principe de
los Apostoles Mate

ARGENTINA

e das águas nasceu a estrela ☆

BRAZIL

Historically the domain of the fresh, vibrant spirit cachaça, Brazilian distillers have recently turned their attention to the unique botanicals the country has to offer, kick-starting a new wave of highly characteristic gins.

AMÁZZONI GIN
SAO PAOLO

Brazil's developing gin scene is spearheaded by Amázzoni Gin, made in the Paraiba Valley around 130km (80 miles) from the centre of Rio de Janeiro on a 300-year-old large farm named Fazenda Cachoeira, which has recently been restored to its original glory back in 1717. Having been a successful coffee plantation in the 18th and 19th centuries, in 1902 it was equipped with the tools and machinery needed for sugar-cane processing, including a stone wheel mill, still used today for milling flour. The *fazenda* has at its heart La Cahoeira, a lagoon, around which the production buildings sit.

The three founders came from very different backgrounds. Arturo Isola had been living in Italy for 30 years before emigrating to Brazil, and is an architect. Tato Giovannoni, an Argentinian, is a mixologist and was key in the development of Príncipe de los Apóstoles Gin, the first ever to count yerba mate (a species of holly) among the botanicals (*see* page 42). Alexandre Mazzaa, the

sole *brasileiro* of the trinity, is a former professional footballer, jazz musician, bartender and international video artist.

This unlikely trio produce a gin that uses juniper berries combined with pink pepper, laurel, lemon, tangerine, coriander and five unique Amazonian botanicals: cocoa, Brazilian chestnut, maxixe (a relative of the cucumber), *Victoria amazonica* (formerly *V. regia*) or giant water lily and cipò-cravo (*Tynanthus elegans*). These eleven ingredients are macerated in neutral grain alcohol and distilled in an alembic cooper pot still (*see* page 22), the first designed and built in Brazil, using the one-shot method (*see* page 29). It is diluted with local spring water to 42% ABV and put into 100% recycled glass bottles.
amazzonigin.com

OTHER BRAZILIAN
GINS TO TRY

YVY DISTILLERY
MINAS BERAIS

Along with Brazil's first dedicated gin distillery Amázzoni (*see* left) is YVY Distillery. Founded by André Sá Fortes, a gastronomy graduate, he opened his first cocktail bar Meet Me at the Yard in Belo Horizonte in 2013. Today, his focus is entirely on the distillery, which uses "spices that historically arrived by sea to Brazil" to make its gin, including YVY Mar, a classic London Dry-inspired Brazilian Dry Gin, bottled at 46% ABV.
yvydestilaria.com.br

WEBER HAUS
RIO GRANDE DO SOL

The H Weber & Cia Ltd a distillery is based in Ivoti in the far south of Brazil near the border with Uruguay, and is the producer of one of the country's most respected brands of cachaça. Their organic gin is the result of two year's work, and uses a botanical mix that includes yerba mate, ginger and fresh cane leaf. It comes in three versions, London Dry Gin WH 48, bottled at 40% ABV, Dry Gin WH 48 Organic, bottled at 44% ABV and Dry Gin WH 48 Pink Organic, also bottled at 44% ABV, distilled in handcrafted copper alembic stills (*see* page 22).
weberhaus.com.br

◔ *Gin production Brazilian-style*

PERU

Home of the complex-flavoured grape-based spirit pisco, Peru's distillers, rather like those of Brazil, are currently exploring the diverse native flora on offer to create highly innovative gins.

LONDON TO LIMA GIN
LIMA

Brit Alex James, a liveryman of the Distillers Company in London, and Peruvian Karena De Lecaros-Aquise were looking to create a product that fused their respective backgrounds and heritages, as well as representing their journey to Peru, and so London to Lima Gin was born. James arranged for two 20-litre (5¼-US-gallon) copper pot stills to be shipped from London to Lima, and the process of making a gin began.

The botanical recipe for the gin takes inspiration from the little-known Andean or spectacled bear, a tree climber whose diet consists mainly of foraged berries, bulbs, honey, fruits, sugar cane and palm hearts. The other key local element is the use of a base spirit produced from grapes, drawing on the Peruvian expertise and experience of making pisco perfected over centuries. Only one grape varietal, Quebranta, is selected, fermented and then slowly distilled in an oddly shaped former pisco still, a 400-litre (106-US-gallon) Portuguese copper pot style named Endeavour that James adapted himself.

Once the base spirit has been distilled, the botanical mix comes into play, including juniper, pink peppercorns, local key lime, Valencia orange, cassia bark, coriander seeds, angelica and orris roots and Peruvian groundcherry (*Physalis peruviana*, also known as the Cape gooseberry), which has a distinctive sweet, almost tart flavour, also helping to bring out sweetness in the citrus elements. Once distilled, the gin is cut with spring water from glacial sources 4,000m (13,125ft) above sea level. When James found his water source, part of the deal with the local community was to install a pipe from the eye of the spring to their local huts, ensuring clean drinking water for the native community. The gin is bottled at 42.8% ABV.
londontolima.com

⊙ *London to Lima bottle mould*

⊙ *The finished article*

BOLIVIA, COLUMBIA AND ARGENTINA

The South American gin revolution continues to develop across the region, with a vibrant cocktail scene developing, bartenders are keen to explore the nation's newly distilled domestic gins with new-found fondness.

GIN LA RÉPUBLICA
LA PAZ

La República Bolivian Dry Gin is distilled at high altitude, 4,000m (13,125ft) above sea level, where boiling point occurs at a lower temperature, which results in a fuller and lighter gin. Non-native botanicals, such as juniper berries, are sourced from the Netherlands and England, but otherwise the ingredients for Andina are mainly from the food markets in La Paz. The distillery uses a 450-litre (119-US-gallon) Charenteis alembic still design (*see* page 22), made by Spanish craftsmen, with a bulb-shaped neck built for a more direct and stronger recovery of botanical flavours, and is directly fired by a wood fire (*see* page 29). Once distilled, the gin is cut with water from the glaciers of the Cordillera Real mountain range, the hard water contributing to the taste of the gin, and bottled at 40% ABV. The distiller also produces Amazónica, which brings together a range of botanicals specific to the Amazon, including acai berry, *cupuazú* (a relative of the cacao tree), *ají gusano* (a small, worm-shaped chilli) and Amazonian tree barks.
master-blends.com

DICTADOR GIN
CARIBE

The expertise of the people behind the super-premium Dictador rum, distilled in Cartagena de Indias, has been cleverly applied to the production of Dictador Premium Columbian Aged Gin, which uses a base spirit made from sugar cane distilled up to five times and comes in two forms. Ortodoxy, which was created by and for the personal consumption of Dictador rum's former president Dario Parra, and uses a secret recipe of berries, peels, roots and spices, while Treasure draws on ingredients such as the local *limón mandarino* (lemon tangerine). Both are bottled at 43% ABV and aged in barrels that once held Dictador rum, Treasure for up to 35 weeks.
dictador.com

PRÍNCIPE DE LOS APÓSTOLES MATE GIN
MENDOZA

One of the first premium gins to be released from Latin America, Príncipe de los Apóstoles Mate is produced in Mendoza at the Sol de los Andes, a place better known for distilling grappa, founded in 2000. Using a wheat base, the gin draws on the flavour of the local yerba mate, a species of holly (*Ilex paraguariensis*) traditionally used to make a tea-like beverage, as a key botanical, alongside peppermint, eucalyptus and pink grapefruit peel mostly sourced from Misiones. It is all distilled in a 200-litre (53-US-gallon) copper pot still and bottled at 40% ABV.
apostolesgin.com

◉ *Label printing at La República*

MIDDLE EAST AND AFRICA

MIDDLE EAST

While the Middle East is not the first destination one would link to gin production, Israel and Lebanon are starting to forge a reputation for some interesting and unusual gins.

ISRAEL AND LEBANON

Both Israel and Lebanon's internationally renowned cocktail scenes mirror the nations' love affair with craft spirits, seeing bartenders eager to explore the range of locally distilled gins, which reflect a passion, innovation and true sense of terroir.

LEVANTINE GIN
TEL AVIV

The craft distillation scene in the Middle East was certainly given a substantial boost back in 2014 when the Milk & Honey Distillery was first commissioned in Tel Aviv by a small team of single malt whisky enthusiasts led by Gal Kalkshtein. The whisky received international acclaim, and hot on its heels was the first craft gin, Levantine, which is created from the same double-distilled base. The recipe consists of juniper and key botanicals that the team source from the local Levinsky market: hyssop, lemon peel, orange, chamomile, verbena, cinnamon and black pepper. A maceration period of 48 hours helps to release the oils and compounds within the botanicals and then a final distillation takes place in a 250-litre (66-US-gallon) pot still before the gin is cut down to 46% ABV and bottled.
mh-distillery.com

AKKO GIN
GALILEE

Founded in 2008, the Jullius Craft Distillery is the project of Yuval Hargil, who initially distilled fruit liqueurs, using grape pomace (seeds and skins) as the base. Hargil's Akko Wild Gin of Galilee (bottled at 40% ABV) comprises 12 botanicals sourced in Israel: juniper from Mount Meron, leaves from the mastic tree, needles from cedars of Lebanon, lemon peel from Kfar Chabad and tangerines from Western Galilee.
jullius.com

PELTER DISTILLERY HAND MADE PINK LADY GIN
GOLAN HEIGHTS

Pelter's excursions into spirits came about in 2013 when the winery's founders Tal and Nir Pelter experimented with distilling several ingredients out of interest just to see what flavours they might uncover. It led them to purchase a 60-year-old alembic still (*see* page 22) originally used in Cognac. After shipping it to the winery, the duo has produced an arak (an aniseed-based spirit), an apple brandy, an eau-de-vie and a gin, which is a distinctly fruity affair influenced by the Mediterranean. The base is from a single distillation of fermented pulp and juice of Pink Lady apples, after which the botanicals are added to macerate for 24 hours before the spirit is distilled again. Key botanicals include juniper, Israeli sage, chamomile, fennel, orris root and dog rose bulbs (bottled at 41% ABV).
pelter.co.il

JUN ARTISANAL LEBANESE GIN
ALEY DISTRICT

The Rechmaya Distillery is located in the village of Rechmaya in the remote hills of the Aley District, about 33km (20 miles) outside Beirut. Produced by husband and wife team Maya Khattar and Chadi Naccour, Jun (bottled at 40% ABV) is produced on a 100-litre (26½-US-gallon) stainless-steel column still named Matilda. The botanicals include organic Lebanese juniper, coriander, ginger, galangal, mastic leaves, rosemary, bay leaves and orange and lemon peels.
rechmayadistillery.com

⊙ *Two of the Middle East's foremost gins*

AFRICA

As a continent, Africa is as geographically diverse as it is from a culinary perspective, providing an extraordinary number of unique botanicals for gin distillers internationally to draw on. Notable examples include Whitley Neill Gin, which uses fruit from the baobab tree, Sacred Gin (*see* page 67), featuring frankincense, an oily gum resin from the tree *Boswellia sacra* native to northeast Africa, and Germany's Elephant Gin (*see* page 103), with its key botanicals of devil's claw and African wormwood. Yet while major gin brands like Gordon's are being produced in some African markets such as Kenya, production of domestic craft gin has still to gain a firm foothold save for a small number of producers and pioneers, South Africa in particular having embraced the craft gin revolution. But that hasn't stopped Uganda, Nigeria and Kenya all being in the top ten gin-consuming nations, according to recent studies.

SOUTH AFRICA

Famous for its brandy production based on the abundance of locally grown grapes, it is no surprise to see South Africa's distillers also turning their hand to gin production, especially given the richness and diversity of native botanicals, of particular note in the Cape Town area.

The botanicals used include locally grown coriander seeds and the peel from organic lemons and oranges, peeled by hand and dried in the sun.

HOPE ON HOPKINS
CAPE TOWN

Leading the way in South African craft distilling is Hope on Hopkins Distillery, an artisanal distillery in the heart of Cape Town producing its own base spirits. Set up by former lawyers and husband and wife team Leigh Lisk and Lucy Beard in 2015, the distillery boasts the first stills to be licensed by the city of Cape Town, named after the founders' grandmothers, Mildred and Maude, plus another pot still called Mouma and a hybrid copper still (*see* page 25), Mad Mary.

Two of their gins, London Dry Gin and Salt River Gin, use a GNS (grain neutral spirit) made from 100% South African-grown malted barley, which is cooked, fermented over several days and then triple distilled on site, while Mediterranean Gin is based on a Western Cape grape spirit. The botanicals used include Tuscan juniper, angelica root, also sourced from Europe, locally grown coriander seeds and the peel from organic lemons and oranges grown in the Cederberg region in the Western Cape, peeled by hand and dried in the sun. Herbs grown in the winelands just outside

Hope on Hopkins has pushed the South African gin movement forward

Franschhoek also feature, along with buchu (*Agathosma*) in Salt River Gin grown on a farm in the Winterhoek Mountains. These are subject to a fourth distillation via vapour infusion (*see* page 20) and cut to bottling strength (43% ABV) with spring water.

Also produced by Hope on Hopkins is A Mari Ocean Gin, *a mari* being the Latin for "from the sea", a partnership between ex-architect Niel du Toit and ex-copywriter Jess Henrich. Using seawater in their distillation process, they produce two main styles of gin, Indian Ocean and Atlantic Ocean. The former takes its flavours from Africa's East Coast, using fragrant East African botanicals such as Swahili lime, Madagascan pink peppercorns and ajwain seeds, as well as turmeric, cardamom and

It is no surprise to see South Africa's distillers turning their hand to gin production, given the richness and diversity of native botanicals.

angelica. Post-distillation, it is infused with chai masala – a mix of Kenyan black tea, cinnamon, black pepper, cloves and ginger – which gives it a golden hue. The Atlantic Ocean Gin shifts the flavour focus to the West Coast of Cape Town and includes "a secret selection of Cape coastal fynbos" (the richly diverse shrubland peculiar to this region), alongside coriander, orange, tangerine, lemon, cardamom, allspice and angelica. Both gins are bottled at 43% ABV.
hopeonhopkins.co.za
amarigin.com

◉ *Gin production at Hope on Hopkins*

SOUTH AFRICA

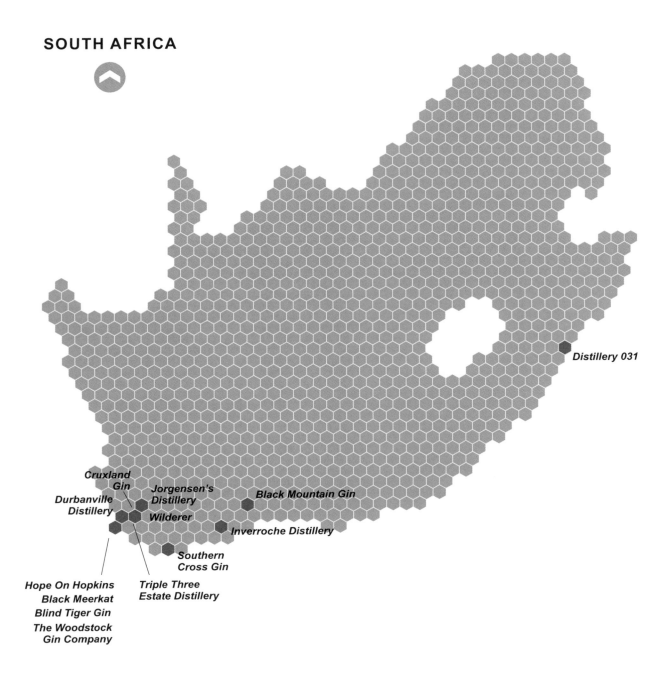

Cruxland Gin

Durbanville Distillery

Jorgensen's Distillery

Wilderer

Black Mountain Gin

Inverroche Distillery

Southern Cross Gin

Hope On Hopkins
Black Meerkat
Blind Tiger Gin

The Woodstock Gin Company

Triple Three Estate Distillery

Distillery 031

BLACK MEERKAT GIN
CAPE TOWN
Mike Sayers and Jayde Maasdorp took the decision in late 2016 to take leave of a combined 40 years in corporate life to make South Africa's first Old Tom gin, Black Meerkat Old Town Gin, based on a traditional Old Tom recipe (see page 21). Starting with a cane spirit that is distilled once using a unique copper catalysation process, 11 botanicals are placed in a Carter-Head still (see page 26) before being distilled in small batches using the vapour-infusion method (see page 20). In a departure from the traditional Old Tom recipe, no sugar or artificial sweetener is added, but sweetness is instead drawn from liquorice root, indigenous rose geranium, star anise and pineapple sage. The gin is bottled at 44% ABV. Their New Harbour Distillery, where the team produce vodka as well as gin, also has a hydroponic greenhouse for growing some of their own botanicals, and the whole site adheres to a strict carbon-neutral philosophy, with all by-products being recycled and reused in the distillery or supplied to city farms as fertilizer, animal feed and general cleaner.
blackmeerkat.com

DURBANVILLE DISTILLERY GIN
CAPE TOWN
Durbanville Distillery was set up by father and son team Robert and Eugene Kleyn, who embarked on an exciting new venture to combine their two greatest passions – engineering and drinks. Their interest was initially sparked while brewing beer with equipment that they built themselves, which led them in turn to the art of distilling.

To produce their Durbanville Distillery Gin (bottled at 43% ABV), the duo unusually engages in the science of cold distillation in a hand-built vacuum still (see page 28) called Eve, possibly the largest spirit-producing vacuum still in the world, which has in recent times been joined by a second still.
durbanvilledistillery.com

TRIPLE THREE GIN
CAPE TOWN
The three gins produced by the Triple Three Estate Distillery, based in Stellenbosch, are somewhat self-explanatory, Just Juniper Berry being distilled with juniper alone, African Botanicals featuring a mix of seven botanicals including the flora of the Western Cape and Citrus Infusion using hand-picked citrus fruit, all bottled at 43% ABV.
triplethree.co.za

THE WOODSTOCK GIN CO
CAPE TOWN
Founded in 2014 by Simon Von Witt, the Woodstock Gin Co creates fynbos-infused (see page 208 and right) South African gins. The recipe for its flagship gin, Inception, includes rooibos, buchu (Agathosma) and wild rosemary, and uses a carefully controlled fractional distillation process (see page 24) from either a beer or a wine base. This leads them on to producing two key varieties of Inception Gin: Inception Beer Base and Inception Wine Base, both bottled at 43% ABV.
woodstockginco.co.za

BLACK MOUNTAIN KAROO GIN
WESTERN CAPE
Black Mountain Gin takes its inspiration from the Swartberg (Black Mountain) range, the tallest (with many peaks over 2,000m/6,560ft) and longest range in the Western Cape province. The Grundheim

Craft Distillery that produces Black Mountain Gin is located just outside Oudtshoorn and was established in 1858, Dys Grundling being the sixth-generation master distiller, making it the oldest independent family-owned distillery in South Africa. Karoo Gin is distilled in the same way as it has always been in a traditional wood-fired (see page 29) Cape pot still in 750-litre (200-US-gallon) batches. The grape-based spirit for the two Black Mountain expressions, Karoo Dry Gin and Karoo Flora Gin, is first double distilled before a selection of ten botanicals – orris, angelica and liquorice roots, aniseed, citrus peels, cardamom, coriander seeds, grapefruit, rose petals and juniper – are macerated in the spirit and finally tripled distilled. Karoo Flora Gin sees another three botanicals – wild aniseed flowers, elderflowers and sweet thorn flowers – added to the mix. Both expressions are bottled at 43% ABV.
blackmountaingin.com

CRUXLAND GIN
WESTERN CAPE
Famous in South Africa for their wine and brandy production, the team at KWV have created Cruxland Gin. Using a grape spirit base and taking a big flavour lead from !N'aabas, aka Kalahari truffles, it is the company's brandy master who developed the recipe, which is made in 500-litre (132-US-gallon) pot stills in Paarl just outside of Cape Town. Other botanicals include South African rooibos and honeybush, along with lemon, coriander, almond, cardamom, aniseed and juniper, which are distilled together, with the truffles having their own distillation. The resulting gin is bottled at 43% ABV.
kwv.co.za/our-brands/view/spirits/7#down

INVERROCHE GIN
WESTERN CAPE
One of the pioneers of South African craft gin, Inverroche Distillery was founded by Lorna Scott and her family at Still Bay in the Western Cape in 2012. The distillery has since grown from a small home industry distilling on a two-litre (4¼-US-pint) still on a kitchen table, to one of the most well-respected craft distilleries in the country, making three gins using a 1,000-litre (265-US-gallon) direct-fired copper pot still, which is filled with hand-pumped water straight from the aquifer beneath the distillery. Their core range of gins comprises Gin Verdant, Gin Amber and Gin Classic (all bottled at 43% ABV), all using a secret recipe drawing on the local fynbos – the flowers, herbs and spices that grow in the Cape Floral Kingdom, one of only six such biomes in the world. As well as cultivating their own botanicals, the company cooperates with local nurseries to propagate plants, re-establish them in their natural habitat and harvest them by hand. Once distilled, the gin is also bottled, labelled and boxed by hand, creating employment for the local community.
inverroche.com/za

JORGENSEN'S GIN
WESTERN CAPE
Jorgensen's Distillery based in Wellington is very much a craft set-up in both ethos and equipment. Established by Roger Jorgensen as an antidote to the major drinks manufacturers in South Africa and their hold on the distilled drinks market, he produces a range of spirits including brandy, vodka, absinthe, limoncello and, of course, gin. Made in small batches of only 180 bottles, the gin is distilled outdoors in a copper

pot still and takes its flavours from juniper harvested from South Africa's only juniper planation in Paarl, angelica, orris, calamus and liquorice roots, rare African wild ginger, coriander seeds and bitter apricot kernels. Add to this *naartjie* (tangerine), Cape lemon peels, buchu (*Agathosma*), rose geranium and grains of paradise that are grown for the distillery in Ghana as part of a beneficial community project. One other exotic botanical, ohandua (*Zanthoxylum ovatifoliolatum*), is harvested by the Himba people of Namibia from the rare Kaoko knobwood in the remote areas of the Kaokoveld. The gin is bottled at 43% ABV.
jd7.co.za

SOUTHERN CROSS GIN
WESTERN CAPE
Made in a lighthouse in the Western Cape, Southern Cross Gin uses a triple-distilled spirit from the Pinotage grape and draws flavour from 21 botanicals, namely African chamomile, blue mountain sage, Overberg buchu (*Agathosma*), *kapokbos* (wild rosemary), *naartjie* (tangerine), rooibos,

blueberries and blackberries, alongside the more conventional fennel, coriander, lemon and orange peel, pepper, clove, cardamom, nutmeg, cinnamon, sage, angelica root, jasmine and Scottish juniper. It also uses seawater from both the Atlantic and Indian Oceans, bottled at 43% ABV.
southerncrossgin.co.za

WILDERER FYNBOS GIN
WESTERN CAPE
Founded by German Helmut Wilderer in 1995 after taking a holiday in South Africa, Wilderer Distillery produces some of the finest grappa from the best available Muscat, Pinotage and Shiraz grapes in South Africa, so it is no wonder the distillery turned its expertise to the art of making gin. Wilderer Fynbos Gin uses a wine-based spirit, water from the Franschhoek Mountains and unique fynbos botanicals (*see* page 208 and left), including buchu (*Agathosma*), honeybush, wild dagga (*Leonotis leonurus*) and devil's claw. The stills, personally selected by Wilderer himself, are made by Kothe

and are 700 litres (185 US gallons) in capacity. The gin is bottled at 45% ABV. Since Helmut Wilderer passed away in December 2016, his son Christian and his longstanding team continue to build on Wilderer's distilling legacy.
wilderer.co.za

D'URBAN GIN
DURBAN
Andrew Rall began his journey into distilling in 2000, after a trip to Scotland left him intrigued by the distillation process and interested in the wide variety of flavours that could come from different single malts. Given that he was based in one of the largest sugar cane-producing nations in the world, rum was Rall's starting point, and in 2007 he converted his garden cottage into a tiny distillery, obtained a home distiller's licence and began experimenting. In 2008, he set up Distillery 031 in Durban, taking the name from the local area dialling code, where he makes a range of spirits as well as a tonic water and a lemonade. D'Urban

Durban Dry Gin is a classic London Dry style made with a blend of ten botanicals including African rosehips, orris root, cardamon, lemon and cassia bark. His barrel-aged gin is a first for South Africa, ageing his D'Urban Gin in French oak barrels. Both gins are bottled at 43% ABV.
distillery031.com

BLIND TIGER GIN
NATAL
Founded in 2017 by Keegan Cook, originally from Cape Town, Blind Tiger Gin is produced using a copper pot still and infused with juniper, coriander, angelica, passion flower and lemongrass. The distillery prides itself on the fact that no batch is ever alike. It is bottled at 46% ABV.
blindtigergin.com

KENYA, UGANDA AND NIGERIA

These countries have historically shown a notable fondness for imported gins, alongside the domestically produced spirit, which continues to grow in popularity over generations.

PROCERA GIN
NAIROBI

Juniper may be the beating heart of every gin, but for Kenya's Procera Gin it couldn't be more significant, as it is named after the rare species of juniper it features, *Juniperus procera*, which only grows at about 1,500m (5,000ft) above sea level in the highlands of Ethiopia and Kenya. The other botanicals used include *ndimu* or Swahili limes and pixie tangerines, both from Kenya. Produced by an operation founded in 2017 by Guy Brennan, the gin is distilled in a 230-litre (61-US-gallon) German Müller still, and bottled at 44% ABV. *proceragin.com*

WARAGI GIN
KAMPALA

East African Breweries Limited (EABL) have been producing Waragi Gin since 1965. Mostly consumed in its home country through small sachets, almost like a juice box, it has become a symbol of Uganda's independence from the British Empire. Using a spirit base made from millet, it is bottled at 40% ABV. *eabl.com/en/our-brands/spirits/uganda-waragi/*

BEST LONDON DRY GIN
LAGOS

Nigeria is the seventh-largest gin-consuming nation according to recent IWSR research (*see* page 147), with brands such as Gordon's being one of the most successful. The Best Distillery in Lagos has existed for over 20 years, producing Best London Dry Gin, bottled at 43% ABV and sold in 30ml sachets as well as regular-sized 70cl bottles. *bestnigeria.com.ng*

REST OF AFRICA

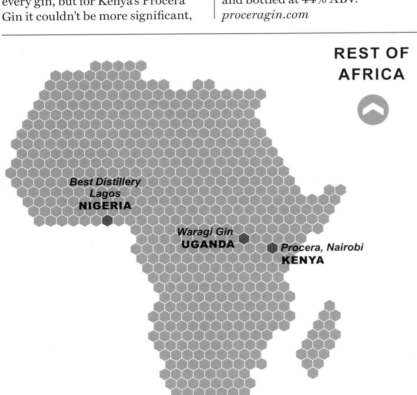

Best Distillery
Lagos
NIGERIA

Waragi Gin
UGANDA

Procera, Nairobi
KENYA

AUSTRALASIA

AUSTRALIA

There is no doubt about it, Australia is currently one of the most vibrant craft gin-producing nations in the world, with many distillers pushing the boundaries of innovation in search of some truly unique flavours. Fortunately, many of the very best Australian gins are available to explore and enjoy beyond the domestic market.

FOUR PILLARS GIN
MELBOURNE

Friends Matt Jones, Cameron Mackenzie and Stuart Gregor founded Four Pillars in late 2013, just as the boom in craft distilling in Australia was kicking off. Now it is well established, with award-winning whisky distilleries and over 50 Australian gins on the market in their home country. Based in the Yarra Valley near Melbourne, which is better known for its winemaking than its gin production, Four Pillars has done some ground-breaking work maturing their gins in ex-wine casks, to bring the two worlds together. However, before the small team could look to purchasing and using wine casks, they first had to develop their signature gin style.

It took around 18 months of test distillations until the team of friends were happy with their formula. They then ordered a 450-litre (119-US-gallon) copper pot still (named Wilma) from famed German producers Carl, and took a further four months in order to fine-tune the recipe, aiming for a contemporary-style gin. The team has slowly expanded production, purchasing a bigger 600-litre (160-US-gallon) still, Jude (after Stuart's mum), and a smaller 50-litre (13¼-US-gallon) version, Eileen, for experimental work. They also have a steam-powered 2,000-litre (528-US-gallon) still named Beth.

◉ *Four Pillars gin is a firm favourite with bartenders*

On their orchestra of stills, Four Pillars produce what they describe as a "modern Australian" gin designed to reflect the blend of cultures in the country by using European juniper, with spices from Southeast Asia through to the Middle East, some native Australian botanicals and citrus from the Mediterranean. The resulting recipe is a mixture of ten botanicals – juniper, cardamom, coriander, lemon myrtle, Tasmanian pepper berry leaf (*see* page 223), cinnamon, lavender, angelica, star anise and whole oranges.

These botanicals are distilled using a wheat base spirit that is sourced from Bomaderry on the south coast of New South Wales, drawing on the production of around 6,000 farmers across the state. This grain spirit is diluted to about 30% ABV and added to their original copper pot still, then the nine dry botanicals are added directly to the pot and the whole oranges are sliced and placed in a botanical basket for the spirit vapours to pass through (*see* page 20). The spirit is then refined through seven separate plates in the column section of the still alongside (*see* page 24).

Each batch of gin takes around seven hours to distil and the resulting gin comes off the still at 93.5% ABV, before being adjusted to a lower ABV, dependent on which expression is being made. Around 460 bottles are produced in each batch. If the gin is destined for their Rare Dry Gin edition, it will simply be cut down to 41.8% ABV and rested to marry for a couple of weeks before being bottled. Their Navy Strength version is diluted to just 58.8% ABV and has the addition of finger limes as an extra botanical. These are placed in the botanical basket during distillation along with the whole oranges. For Spiced Negroni Gin (bottled at 43.8% ABV), grains of paradise are added to the dry botanical mix, with fresh blood oranges and ginger in the botanical basket.

Their most unusual product draws its inspiration from the local winemakers. In 2015, Four Pillars took the bold step to steep some Yarra Valley Shiraz grapes in high-proof Rare Dry Gin for eight weeks, in the same way that sloe gin is produced. The fruit was then pressed and the juice blended with more Rare Dry Gin. Bottled as Bloody Shiraz Gin, it is released on a vintage basis, bottled at around 37.8% ABV. Four Pillars also produce a series of limited-edition cask-aged gins that have featured both sherry and chardonnay editions.
fourpillarsgin.com.au

⊙ *Four Pillar's Cameron Mackenzie*

AUSTRALIA

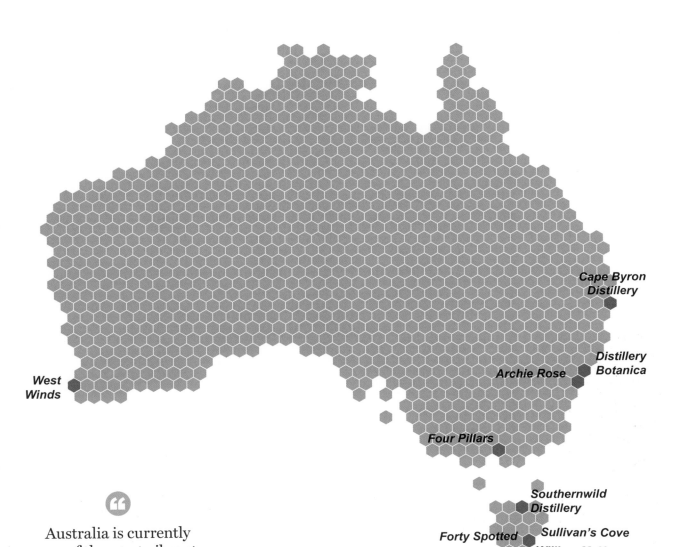

West
Winds

Archie Rose

Cape Byron
Distillery

Distillery
Botanica

Four Pillars

Southernwild
Distillery

Forty Spotted

Sullivan's Cove

William McHenry
Distillery

Australia is currently
one of the most vibrant
craft gin-producing
nations in the world.

ARCHIE ROSE GIN
SYDNEY

When founder of the Archie Rose Distilling Co. Will Edwards decided he wanted to produce, in his words, "something tangible" in his chosen location of Sydney, he first had to contend with the fact that no one had set up a distillery in the city in more than 160 years. He finally achieved his aim in 2014, but not before waiting exactly 364 days from when he commissioned craftsman Peter Bailly, Australia's only still maker, to create the stills to his exact specifications, hand-hammering and fabricating copper specially shipped in from Europe.

The three copper pot stills are used to make a range of gins as well as whisky and vodka. The core Archie Rose Signature Gin (42% ABV) features 14 different botanicals, including native Australian blood lime, dorrigo pepper leaf, lemon myrtle and river mint, together with a pronounced juniper element. Alongside is a Distiller's Strength edition, currently bottled at

52.4% ABV. The distillery also releases series of limited editions, such as their Summer Gin Project, with two different expressions featuring sustainably sourced, locally-foraged ingredients. The Bush version is inspired by the Australian summer and uses native waxflower, pink peppercorns, wild farmer's friend and native thyme, with herbal and eucalyptus notes. Although sold out, you can probably still find this release in a few bars if you look out for it. The Coast version draws on strawberry gum, sea lettuce, peach and coconut. Both expressions are bottled at 40% ABV.

Archie Rose also offers the concept of tailored spirits, with their website presenting a range of botanicals to choose from for building on the Signature Gin. From a maximum of five botanicals, they suggest concentrating on three, and once the botanicals are selected, they will adjust the strength of each botanical for a balanced bespoke result. *archierose.com.au*

○ *Barrel ageing gin at Archie Rose*

Archie Rose also offers the concept of tailored spirits, with their website presenting a range of botanicals to choose from for building on the Signature Gin.

MCHENRY GIN
TASMANIA

Founded by William (Bill) McHenry in 2012, the McHenry Distillery sits on the side of Mount Arthur on the Tasman Peninsula, which stands over the village of Port Arthur and opens southward into the Great Southern Ocean, making it Australia's southern-most distillery and the southern-most family-run distillery in the world. The original expression, a Classic Dry, took McHenry six months and over 25 versions before he was happy with the results. It is made in a 500-litre (132-US-gallon) pot still, using citrus peel, star anise, coriander seeds, cardamon and orris root to accompany the juniper heart, macerated for 24 hours in a natural spirit distilled from sugar cane and bottled at 40% ABV. This is accompanied by a Navy Strength version at 57% ABV. McHenry also produces a barrel-aged edition (40% ABV), where resting in a 200-litre (53-US-gallon) barrel formerly used for the maturation of Russell's Reserve bourbon whiskey combines with the unique cool, moist, maritime environment to create a gin with an exceptional depth of flavour. *mchenrydistillery.com.au*

THE WEST WINDS GIN
WESTERN AUSTRALIA

As the story of gin itself starts with adventure on the high seas and importing and exporting exotic herbs, spices and other botanicals, so does that of The West Winds Gin, based in Margaret River. It was the west winds that accidentally swept some of the earliest settlers to this part of the world, on a Dutch East India Company (*see* page 16) ship navigating away from South Africa back home to the Netherlands. The group of four friends, Jeremy Spencer, Jason Chan, Paul White and James Clarke, who founded the operation in 2010 chose their location carefully, looking for a place that would best reflect Australia and with land fertile enough to provide them with the local botanicals, such as wattle seed, myrtle and bush tomato required to link their gin to the land. The team also needed a quality water source and chose rainwater from the coastal Margaret River area to provide

them with fresh, pure water. They initially installed a small 150-litre (40-US-gallon) copper pot still, which has since been expanded to 600 litres (160 US gallons), to produce their first one-shot gins (*see* page 29), released in 2011: The Sabre, a citrus-led London Dry featuring wattle seed and lemon myrtle, bottled at 40% ABV, and The Cutlass, at the higher strength of 50% ABV, made with Australian bush tomato and cinnamon myrtle. The team soon added The Broadside, at 58% ABV, which contains sea parsley seasoned with sea salt from the local coast, and The Captain's Cut, at 63% ABV, drawing on pink grapefruit, sage and thyme.
thewestwindsgin.com

> The story of gin itself starts with adventure on the high seas and importing and exporting exotic herbs, spices and other botanicals.

The wild coast of Australia, the inspiration for The West Winds Gin

OTHER AUSTRALIAN GINS TO TRY

BROOKIE'S BYRON DRY GIN
NEW SOUTH WALES

Cape Byron Distillery is located at the heart of the Brook family's 40-hectare (96-acre) farm in the hinterland of Byron Bay, hidden among the macadamia orchard and rainforest that the Brooks have regenerated. The distillery was purpose-built on one of the only bare plots of land remaining. Inside is George, their custom-made 2,000-litre (528-US-gallon) copper pot still, in which they produce Brookie's Byron Dry Gin using the one-shot method (see page 29) and vapour infusion (see page 20) of 26 botanicals, 18 of which are native. Of these, the most interesting are sunrise finger limes from Byron Bay, blood limes, kumquats, two types of myrtle and, of course, their own macadamia nuts. To balance such a complex recipe, help to craft their gin was at hand from a distilling legend, Jim McEwan, who has a long history of making Scotch whisky and also produced the first gin from the Isle of Islay, The Botanist (see page 80) on Scotland's west coast. The gin is bottled at 46% ABV.
capebyrondistillery.com

DISTILLERY BOTANICA
NEW SOUTH WALES

On the Central Coast of New South Wales lies Distillery Botanica, a boutique distillery headed up by Philip Moore. Set among 1.2 hectares (3 acres) of gardens, Moore purchased the distillery over a decade ago after founding and managing Renaissance Herbs, Australia's largest wholesale herb nursery, for over 20 years where he grew close to a million plants per annum. Now his tools are a copper pot still and a rectifying column still (see page 24) on which Distillery Botanica gins are produced. These include Moore's Dry Gin (40% ABV), a classic juniper-led Dry, and Distillery Botanica Dry Gin (42% ABV), where individual distillations of fragrant floral botanicals such as murraya, jasmine and orange blossom are blended together.
distillerybotanica.com

DASHER + FISHER GIN
TASMANIA

Produced by Southernwild Distillery on the northwest coast of the island, Dasher + Fisher Gin is named after the two rivers that run from the local mountains, filled with melted snow water, through the rich hinterland to the pristine coast of Tasmania's northwest. It is this pure water, along with botanicals sourced from the many local growers, that is used in the gin, which comes in three expressions. Mountain Gin (45% ABV) is a London Dry style featuring 11 botanicals, including Tasmanian highland pepper berries (see right) and liquorice root. Meadow Gin (45% ABV) uses 15 botanicals built around lavender and oranges picked from local gardens and fields, while Ocean Gin (42% ABV) draws on 12 botanicals including wakame seaweed from the Tasman Sea. Ocean Gin and Meadow Gin are produced using a single-shot distillation process (see page 29) involving both maceration and vapour infusion (see page 20), with Mountain Gin using 100% maceration before distillation.
southernwilddistillery.com

FORTY SPOTTED GIN
TASMANIA

Tasmania could easily be described as the powerhouse of Australian distilling, despite its relative remoteness, and one of its flagship gins is Forty Spotted, made at the award-winning Lark Distillery. The gin draws flavour from more traditional botanicals such as coriander and lemon peel, along with Tasmanian pepper berry or *Tasmannia aromatic* (or *T. lanceolata*), whose unusual characteristics add a citrus-like zing. Produced using the steeping method, each botanical is individually left in high-strength spirit before distillation to ensure maximum extraction of flavour, and is bottled at 40% ABV. As for the gin's name, it comes from Tasmania's rarest bird, the forty-spotted pardalote or *Pardalotus quadragintus*.
fortyspotted.com

HOBART NO.4
TASMANIA

Fellow Tasmanian whisky distillery Sullivans Cove produces Hobart No.4 Gin using a Tasmanian single malt base spirit made with 100% local barley, which is then enriched with four native Australian botanicals – lemon myrtle, anise myrtle, wattle seed and Tasmanian pepper berry (see left). It is bottled at 44% ABV.
sullivanscove.com

NEW ZEALAND

Sharing with Australia a desire to develop gin with its own national style, New Zealand's distillers are passionate about the process: from using the purist water to seeking out the most unusual local botanicals.

SCAPEGRACE GIN
SOUTH ISLAND

Scapegrace is one of the newest gin producers on the market, launching their gin in 2014 into a booming market. A classic London Dry style, the gin is distilled using an original 19th century 3,000-litre (793-US-gallon) John Dore copper pot still, which found its way to New Zealand via boat from the UK in the middle of the last century. After being decommissioned and left to rust, the team at the distillery restored it and put it to good use making gin.

Originally called Rogue Society, founders Daniel Mclaughlin, Mark Neal and Richard Bourke faced their first major challenge not with restoring the old still or finding the right mix of botanicals but with their name when they discovered when trying to export to the EU that the trademark for "rogue" in drinks was already in use by an American beer brand. Needing something different and memorable, they hit upon the ancient word scapegrace, meaning "free-spirited" or indeed "rogue".

Produced by master distiller John Fitzpatrick, the core expression, Scapegrace Classic, is built around the 12 classic botanicals of juniper berries, lemon and orange peels, coriander seeds, cardamom pods, nutmeg, cloves, angelica, liquorice and orris roots, cinnamon sticks and cassia bark, with a 13th botanical, dried Moroccan tangerine peel, added to the navy-strength Scapegrace Gold expression, giving it a heavy citrus, tangy note and rich mouthfeel. Both are built on a wheat-based spirit of 96.2% ABV. The botanicals are macerated for 24 hours prior to double distillation, resulting in a final spirit strength of around 78.9% ABV. Once distilled, the gin is cut to drinking strength using water sourced from one of the world's last natural aquifers close to the distillery, which is fed from the country's Southern Alps, the only native ingredient in the bottle. Scapegrace Classic is bottled at 42.2% ABV, and Scapegrace Gold at 57% ABV.
scapegracegin.com

NEW ZEALAND

Denzien

Scapegrace

Cardrona
Distillery

THE SOURCE GIN
SOUTH ISLAND
To visit one of the world's most southerly distilleries requires a trip over to New Zealand. Desiree Whitaker, a former dairy farmer from South Canterbury, sold her farm in May 2013 to look for a site to distil in and settled in the Queenstown-Lakes District (their address is "Between Wanaka and Queenstown"), setting up the 100% family-owned and operated Cardrona Distillery in 2016 to start making gin, whisky and other spirits. Leading the distillery team, Whitaker uses copper pot stills from Forsyths in Rothes, Scotland, to distil the gin. The Source uses locally foraged rosehips together with juniper, coriander seeds, angelica root and lemon and orange zest, which are vapour distilled (*see* page 20) into a malt spirit produced at the distillery, and is bottled at 47% ABV. *cardronadistillery.com*

DENZIEN GIN
NORTH ISLAND
Founded by Eamon O'Rourke and Mark Halton, the Denzien Urban Distillery is based in the heart of Wellington, using a Kothe copper pot still, local rainwater, native botanicals and a sustainable whey-based ethanol to make its classic juniper-forward Te Aro Dry gin, which comes in at 42% ABV. *facebook.com/ denzienurbandistillery*

ASIA

Asia's thirst for gin has been a relatively reserved affair, at least from a domestically produced perspective. Across Northeast Asia, shōchū (Japan), soju (Korea), gaoliang or kaoliang (Taiwan) and baijiu (China) have been the dominant domestic white spirits, giving little room for major growth in domestic gin until now, with just a handful of notable craft operations opening up in the past five years. However, the craft market is beginning to show signs of a potential boom, especially in Japan (see page 229). China is also witnessing the embryonic growth of the craft gin scene, with several new micro home-grown brands turning the heads of bartenders in the major cities such as Shanghai.

JAPAN

For the past century, Japan has embraced foreign spirits, taking its famed dedication and attention to detail into the production of domestic whisky by storm. In fact, Japanese whisky is now the benchmark against which all other New World whisky makers are measured and has set the bar for the ultra-premium spirits sector.

The Japanese were likely to have had their first taste of gin in the mid- to late 18th century when Dutch traders entered the island of Dejima off the harbour of Nagasaki, but mostly consumed only by those who had settled there. It has been suggested that there were attempts to produce a local gin-like spirit as early as 1812, but there are no records to confirm whether it was a success or whether the strict conditions under which the settlers lived in the Edo period would have indeed allowed it to flourish.

Now world famous for its skills in whisky distilling, the industry was built on the work done by Masataka Taketsuru, whose trip to Scotland to study chemistry in 1918, and through his relationship with Shinjiro Torii, spawned Japan's first whisky distillery, Yamazaki. However, had Taketsuru-san visited Scotland today with its thriving gin scene, he may well have returned to make gin rather than whisky.

It is well over 90 years since the first whisky was made at the Yamazaki Distillery in 1923, but also over 80 years since one of Japan's first official gins, Suntory's Hermes Gin, was released in 1936. But in the intervening period, the domestic market for gin simply tailed off, while whisky production boomed. Today, however, it is a very different story, with more than a dozen distilleries currently producing gin, focusing on a huge diversity of local botanicals and base spirits, including rice-based sake, which brings an almost Dutch genever-style flavour (*see* page 18) to the resulting gin.

THE KYOTO DISTILLERY
KYOTO

The Japanese gin revolution kicked off in October 2016 in the city of Kyoto when the first bottles of KI NO BI Kyoto Dry Gin were filled by hand, ready to lay the path for one of the most exciting new distilling arenas in the world. With a desire to create a gin influenced by the country itself, The Kyoto Distillery's starting point was to use local botanicals wherever possible, and they found that the best way to do this – which has become something of a tradition across the Japanese gin scene – was to create smaller batches of botanical distillates and then skilfully blend them together.

The key botanicals in KI NO BI are yellow yuzu sourced from the north of Kyoto, hinoki wood, bamboo

⬤ *Local Kyoto gin being served in a bar in the city*

Kyoto gin kick-started the Japanese craft gin movement

leaves and gyokuro tea from the Uji region, and green sanshō pepper berries. Building on a rice-based spirit, the botanicals are separated into six different categories: base (juniper, orris, hinoki), citrus (yuzu, lemon), tea (gyokuro), spice (ginger), herbal (sanshō pepper and *kinome*) and fruity and floral (bamboo leaves and shiso leaves). Each category is distilled individually and then blended together with water sourced from the famous sake brewing district, Fushimi, before being rested. When ready for bottling, the same water is used to reduce the product to the chosen bottling strength of 45.7% ABV.

Since the launch of KI NO BI, other expressions have been released by the distillery, most notably an

KI NO BI gin from Kyoto distillery

aged version, KI NOH BI, which has spent time maturing in a cask from the legendary but sadly closed Karuizawa whisky distillery. Carrying notes of vanilla, cardamom and ginger, with a finish that is distinctly oak driven and very much whisky influenced, it is yet another example of how the innovation and creativity within Japan's distilling scene could well see this country developing some of the finest gins on the market in the coming years. *kyotodistillery.jp*

JAPAN

9148 Gin,
Benizakura Distillery

Nikka Coffey
Gin

Meirishurui
Wa Gin

Ki-No-Bi,
Kyoto Distillery
Roku Gin

Sakurao Gin
Kozue Gin

WA-BI Gin, Tsunuki/Hombo
Shuzo Distillery

in the gin, such as sakura flower (cherry blossom) and a vigorous direct copper pot still charge of the citrus botanicals (*see* page 22), some of which come from domestically harvested yuzu.

Roku uses six Japanese botanicals, each harvested at the peak of their particular growing season to achieve the best possible extraction of flavour: sakura flower and sakura leaf in the spring, sencha and gyokuro tea in the summer, sanshō pepper in the autumn and yuzu in the winter. These elements are combined with a core recipe of eight more classical botanicals: juniper, coriander, angelica root, angelica seeds, cardamom, cinnamon, bitter orange peel and lemon peel. The gin is bottled at 43% ABV. A special Travel Retail Select Edition that contains a higher proportion of sakura in the recipe than the regular release is also available.
suntory.co.jp/wnb/rokugin/en/

ROKU GIN
OSAKA

Roku marks Suntory's serious intentions within the rapidly expanding premium gin market, since although it also produces the more mass-market Suntory Extra Dry and Smooth 37 (only available domestically), Roku is very much the more visible, produced at the operation the company established in Osaka to cater for more experimental and boutique projects. Four distinct types of pot still are used, in which each individual botanical is distilled separately before being blended together to preserve the subtle differences in extraction, including a more delicate vapour infusion in a stainless-steel still for the more floral elements

◉ *Suntory's foray into gin with Roku*

NIKKA COFFEY GIN
SENDAI

The history of Japanese distillation would have been significantly poorer had it not been for the interaction between Shinjiro Torri and Masataka Taketsuru back in the early 1920s when they came together to found what would eventually become the Yamazaki Distillery. In the early 1930s, Taketsuru left the partnership to set up the Nikka company on Hokkaido and then the Miyagikyo Distillery in Sendai in 1969. It is here where Nikka's Coffey Gin is now produced, using the same pair of column stills, sometimes known as Coffey stills after Aeneas Coffey who invented the still back in 1830, which were imported from Scotland in the 1960s.

Nikka's gin is made by taking a broad range of botanicals, some native to Japan and some more classic, which are effectively divided

> Nikka's gin is made by taking a broad range of botanicals, some native to Japan and some more classic.

into three groups: sanshō pepper; fruit; and herbs and spices. The herbaceous/spicy botanicals are distilled in a regular copper pot still, but the citrus elements and pepper are distilled at a low pressure to maintain more of their delicate flavour. The citrus botanicals include yuzu, *kabosu* (which look like limes, but are closely related to yuzu), *amanatsu* (a larger fruit, similar to grapefruit) and *shikuwasa*, a sour citrus fruit native to Okinawa and Taiwan. This makes for a very citrus-forward gin when combined with the other botanicals (lemon and orange peels, coriander seeds, tangy apple, juniper and sanshō pepper), with the juniper playing more of a supporting role in what is a complex gin, bottled at 47% ABV. Nikka also produces a little-known, more traditional gin called Wilkinson that is only available domestically.
nikka.com

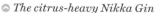

◉ *The citrus-heavy Nikka Gin*

OTHER JAPANESE GINS TO TRY

SAKURAO GIN
HIROSHIMA

The newly commissioned Sakurao Distillery opened in Hiroshima in 2018, but with a heritage of blending whiskies dating back to the 1930s, mostly using imported spirits. The first batch of its Original Japanese Dry Gin is a recipe that uses a high proportion of juniper together with hinoki (Japanese cypress), green tea, ginger, *aka shisho* (red perilla) and fresh citrus grown around Hiroshima including green lemon, sweet summer orange, navel orange, yuzu and *dai dai* (bitter orange), which are simultaneously macerated or vapour infused in a German hybrid pot/column still (*see* page 25). A Limited version brings together 17 botanicals, with a broader focus on Japanese horticulture: Japanese juniper berries and leaves from Hiroshima, sakura flower (cherry blossom), *kinome* (sanshō pepper leaves), wasabi and even oyster shells, which the distiller says add an additional saline note to the finished gin. The recently released Hamagou edition is a more herbaceous expression. All three gins are bottled at 47% ABV. *sakuraodistillery.com/en/ sakurao/*

KOZUE GIN
WAKAYAMA

Nakano is the maker of Kozue Gin at its Fujishiro Distillery in Kainan, a company that has been in the soy sauce business since the 1930s, as well as producing plum wine, *shōchū*, sake and *kibaichu*, which is a distillate from the umeshu plum. The gin brings together imported European juniper and several botanicals that grow abundantly in the Wakayama Prefecture where

the distillery lies, which include *koyamaki* or Japanese umbrella pine (which isn't actually a pine but an ancient species of evergreen tree estimated to have been in existence for over 230 million years), mandarin and lemon peels and sanshō pepper. It is bottled at 47% ABV. *nakano-group.co.jp*

MEIRISHURUI WA GIN
IBARAKI

This successful winemaker and distiller has been in the drinks business since the 1950s, creating sake, distilled *shōchū*, plum wines and other liqueurs. The distillery's latest creation is WA GIN, released in August 2017, and is arguably the first Japanese craft gin to create a base spirit from *shōchū* – in this case, a ten-

year old example, distilled from Japanese rice sake. The spirit is then redistilled with a handful of classic botanicals: juniper, lemon and orange peels and cinnamon. The *shōchū* gives the overall gin an additional fermented, slightly starchy herbaceous note, along with a sharp citrus note in the background. It is bottled at 45% ABV. *meirishurui.com*

9148 GIN/BENIZAKURA DISTILLERY
HOKKAIDO

The most recent distillery to have opened in Japan and the second on Hokkaido (the other is Nikka's Yoichi – *see* page 232 or opposite), Benizakura Distillery entered the craft gin market in April 2018, with

9148-0100 (45% ABV), a limited run of just under 600 bottles, which was designed to be distinctly umami led, using dried shiitake mushrooms, dried radish, locally sourced hidaka kelp, juniper, coriander, cinnamon, angelica, lemon peel, blueberries, rose petals, black pepper, cardamom, white pepper and clove. It has since unveiled further batches with numerically inspired recipe names, including 1922 Sapporo, a homage to the city of Sapporo, using ten different botanicals from the city's different wards including cucumber, mountain wasabi, mint, lilac, tomato, lavender and cherry, bottled at 42% ABV. *hlwhisky.co.jp*

WA BI GIN
KAGOSHIMA

Hombo Shuzo has been distilling whisky since 1960, but its product range has only been available domestically until recently. The company began a foray into craft distillation in 2015 by opening up the Tsunuki Distillery, a separate 90,000-litre (23,800-US-gallon) facility, to make both gin and more experimental whiskies. WA BI GIN is one of the first craft spirits through the gate and combines juniper, yuzu, bitter orange from Hetsuka, lemon peel, kumquat, Saigon cinnamon leaf, shell ginger leaf (*Alpinia zerumbet*, a tall perennial plant native to East Asia), green tea and the Japanese herb perilla. It is bottled at 45% ABV. Having proved a success in Japan, it has been followed up with a Juniper Strength version, which contains juniper as the single botanical and is bottled at 50% ABV. *hombo.co.jp*

CHINA

China's dominant spirit of choice is *baijiu*, an intensely flavoured, high-strength white spirit made by naturally fermenting different grains such as wheat, barley, sorghum and sometimes rice and beans, either in chambers under the ground, in clay pots or in a mixture of the two. It produces a spirit like no other when distilled – a funky mix of savoury, fruity, herbal and sometimes medicinal flavours. Its success is astronomical – one brand, Kweichow Moutai, was reported as being the world's most valuable spirits brand in 2018.

The popularity of *baijiu* in the domestic market has meant that it is difficult for gin to gain a footprint outside the major cities. However, with over 21 million new drinkers of legal age entering the market each year, the opportunity for imported brands such as Tanqueray, Gordon's and Beefeater is promising, and so is the potential for China's very own domestic production of craft gins, a scene that has slowly been bubbling up since 2017.

PEDDLERS GIN
SHANGHAI

The very first of these new brands is Peddlers Gin. Launched in early 2018 by Ryan Mcleod and two friends, the trio spent over three years developing a recipe and techniques before settling on a formula that suited the ethos of the gin: to be as exotic as the city of

China's very own domestic production of craft gins is a scene that has slowly been bubbling up since 2017.

The unique Peddlers Gin from China

⊙ *Dragons Blood, a new horizon for gin*

province led them to create a gin with a local distiller that reflected the diversity of flavours found there and includes lemons sourced from Hainan, locally grown Hunan peppers and coriander, alongside Chinese juniper from the Shandong province, giving another element of authenticity to the concept. Post-distillation in a grain spirit produced in Yunnan province, the gin is additionally infused for 48 hours with crushed coriander seeds and lemon peel, which gives it a slightly golden hue.
crimsonpangolin.com

DRAGON'S BLOOD GIN
INNER MONGOLIA

Dragon's Blood was founded in March 2018 by New Zealand chef Daniel Brooker, who has pieced together the distillery from scratch in the city of Chifeng. The gin brings together locally sourced botanicals such as gold rosebuds and wild bush pepper, and is made using a mixture of distillation and compounding (*see* page 20), which gives the spirit its distinctive dark red colour (bottled at 47% ABV).
facebook.com/dragonbloodgin/

Shanghai. The recipe is a complex and spicy mix of 11 botanicals centred around juniper from the northern Hungarian highlands, which is macerated in a neutral grain alcohol for ten hours before distillation takes place. The juniper is joined by Sichuan pepper from the small village of Qingxi, Buddha's hand or fingered citron from Yunnan province, East Asian mint from southeast China, lotus flower from the north, angelica from the northeast, liquorice from an organic farm in the Guangdong province, cubeb berries from Java, coriander seeds from northern India, cassia bark from Yunnan near the

Tibetan border and finally Xinjiang almonds from near the border with Kyrgyzstan. The gin is vapour infused in a small copper alembic still (*see* page 22) and the spirit run only yields around 20 bottles per batch, bottled at 45.7% ABV.
peddlersgin.com

CRIMSON PANGOLIN GIN
HUNAN

Distilled and bottled in Changsha, Crimson Pangolin Gin is a concept dreamed up in early 2017 by ex-pats Helena Kidacka and David Munoz, who are based in Shanghai. Their love of the cuisine from Hunan

KAVALAN GIN TAIWAN

Taiwan is a country already well versed in producing Western-influenced spirits to great acclaim. The country's first whisky distillery, Kavalan opened back in 2005, with spirit running from the stills on 11 March 2006. Since that time, the distillery has gone on to produce some of the most awarded whiskies in the world, winning legions of devotees for its attention to detail and complex, varied single malts. So it was with great interest when master distiller Ian Chang, himself a multi-award winner for his innovative work in spirits, took on the role of producing Taiwan's first craft gin. The distillery, which was expanded in 2016, had in 2008 taken the decision to install some additional German-made stills to meet the increasing demands for its whisky, but finding the spirit too light for its purpose, decided to use them for more experimental purposes and in 2012 began the first trials of manufacturing a gin. The recipes went through scores of iterations and botanical trials until Chang and his team were happy with the results and the

gin finally got the green light to be released in September 2018.

The base spirit of the gin begins life in exactly the same way that the distillery produces its single malt whisky. Malted barley is mashed and fermented into a strong beer of around 8–8.5% ABV. But instead of being distilled twice, it receives an additional third distillation to bring the strength up to around 65–70% ABV, when botanical distillates and essences are added in or cold compounded (see page 20).

The botanical recipe for Kavalan Gin is a mixture of classics – juniper, coriander seeds and aniseed – and three more fruit-driven ingredients, which reflect what is readily available in Yilan, where the distillery is based. These are kumquat peel, dried red guava and dried star fruit, which brings an almost cherry-like tangy note on the palate, with the coriander delivering a slightly spicy citrus touch. It is bottled at 40% ABV.
kavalanwhisky.com

INDIA AND SRI LANKA

As in Japan, the Indian consumer has fallen head over heels in love with domestically produced whisky. However, it is classified as a very different type of spirit to the whisky produced elsewhere, mostly using a base of molasses rather than malted barley, bringing it more in line with rum. As a result, the Indian craft gin market is still very much in its infancy, with only a handful of small brands producing independently owned products. These are unlikely to dent the huge sales of the domestically distilled McDowell's Blue Riband Extra Dry, which was first introduced back in 1959 and continues to hold a major market share, along with other more well-known brands such as Gordon's, Tanqueray (*see* page 82), Bombay Sapphire (*see* page 69) and Finsbury – not a high-profile brand in the UK where it is made (at the Langley Distillery – *see* page 75), but clearly popular with the Indian palate.

Since India comprises 29 states and seven union territories, each one governed by different rules on the production and distribution of alcohol (several enforcing a total prohibition of alcohol), market-specific gins are popular, such as Moonwalk Gin, a grain-based spirit with juniper flavouring, available only in Haryana.

The Indian craft gin market is still very much in its infancy, with only a handful of small brands producing independently owned products.

◉ *Gin from the home of spices*

● *Gin production at Näo gin*

INDIAN GINS TO TRY

NÄO SPIRITS
GOA

Bar owners and friends Anand Virmani and Vaibhav Singh launched India's first craft gin, Greater Than London Dry Gin, back in 2017 after establishing their company two years prior to that. They felt that there was a gap in the market for a premium offering that represented the growing appreciation of fine spirits in India. Greater Than is made as a multi-shot gin (see page 29) in monthly batches using a wheat-based neutral grain spirit, which is then infused with a number of imported classic botanicals: Macedonian juniper, German angelica root, Spanish orange peel and Italian orris, along with Indian lemongrass, ginger, fennel seeds, coriander and chamomile flowers. The botanicals are macerated and then distilled in a 1,000-litre (264-US-gallon) pot still before being bottled at 42.8% ABV.

NÄO's other gin is a different affair altogether. Hapusa takes its name from the Sanskrit word for juniper and is currently the only gin in the world to use juniper native to India, grown in the Himalayas. The duo undertook the task of spending three days scavenging through the markets of Khari Baoli in Delhi when they finally struck gold. Hapusa is a single-shot gin (see page 29) made on the same still as Greater Than, but with the Himalayan juniper. It includes mango, ginger, coriander seeds, a small amount of turmeric, cardamom, almonds and the final key ingredient *gondhoraj lebu*, a variety of lemon that is indigenous to east India, and a cross between a mandarin and a lime. Hapusa is bottled at 43% ABV.
naospirits.com

STRANGER & SONS GIN
MUMBAI AND GOA

Sakshi Saigal, Rahul Mehra and Vidur Gupta put their business backgrounds aside and allowed an element of passion to flow through when the trio developed the Third Eye Distillery in Mumbai where they produce Stranger & Sons Gin. It has a recipe of nine botanicals and is distilled in a still designed in and shipped from the Netherlands. Apart from the juniper, which comes from Macedonia, the other herbs and spices are all sourced locally to the distillery. Stranger & Sons (bottled at 42% ABV) is an intensely citrus-heavy gin, which is unsurprising given that it contains two kinds of limes, alongside further citrus from *gondhoraj lebu* (see left).
instagram.com/strangerandsons/

JAISALMER INDIAN CRAFT GIN
UTTAR PRADESH

Pronounced *Jessalmeer*, Jaisalmer Indian Craft Gin is small-batch triple-distilled in a copper pot still by master distiller Anup Barik at Rampur Distillery – the makers of Rampur Indian Single Malt Whisky. Located in the foothills of the Himalayas, the distillery is one of India's oldest, tracing its roots back to 1949. The recipe uses seven of its 11 botanicals to highlight all the regions of India. Coriander and vetiver are grown in the fields around Jaisalmer in the north; sweet orange comes from central India; cubeb berries and lemongrass are sourced in southern India; Darjeeling green tea hails from eastern India; and lemon peel is brought in from western India. Added to these are angelica root, liquorice and caraway seeds, with the juniper berries coming from Tuscany. It is bottled at 43% ABV.
jaisalmergin.com

ROCKLAND DRY GIN
SRI LANKA

Sri Lanka is a country blessed with a rich heritage of spirit production, famed for producing Ceylon arrack by fermenting and then distilling the sap of coconut flowers before ageing the resulting spirit in oak. But it comes as something of a surprise to find a history of gin production at what was the first commercial distillery to be established in the country. Set up to produce arrack in 1924, at the outbreak of World World Two regulations dictated that Rockland Distillery switch to making medicinal alcohol to support the war effort. But post-war, the distillery was free to create their Rockland Dry Gin, which remains very much in production today, being the biggest-selling gin in Sri Lanka, with the third generation of the family now running the company. Rockland (bottled at 38% ABV) is a simple botanical balance of juniper, coriander, lemongrass, ginger and Ceylon cinnamon. A distinct lemon version (bottled at 38.5% ABV) is also available, which is post-infused with lemon essence, giving a sharper citrus burst. In 2015, a gin called Colombo No. 7 was released, drawing its inspiration from an original recipe developed by the founders of Rockland, using the highly potent curry leaf as a key botanical. Colombo No. 7, bottled at 43.1%, is currently distilled in the UK, so isn't strictly a Sri Lankan gin. However, it certainly oozes plenty of provenance and local charm, so is worth seeking out.
rockland.lk
colombosevengin.com

SINGAPORE

Singapore has long been associated with its very own classic gin cocktail (*see* page 54 for a more detailed description), so the spirit is very much ingrained in the fabric and culture of the city state. Today, Singapore is witnessing a strong gin renaissance influenced largely by its internationally renowned bar scene, which has taken the cocktail world by storm. By way of example, take a visit to Atlas, a dedicated gin palace, and you will find over 1,200 different gins from more than 40 different countries. And while the majority may be European or US gins, there has been a flurry of local distilling activity over the last two years, with the beginnings of a domestic craft gin scene surely just around the corner.

⚉ *The classic Singapore sling cocktail*

BRASS LION SINGAPORE DRY GIN
SINGAPORE

Brass Lion Distillery is Singapore's second microdistillery and tasting room, which was opened in September 2018 by Jamie Koh, the businesswoman behind two successful bars in the city. Koh's journey began seven years ago, when she began exploring gin production from Europe and the USA, learning the craft of distillation along the way. Brass Lion Singapore Dry Gin is based around a German Arnold Holstein pot still with a separate column still (*see* page 22), and its botanicals reflect the modern culinary approach that Singapore is famous for without moving too far into the esoteric. Torch ginger flower, galangal, kaffir lime leaves and dried mandarin peel form the heart of the recipe alongside juniper, combined with 18 botanicals including tamarind, lemongrass, pomelo peel, chrysanthemum flowers, cardamom, cubeb berries and angelica root. It is bottled at 40% ABV.
brassliondistillery.com

TANGLIN ORCHID GIN
SINGAPORE

Tanglin Distillery is the first gin distillery in Singapore and the first new distillery for more than 40 years. Founded by Andy Hodgson, Tim Whitefield, Chris Box and Charlie Van Eeden, the name comes from the

Tanglin district, these days a smart residential suburb, but back in the 17th century it was a wild jungle inhabited by tigers, with a number of plantations growing pepper, nutmeg and gambier, an astringent shrub. It is the combination of some unusual botanicals: Indian amchoor or powdered green mango, orchid flowers and stalks from *Dendrobium nobile Lindl.*, which is widely used in traditional Chinese medicine, whole vanilla pods from the vanilla orchid and organic oranges. These are blended alongside the more traditional coriander seeds, juniper and liquorice and angelica roots. Using a base of Australian GNS (grain neutral spirit) made from wheat from a farm in New South Wales, the spirit is cut to around 38% ABV and filled into a 250-litre (66-US-gallon) Polish Genio still (*see* page 29). The distillation occurs over a ten-hour period and the final gin is reduced to 42% ABV and bottled without chill filtration (*see* page 29).
tanglin-gin.com

THE PHILIPPINES

The Philippines is quite simply an extraordinary place when it comes to the world of gin. It has embraced the spirit like no other country and to date is still the largest consumer of gin by volume than any country in the world. In many respects, its passion for gin can probably be traced back to the 1700s, specifically 1762–4, when the British occupation of Manila meant that distilled gin from London and Holland was imported regularly to satisfy the thirsts of those living in the capital. It later became a mainstay for Spanish settlers and a few members of the Filipino elite, so much so that in 1834 the first dedicated distillery, Ayala, was founded in the Quiapo district of Manila and began to produce Ginerba San Miguel, a brand name that even today continues to define the gin category worldwide. The brand's now iconic label, an image of St Michael vanquishing Lucifer, more widely known as *Marca Demonio*, was created by Filipino artist Fernando Amorsolo back in 1917, who went on to become arguably the most highly regarded artist from the country. It is an image that still adorns every bottle of Ginerba San Miguel, further reinforcing the spirit's status as a national treasure.

The sugarcane grown in the Philippines provides the base for some local gins

GINERBA SAN MIGUEL
MANILA

It isn't surprising that San Miguel is made from a base of sugar-cane spirit, given its abundance on the islands. The sugar is refined on the island and then distilled into alcohol at the Bago Distillery, an industrial-scale operation that is the home of San Miguel. The proprietary brand is a cold compounded gin (*see* page 20), with a number of essences added to the spirit before it is diluted and bottled at 40% ABV. The recipe is not in the public domain, but given its modest price, it is certainly a very standard product. A more upmarket version – San Miguel Premium – was released to compete with the other popular imported gins, such as Gordon's and Gilbey's, which has a dominant juniper note and a citrus tang, along with delicate notes of spice, bottled at 35% ABV. One of the most popular serves is the GinPom: a mixture of gin, water and powdered pomelo-flavoured juice. *ginebrasanmiguel.com*

CROWS HAND-CRAFTED GIN
MANILA

At the other end of the scale, a tiny operation called the Crows Craft Brewing & Distilling Co. released what was the Philippines' first craft gin in 2017, Crows Hand-Crafted Gin (bottled at 45% ABV). The minuscule output of just 60 bottles per batch (and an even more scarce oak-aged, ten-bottle batch edition called Barrel Reserve) using 23 botanicals, including juniper, orange peel, cardamom, orris root, rosehips, lavender, angelica and cassia bark, meant it was only stocked in a few bars in Manila. Crows have opened a second distillery in San Francisco. *crowscraft.com*

MALAYSIA AND VIETNAM

The year 2018 saw the birth of two other new gins in the Southeast Asian region from Malaysia and Vietnam.

JIN
MALAYSIA

The bartenders from Locker and Loft, located in the neighbourhood of Damansara Kim in the city of Petaling Jaya, decided to create Malaysia's first new craft gin simply called Jin. This is not a distilled spirit, but a compounded infusion (*see* page 20) of some 16 botanicals including juniper, star fruit, guava, pomelo, dried jackfruit, dates, roselle, rosemary, sapodilla fruit, lemon peels, cardamom, kaffir lime, dried chrysanthemums and basil leaves, which gives a distinctly fruity flavour upfront leading into some more familiar juniper/citrus notes. It is only available at the bar.
lockerandloft.com

FURBREW GENEVA GIN
VIETNAM

Brewer Thomas Bilgram from the renowned Hanoi-based craft brewery Furbrew created Vietnam's very first craft gin around the concept of using waste beer as the base ingredient. After experimenting on a small scale, he partnered up with a local distiller to distil a blend of 4,500 litres (1,190 US gallons) of unusable beer into a spirit base, which gave him just 500 litres (132 US gallons) of spirit to explore. Juniper and kumquat peel are the only botanicals listed in the recipe, to retain some of the natural hop-driven flavour from the spirit, which runs from the still at 68% ABV before being reduced and bottled at 43% ABV.
furbrew.vn

Asia is a rich source of incredible herbs and spices

THAILAND

Inspired by the success of the burgeoning craft beer scene in Thailand, several distillers are now getting in on the act of making craft gin in various locations across the country, exploring a unique combination of botanicals and base alcohol sources.

IRON BALLS GIN
BANGKOK

A R Sutton & Co Engineers microdistillery was founded in 2015 by renowned Australian bartender Ashley Sutton, and his first gin, Iron Balls, is as pioneering as it is unusual. Given that the distillery was the first to be licensed in Bangkok for a little over 30 years, the desire

Thailand's idyllic landscape: perfect for exotic botanicals

to create something completely out of the box yet representative of the distillery's locality must have weighed highly when creating the recipe. If that was indeed the case, then Iron Balls has achieved its objective. Its base ingredient is a mixture of coconut and pineapple, which is fermented to create a sweet liquor of around 13% ABV and then column distilled into a spirit (*see* page 24). The botanical recipe is a closely guarded secret, but the flavour gives hints of juniper, some warming cinnamon and ginger, a lighter citrus note and some herbaceous/citrus coriander. However, the most overriding flavour is a sweet fruity note like no other gin, which is distinct but not overpowering and highlights the unique importance of the base spirit. It is bottled at 40% ABV.
ironballsgin.com

PAPER LANTERN GIN
CHANG MAI

Despite being a distinctly Singaporean gin, conceived and launched in 2016 by husband and wife team Rick Ames and Simin Kayhan-Ames, who live and run the brand from the city state, Paper Lantern Gin is actually distilled in Chang Mai, using a base alcohol created from rice. The key botanicals are Sichuan peppercorns, along with ginger, lemongrass, galangal and makhwaen seeds or prickly ash, a common spice in northern Thai cuisine. It is bottled at 40% ABV.
drinkpaperlantern.com

ESSENTIAL TERMS

The distillation process is often described as "alchemy" – a balance between creativity and science, using practices and skills that have stood the test of time for centuries. Below is a list of terms that are essential to any distiller and worth bearing in mind when navigating your way through this Atlas and the world of gin.

ABV

Stands for alcohol by volume – the standard measure for the amount of alcohol contained in a spirit, expressed as a percentage of volume (*see* **Proof**, an additional measure used in the USA). Some gins are deliberately bottled at higher volumes, such as navy strength (typically 57% ABV or higher – *see* page 21), for a bolder, more intense flavour.

BOTANICALS

The seeds, herbs, roots, fruit and berries, including the essential juniper, that provide one of the core blocks of flavour in any gin, ranging from the "classics" (*see* page 42) to the exotic.

CHILL FILTRATION

A process to remove certain fatty compounds (lipids) from gin that cause it to turn cloudy when exposed to colder temperatures. Some distillers choose not to chill filter their gin, claiming that these compounds give additional texture and flavour to the spirit.

CONDENSER

A vital piece of equipment that turns hot spirit vapour back into a clear liquid after it has been distilled. Usually seen partnered with a **still**.

CUT POINTS

The key points in the distillation process when the distiller collects or retains the desirable proportion or "heart" of a spirit **distillation run** to be distilled further, discarding the remainder of the spirit up to that point, which contains unwanted and toxic substances. The cut point in the earlier stage of distillation is often called "the heads" and in the final stage "the tails".

DIRECT CHARGE

A process whereby the **botanicals** (either mixed into a specific recipe or individually) are loaded into the pot of a **still** with spirit ready to be distilled.

DISTILLATION RUN

The process of distilling a batch of gin. The amount of time distillers take to run their distillation batch varies hugely and depends on the type of botanicals used, the size of the **still** and the desired intensity of flavour, but on average it takes around five to six hours.

ETHANOL

Also known as ethyl alcohol, this is the type of alcohol that can be consumed, the core of every spirit. Distillers work hard to remove methanol – a toxic chemical created in the distillation process (*see* **Cut Points**).

FERMENTATION

The all-important chemical reaction where yeast begins to consume the natural sugars in the mash of grain, molasses or wine, turning them into alcohol, which is then distilled.

FIELD-TO-GLASS/GRAIN-TO-GLASS

Terms used by distillers when every aspect of gin making is effectively controlled by the distiller: from the production of the base alcohol, through using often locally grown or sourced botanicals to distilling and bottling on site.

FLOOR MALTING

A largely historical process, practised by only a handful of distilleries today, where barley is malted on a traditional stone malting floor by adding water and turning it by hand over a number of days until the grains

germinate. The modern process of malting barley is an industrial one, but the traditional craft of floor malting is something distillers are beginning to revisit.

FRACTIONAL DISTILLATION
The process of taking different elements or **cut points** from a spirit – that is, separating it into its constituent parts (fractions) – by distilling it in a column **still** fitted with a series of plates (*see* page 24).

FYNBOS
The name given to the belt of natural shrubland in the Eastern and Western Cape of South Africa, a term distillers in the country often use to denote the type of locally sourced botanicals featured in their gins.

GNS
Stands for grain neutral spirit (alternatively termed neutral grain spirit) – the most widely used spirit base in the production of gin internationally. The grain can be anything from corn (maize), wheat, rye or other cereal, which is distilled up to around 98% **ABV** to become odourless and flavourless.

LONDON DRY
A style of gin production where all the botanicals are distilled in the spirit (or the vapour) rather than using post-distillation additives. Not exclusive to London, the term applies to gins produced all over the world (*see* page 20).

MACERATION
The process whereby botanicals are initially steeped in neutral alcohol for a period of time, ranging from a few hours to often 12–48 hours but sometimes up to a year, to extract flavour and aroma before distillation begins. This can occur within the pot **still** itself or in specific maceration vessels.

MASH/MASH BILL
The grain or mixture/recipe of different grains used in the first stages of alcohol production. Wheat, corn (maize), rye, barley and other cereals are used singularly or combined to produce a **GNS** (grain neutral spirit), which is then redistilled with **botanicals** to produce gin.

MULTI-SHOT
A process whereby a highly flavoured, high-strength gin concentrate is produced, which is subsequently cut with neutral spirit and diluted with water to a bottling strength.

NEW WESTERN
Refers to the style of gin being made predominantly in North America, where **botanicals** such as citrus fruit or specific spices are used to create the central (but not predominant) flavour, partnering rather than focusing solely on the juniper as the lead botanical.

NON-GMO
This term is applied to grains and spirit that are produced without the use of genetically modified organisms.

ONE/SINGLE-SHOT
A process whereby a single batch of gin is produced, usually at a very high strength (70–80%+ **ABV**) using a balanced **botanical** recipe, then diluted with water down to around 40% ABV before being bottled.

PROOF
A measure for the amount of alcohol contained in a spirit expressed as a degree, equal to twice the **ABV**, often used in the USA in addition to the obligatory ABV. The term relates back to when distillers would "prove" the strength of their spirit by mixing it with gunpowder – if it still ignited, it passed the test (*see* page 21).

RECTIFICATION
The process of strengthening the alcohol content of a base spirit by redistilling it in a column **still** or, occasionally, a pot still.

STILL
The individual vessels in which gin is distilled, where a base spirit is heated from below, turned into a vapour and then condensed back into a liquid again. Traditionally, a copper pot still is used in most forms of distillation because copper is a very malleable metal and also an active element for drawing out flavour compounds in a spirit. (*See* Types of Gin Still, page 22)

STRIPPING
Also known as purification, where a high-strength base alcohol is produced by essentially stripping the impurities and liquid volume out of a lower-strength spirit to leave only trace elements of flavour and aroma.

VAPOUR INFUSION
The method of distilling gin where **botanicals**, sometimes the more delicate floral ones, are hung in a basket or on a perforated tray in the neck of a still to allow the spirit vapours to pass through them before being condensed back into a liquid.

INDEX

PICTURE ACKNOWLEDGMENTS

The publishers would like to acknowledge and thank the following distilleries and drinks companies who have kindly supplied images for use in this book.

5l The Botanist; 6 Kongsgaard; 7 La Insoportable Brewery and Distillery/Alum Gálvez; 8al Wilderer Fynbos Distillery; 8b Koval Distillery; 12ar Caledonia Spirits/photo Jesse Schloff; 13l The Botanist; 13br The Boatyard Distillery; 20 Distillerie du St Laurent; 34 Monkey 47; 53b Double Dutch; 63 Beefeater Gin; 64 Beam Suntory Inc/Sipsmith; 67 Marylebone Gin; 68al & ar Hepple Gin/Tom Bunning; 68b, 69 Bombay Sapphire/Hype Photography; 70 Warner's; 73 Southwestern Distillery; 74 Hepple Gin; 76 The Oxford Artisan Distillery; 77 Wheadon's Gin; 87 Dingle Distillery; 89 Jawbox Gin/Perfect Swerve; 90 The Boatyard Distillery; 91 Ballyvolane Spirits; 98a Filliers; 99 Rutte Gin; 100, 101, 102 Monkey 47; 103 Elephant Gin; 104a & b GinSTR; 105 Berliner Brandstifter; 106 Rick Gin; 107a Xellent Gin; 107b 5020 Gin; 108 Distillerie du Paris/Emilie Albert; 109,110a Citadelle Gin; 110b G'Vine Gin; 112 Audemus Spirits; 113a & b Le Gin C'est Nous; 116 Beam Suntory Inc/Larios; 118, 119 Gin EVA; 121 Malfy Gin; 123a Wolfrest Gin; 123b Bottega SpA; 125 Three Graces Distilling; 130b, 131 Nordisk Braenderi; 132 Kyro Distillery/Veera Kujala; 134a Thoran Distillery; 134b Eimverk Distillery; 135 Oslo Handverksdestilleri; 139a & b Liviko Distillery; 143 Žufánek Distillery; 144 Distillery Duh u boci; 145l Henkell & Co Distillers; 145r Rodionov & Sons; 147 Ladoga Group; 153, 154 New York Distilling Company; 155a & b Philadelphia Distilling; 156a Iron Fish Distillery; 156b Fleischmann's Gin; 159 Caledonia Spirits/photo Jesse Schloff; 160a Letherbee Distillers; 161, 162a FEW Spirits; 164, 165 Treaty Oak Distillery; 166a Letherbee Distillers; 166b North Shore Distillery; 169, 170a & b St George Spirits/Ben Krantz; 171 Hotaling & Co.; 172a Distillery No. 209; 175 Copperworks Distilling; 176 Cutwater Gin; 177a Old Harbor Distilling Co; 177b Mulholland Distilling; 180, 182 Distillerie du St Laurent; 181 Okanagan Spirits; 184a Strathcona Spirits; 184b Ampersand Gin; 189 Gin Katun; 190a & b La Insoportable Brewery and Distillery/Alum Gálvez; 192a, 193 Fazenda Cachoeira Distillery; 194, 195l & r London to Lima Gin; 197, 203l Rechmaya Distillery; 203r Jullius Craft Distillery/Ilya Melinkov; 207 Hope on Hopkins/Mapodile Mkhabela; 208l & r Hope on Hopkins/Retha Ferguson; 211a Wilderer Fynbos Distillery; 211b Blind Tiger Gin; 216b, 220l Archie Rose Distillery; 217l & r, 218 Four Pillars Gin/Anson Smart; 220r, 221a & b William McHenry Distillery/Peter Jarvis; 222a & b The West Winds Gin; 223 Cape Byron Distillery; 230a & b Kyoto Distillery; 231 Beam Suntory Inc/Roku Gin; 233 Benizakura Distillery; 235 Peddlers Gin Co; 236a Dragon's Blood Gin; 237ar Kavalan Gin; 240, 241b NAO Spirits; 241a Jaisalmer Indian Craft Gin; 242a Tanglin Distillery; 245b Paper Lantern Gin; 247a La Insoportable Brewery and Distillery/Alum Gálvez; 247b Gin La Republica; 248a Cape Byron Distillery

Additional photographic credits

5r Folio Images/Alamy Stock Photo; 8ar dpa picture alliance/Alamy Stock Photo; 10 puk khantho/Unsplash; 14 Museum of London/Bridgeman Images; 15 Library of the University of Leiden, MS BPL 14A, folio 115v; 16 United Archives/Alamy Stock Photo; 17a World History Archive/Alamy Stock Photo; 17b Maurice Collins Images/Mary Evans Picture Library; 19 Illustrated History/Alamy Stock Photo; 21 Chronicle/Alamy Stock Photo; 32 Florilegius/SSPL/Getty Images; 33 Ppy2010ha/Dreamstime.com; 35 Gary Kavanagh/iStock; 36 Simon Grosset/Alamy Stock Photo; 38 Wellcome Images; 56 E K Yap; 60, 85 redmark/iStock; 62 Cath Harries/Alamy Stock Photo; 72 David A Eastley/Alamy Stock Photo; 78 lucentius/iStock; 79 urbanbuzz/Shutterstock; 86 hugo-kemmel/Unsplash; 92 mammoth/iStock; 94 fiLigor/iStock; 95 Lordprice Collection/Alamy Stock Photo; 97 Jan Fritz/Alamy Stock Photo; 98b enricobaringuarise/Shutterstock; 114 Factofoto/Alamy Stock Photo; 120 Aleksandar Georgiev/iStock; 124 Milan Gonda/Alamy Stock Photo; 126 guillaume-briard/Unsplash; 130a ClarkandCompany/iStock; 136 Gilly/Unsplash; 140 jarino47/iStock; 146 GeorgeK/iStock; 150 M B Rubin/iStock; 152 dhughes9/iStock; 158, 162b enricobaringuarise/Shutterstock; 160b luvvstudio/iStock; 168 franckreporter/iStock; 172b Lara Hata/iStock; 174 Jeff Spicer/Press Association Images; 178 Erica Ellefsen/Alamy Stock Photo; 188 Photoservice/iStock; 192b Kiyoshi Takahase Segundo/Alamy Stock Photo; 196 Sébastien Lecocq/Alamy Stock Photo; 200 irisphoto2/iStock; 202 M Sobreira/Alamy Stock Photo; 204 David Clode/Unsplash; 206 all Nic Bothma/EPA-EFE/Shutterstock; 212 J F Jacobsz/iStock; 216a Bruce Aspley/iStock; 225 primeimages/iStock; 228 Prasit Rodphan/Dreamstime.com; 229 rolandoemail/Pixabay; 232l enricobaringuarise/Shutterstock; 232r igaguri_1/iStock; 234 BluHue/iStock; 238 Image Broker/Alamy Stock Photo; 239 Macduff Everton/National Geographic Image Collection/Alamy Stock Photo; 242b Alan Keith Beastall/Alamy Stock Photo; 243 vincentlecolley/iStock; 244 aluxum/iStock; 245a IakovKalinin/iStock

12a, bl & br, 13ar, 50, 52 all, 53a, 66 photographed at East London Liquor by Simon Jessop, simonjessop.com

80, 83, 115, 213, 236b, 237al & b, 248b photographed by Neil Ridley and Joel Harrison

ACKNOWLEDGMENTS

THE AUTHORS WOULD LIKE TO THANK THE FOLLOWING PEOPLE:

Giorgio Bargiani and Agostino Perrone at The Connaught Bar

Denise Bates, Leanne Bryan, Juliette Norsworthy and the team at Octopus Publishing

Jamie Baxter

Bev, Dimple, Georgina, Louise, Pip and the IWSC team

Jared Brown and Anistatia Miller

Nate Brown

Martine Carter

Ian Chang

Nicholas Cook and The Gin Guild

Charlie Critchfield and all at Remarkable TV

Alex Davies

Dawn Davies and the Speciality Drinks team

Philip Duff

Ben Ellefsen, Atom Brands

Berry Bros. & Rudd (for inventing the concept of the Three Martini Lunch)

James Goggin, Alexis Self, Michael Vachon and the Maverick Drinks team

Victoria Grier

Gus and the team at The Union Club

Raissa and Joyce de Haas

Nicole Hatch and *The Telegraph* Gin Experience team, including Susy Atkins

Jon Hillgren

Simon Jessop

Melanie Jones at Singapore Tourism Board

Allen Katz

Lola Lau

Nico Liu

Joe McGirr

Alessandro Palazzi at Dukes Hotel

Chris Papple

Desmond Payne MBE

Jo Richardson

Caroline, Lois and Honor Ridley

David T Smith

Emma Stokes

Olivier and Emile Ward

Olly Wehring

Luke Wheadon

Alex Wolpert

Liquoria Limantour in Mexico City

The team at Kyrö in Finland

Sipsmith Distillery